Small Christian Communities:

A VISION OF HOPE FOR THE 21st CENTURY

Revised and Updated

Thomas A. Kleissler

Margo A. LeBert

Mary C. McGuinness

PAULIST PRESS
New York/Mahwah, New Jersey

We invite you to duplicate, without permission, *only* the following materials from *Small Christian Communities: A Vision of Hope for the 21st Century:* the samples that conclude Chapters 5 and 9 as well as the Appendix.

NIHIL OBSTAT:
Reverend Monsignor Robert E. Harahan, S.T.D.
Archdiocese of Newark Theological Commission
Censor Librorum

IMPRIMATUR: Most Reverend Theodore E. McCarrick, D.D., *Archbishop of Newark*

Cover design by Lynn Else.

Book design by Saija Autrand, Faces Type & Design.

Interior illustrations are taken from the first two volumes of *SPECIAL TOUCH for your Creative Needs,* published by The Communications Office, Sisters of St. Joseph of Carondelet, 11999 Chalon Road, Los Angeles, California 90049, 213-272-8016.

Library of Congress Cataloging-in-Publication Data

Kleissler, Thomas A., 1931–
    Small Christian communities: a vision of hope for the 21st century (revised and updated) / Thomas A. Kleissler, Margo A. LeBert, Mary C. McGuinness.
        p. cm.
    Includes bibliographical references and index.
    ISBN 0-8091-4157-4
    1. Christian communities—Catholic Church.   2. Prayer groups—Catholic Church.   3. Laity—Catholic Church.   4. Catholic Church—Adult education.   5. United States—Religion—1960-
I. LeBert, Margo A., 1947-1997 . II. McGuinness, Mary C., 1933- . III. Title.
BX2347.7.K44 1997
250—dc21   97-33717
                                                                                                                    CIP

Published by Paulist Press
997 Macarthur Boulevard
Mahwah, New Jersey 07430

www.paulistpress.com

Printed and bound in the
United States of America

Contents

We dedicate this book to our parents,
Elizabeth and Edwin Kleissler,
Cleo and Elden LeBert,
Mary M. and Richard M. McGuinness,
and to our families
who nurtured us
in our first experience of small community
and to countless others
who over these last few decades
have touched our lives so much
by enriching our growing appreciation
of the dynamic vitality
in small Christian communities

Acknowledgments

We wish to acknowledge the thousands of small Christian community members whose experience over the years has contributed to this work. Because of their faith, insights, stories, and struggles our lives have been enriched.

We express special gratitude to the past and present members of RENEW International, especially those who serve in our Small Christian Community Department, and to our predecessors who served in the SCC Department of the Archdiocese of Newark whose individual and cumulative efforts have contributed greatly to this work. This book was enlivened through their prayers, ideas, reflections, critique, support, and enthusiastic work for the renewal of our church.

We are grateful for all those who shared their faith stories with us and gave us permission to use them. All stories used in this work are true. However, we have chosen to use only first names; in a few cases, names have been changed to protect the anonymity of the person.

We acknowledge with gratitude those whose direct feedback and guidance have helped and sustained our efforts.

We especially thank Fathers John Russell, O. Carm., and James M. Cafone whose wisdom, careful reading, and loving patience have guided us in so many ways; Ansgar Holmberg, CSJ, and Marion Honors, CSJ, for permission to use their inspiring artwork; and all those who allowed us to use their stories.

In addition, we offer heartfelt gratitude to Julie Jones, whose graciousness, research, and diligent work saw us through long hours of revisions.

We also wish to thank Paul McMahon, our editor at Paulist Press, for his untiring patience, consistent support, and helpful guidance throughout this project.

Finally we are grateful to all who read this book, share its vision, and strive to enliven the church and transform the world through small Christian communities.

Preface

In 1994, Father Bernard Lee, MA, a theologian at Loyola University, New Orleans, invited me to join him in a study of small Christian communities in the Catholic Church in the United States. The Lilly Endowment of Indianapolis provided us a grant, and we began our formal study of small Christian communities (SCCs) in the Catholic Church in the winter of 1995. Father Lee had become convinced that a study encompassing both sociological and theological methodologies would reveal the SCC movement to be one of the truly dynamic outgrowths of Vatican II, and a harbinger of the church to come in the Third Millennium. At that time I knew little about RENEW, and even less about the other organizations that were then active in encouraging the formation and development of a wide range of types of SCCs in the Catholic Church. But my own participation in one small community led me to believe that the study might indeed prove fruitful.

By the time I was invited to write this preface in the spring of 1997, my colleagues and I had come to appreciate the dynamism that characterizes the SCC movement in the church today. Most important, we have come to realize the central role that the RENEW International Service Team has played in helping to bring this vision to reality from coast to coast and throughout 130 of the church's 186 dioceses in the United States. For example, 44 percent of six different types of SCCs said that they had participated in RENEW in their parish. Also, the great majority of those who had participated in RENEW said that it was one of the important influences on their decision to join a small community following their participation in RENEW.

This revised and updated edition of *Small Christian Communities: A Vision of Hope for the 21st Century* is a rich source of practical information about how to make the vision of the parish as "a community of many small communities" come alive in today's parish. One of the things that struck me most forcefully as I read the book was how well it mirrored the reality we were encountering in our site visits to, and interviews with, leaders of SCCs. The book, then, is much more than a vision. It is a document not only rich in helping newcomers over the hurdles that are most surely a part of life in many parishes, but one rich in examples of how people like you have found both personal and social fulfillment through their participation in SCCs. Our research findings show that the overwhelming majority of SCC members say it has been a "deeply satisfying experience," while majorities also identified their SCC participation as providing them with:

- the primary source of spiritual nourishment,
- a new way of participating in the parish, and
- a new way of being *church.*

In this brief overview, it is not possible to single out all the ways in which this book provides the processes that lead to the enrichment of parish life. Suffice it to mention Chapter 9, in which the authors address the challenging problem of reaching out to thousands of people who are yearning for something more than just the forty-five minute weekend Mass to satisfy their spiritual yearnings. The chapter is rich in examples, suggestions, and a variety of models that are known to be successful in bringing newcomers into the movement. Again, our research supports their models, their suggestions, their ability to face and address the hard questions about how to draw people, especially young people, into a small community. Our research has found that two out of three SCC members say that, in addition to the influence of the parish RENEW process, they found the encouragement of friends very influential. Perhaps most important, three out of four SCC members acknowledged that they were also greatly influenced by the fact that they were seeking support and growth in a small group. This latter finding supports an earlier study (Robert Wuthnow, *Sharing the Journey,* New York: The Free Press, 1994) of the national population of the United States, in which 40 percent of all adults said they belonged to at least one small group, and that it provided them with support and meaning.

In Chapter 16, the authors state boldly that "for small Christian com-

*Something More
Sharing Something More*

*SCC … "sharing something more
Belonging to something more*

munities to be worthy of their name, carrying out the mission of Christ must always be kept central." They explore in detail why it has proven so difficult to get people to participate in concrete actions. That indeed has been our finding to date. While the U.S. bishops and a number of independent Catholic groups such as NETWORK and Center of Concern have become steady voices throughout the country to strengthen actions in support of the church's social teachings, most small communities are far from that stage in the process of living out the vision. The findings from our research indicate that less than a quarter of SCCs address social issues on a regular basis at their gatherings; and a smaller number have found the strength to allow themselves to be sent forth to live and preach the Good News of Jesus. For those who are willing to read about the experiences of others who have dared to do so, Chapter 16 offers both encouragement and reward.

Interspersed throughout the book are references to the IMPACT Series, which strives to help SCCs connect with the social teachings of the church. These materials cover a wide range of human and social issues, for example, there are booklets on strengthening family life, morality, nonviolence, interracial harmony, hunger, civic responsibility, ecology, and the life issues of abortion, euthanasia, capital punishment, and domestic violence. Through the social inquiry approach of *observe, judge, act,* RENEW International hopes that SCC participants will not only be led to prayerful reflection and fruitful sharing, but also to concrete actions that positively influence human attitudes and behavior.

In his annual report on *Religion in America* (The Princeton Religion Research Center, 1996), George Gallup reflected on what he called the dynamic growth of small faith groups across religious denominations in the United States. He estimated that between 30 percent and 40 percent of adult Americans belong or have belonged to these groups (which include RENEW and the diverse groups that are part of our study) in the past ten years. In Gallup's words, the development of these small groups "can help meet two of the great desires in the hearts of Americans: the desire to find deeper meaning in our world, and the desire to build deeper, more trusting relations with other people in our often impersonal and fragmented society" (p. 12).

The SCC movement led by RENEW International not only promotes deeper meaning and more trusting relations, but also provides the means by which we are sent to live the gospel at local, state, national, and even international levels. This is the process by which we become a community of communities.

William V. D'Antonio, Ph.D.
Principal Researcher,
Small Christian Communities Project,
Catholic University

Abbreviations

Documents of Vatican II are abbreviated according to the two first words of the Latin text.

AA   *Apostolicam actuositatem:* Decree on the Apostolate of the Laity.

AG   *Ad gentes:* Decree on the Church's Missionary Activity.

CD   *Christus Dominus:* Decree on the Bishops' Pastoral Office in the Church.

DV   *Dei Verbum:* Dogmatic Constitution on Divine Revelation.

GS   *Gaudium et spes:* Pastoral Constitution on the Church in the Modern World.

LG   *Lumen gentium:* Dogmatic Constitution on the Church.

OT   *Optatam totius:* Decree on Priestly Formation.

PO   *Presbyterorum ordinis:* Decree on the Ministry and Life of Priests.

SC   *Sacrosanctum concilium:* Constitution on the Sacred Liturgy.

Introduction

Today, more than ever, we believe there is a real call to holiness. If the church is to be a transparent light to the world, we all need to become genuine, sincere and holy people. We believe that small Christian communities (SCCs) are a dynamic, grace-filled way to grow in the spiritual life. For it is in SCCs that we, the authors, particularly have grown spiritually and have seen people grow in a holistic spirituality.

Small Christian communities are a source of great hope in the church today. Because the notion of community is essential in understanding the mystery of God's presence in our church, *Small Christian Communities: A Vision of Hope for the 21st Century* points to the value of small communities and envisions the dynamic possibilities of a parish that places a pastoral emphasis on their development. This work focuses on parish-based small communities as a means by which the gospel values of Jesus may be lived and proclaimed effectively.

The time has come to acknowledge the spiritual potential of small communities.

Today, we are also being invited to a deeper understanding of the nature of the Christian vocation and a fuller appreciation of ministry, both ordained and non-ordained. With fewer and older priests, the challenge is greater than ever for lay people to assume their full baptismal role in the church.

It is time to explore fully the possibilities that a much higher percentage of parishioners is ready to be involved conscientiously in the work of evangelization, of integrating the gospel into all areas of their lives, and of bringing Christian values to impact upon our world. The Catholic parish of the 21st century could indeed become "a community made up of many small communities" as recommended by John Paul II.

One way of renewing parishes . . .
might be to consider

the parish as a community of communities.
It seems timely therefore
to form ecclesial communities . . .
that allows for true human relationships.
(*Ecclesia in America* 41)

If this is the right vision, the pastor and staff need to give priority to it. With so much else going on, they need to discern and select outstanding leadership for the Core Community, give moral support and encouragement, and entrust the leaders with the implementation of the vision.

Ten million people have participated in RENEW small groups over the past 25 years. Many dioceses have reported that as a diocesan average 30 percent to as high as 47 percent of active Catholics have participated in these groups.

Many people who have been in these groups continue to meet on a regular basis. Through their desire to grow spiritually and the commitments they make to one another, they might rightfully become continuing small Christian communities. The remarkable growth of small groups and communities in our time and the highly positive diocesan evaluations of RENEW small groups in terms of the spiritual growth of parishioners motivate us to encourage and expand this type of vibrant faith experience.

We feel a sense of responsibility to aid this ongoing journey by sharing what has been learned through RENEW International's experience, not only for the benefit of those following through from the RENEW process, but also for the benefit of all interested in small communities. *Small Christian Communities: A Vision of Hope for the 21st Century* thus offers guidance to pastors and parish leaders in the development of parish-based small groups and communities.

We envision small communities as part of the larger parish, indeed of the whole Catholic Church, the People of God, its tradition, teaching, leadership, and guidance. This book does not address free-floating communities, but rather parish-based communities that play an important role in parish life and exist in relationship to the authority of the local pastor and bishop. These small communities benefit from their role in the larger Catholic Church by living the life of the Spirit.

While speaking of the value of small communities, we do not intend to make that value exclusive or to devaluate other experiences. If an imbalance exists today, it is probably that small Christian communities receive too little attention from parish leadership. In view of the potential spirituality they offer, it is not unreasonable to suggest that 10 percent to 20 percent of the time and energy expended by parish leadership be focused in assisting small communities. Rather than showing signs of neglecting the overall parish, such action would demonstrate a pastoral effort that would redound to the good of the entire parish.

No dynamic in and of itself can renew the church. Ultimately, it is the Spirit of God who renews the church. Yet we believe that the recent increase of small communities is one of the more significant events of our age to encourage the renewal of the church and the transformation of the world.

Through this work we enter into dialogue with all others who are in small Christian communities or who desire to foster and develop them for the renewal of our church and the transformation of the world.

Ultimately community is a gift. It is not human effort that will build small Christian communities. It is the Spirit of God working in and through all of us who will set hearts aflame and bring us into communion with one another, with all creation, and with God.

The love of Christ impels us! (See 2 Corinthians 5:14.)

Sharing something more
Something more
Belonging to something more

How To Use This Book

Essentially *Small Christian Communities: A Vision of Hope for the 21st Century* is a pastoral work. It is divided into three parts.

Part I: Foundations for Small Christian Communities
Part I conveys historical, theological, ecclesiological, and spiritual foundations of small Christian communities.

Part II: The Pastoral Direction and Its Implementation
Part II presents the pastoral direction of the parish as "a community of many small communities." It offers various approaches that facilitate healthy small community development along with many concrete "how to" steps. It is valuable to **all** who are interested in exploring the development of small communities in the parish.

Part III: Concrete Approaches
Part III highlights concrete approaches in bringing about the fullness of the pastoral direction. It explores the benefits that will occur in family life and in the faith life of all parishioners.

Obviously, everyone will benefit from reading the entire book. *Certain areas have been particularly helpful for specific audiences,* for example
- A must reading for **small community members and leaders** are two sections in Chapter 7, "Commitment of Small Christian Community Members" and "Essential Elements of Small Community," and Chapter 3 on spirituality.
- **Small community leaders** will find in Chapter 10 not only criteria to see if they are on target, but a good reflection piece for an "examen of consciousness for leaders." They will also find key ways of helping small community members be more involved in the mission of Jesus in both Chapters 13 and 15.

- The **pastor and staff** will find in Chapter 11 fifteen ways to support the development of small communities, guidelines to enhance their participation in SCCs, and a section on managing time. **Core Community members** will find the chapter helpful to understand better the role of pastor and staff.
- **Core Community members** will find every chapter in Part II beneficial. For example, the section on Sign-Up Sunday is useful not only when beginning seasonal small groups but in an ongoing way, specifically in inviting new members.
- **Workshop presenters** on prayer (Chapter 14) or mission (Chapter 15) will find ample material to develop their sessions.
- **All** will benefit from what has been called the "jewel" of a chapter on prayer (Chapter 14).

To encourage dialogue and understanding, reflection, and faith sharing, questions are provided after each chapter. **Parish Core Communities, staffs, ministerial communities,** or **SCC members** may enjoy the opportunity to share their insights. The following direction can be used after the Scripture reading: *Take a few minutes to savor a word, a phrase, a question, or a feeling that rises up in you. Reflect on this quietly or share it aloud. How does this affect me?*

In addition, the following questions can be used with any chapter: *What statements have been encouraging to me in this chapter? Why? What statements have been challenging to me? Why?*

PART I

Foundations for Small Christian Communities

1. Small Christian Communities: A Source of Parish Renewal

We live in the rarest of moments. Today we are called to analyze what has taken place in the course of history and project possibilities to shape the future. Tumultuous events and constant change have been the hallmarks of our time. Yet a continuing and ever-constant element of our lives has been the enduring love that God has for us.

Over the course of the church's history small communities have played a significant role in proclaiming and developing that love. Small communities have enabled believers to search for the face of God and to develop a more profound union with God and one another. They have also been a means for renewing and expanding the church. They offer greater hope than ever that Christians will deepen their love for God, for one another, and for all of creation, and in so doing they will renew the face of the earth.

The following is an example of how one parish filled with many small Christian communities helped to renew the face of the earth:

> When disaster strikes, people usually respond well. But if they have been sharing their faith in community, the response is total and immediate. This is what the people of Our Lady of Lourdes Church in Otway, Ohio, found out when a number of Appalachian creeks flooded their community for twelve hours.

Three days after the flash flood hit, the parish appealed to St. Elizabeth Seton parish in nearby Pickerington for help. That afternoon, according to Rosie Owens of the Seton parish, the small faith-sharing groups launched "a telephone chain," and by eight the next morning "had six adults packed to go to Otway with enough supplies to fill one van and two cars." With the help of brooms, mops, shovels, buckets, gloves, and disinfectants, they cleaned what could be salvaged in the church and disposed of what was lost.

That was only the beginning. A new round of phone calls started on Friday and "by Saturday we had so many supplies we had to borrow a nineteen-foot U-Haul to transport them," said Rosie. Then, on Sunday "thirty-two adults and thirty youth gathered at Seton at six forty-five A.M. to go to Otway" to help not only the church but members of the community as well.

Father John Stattmiller, the pastor at Our Lady of Lourdes, referred to that Sunday as "Rejoicing Sunday." Following the Mass, the "good neighbors" went out to the community in crews. Some pulled up carpet and tile in homes, some cleaned along the streets and creeks, and others organized foodstuffs and supplies and helped to distribute them to the local people. Recalling the challenge, Rosie said, "Without the faith-sharing groups, Seton parish would not have been able to respond so quickly. The structure of the groups allowed us to call approximately five hundred people in a few hours."

"Even in the midst of disaster," said Rosie, recounting the devastation, "miracles are evident." To her it was the faith of people who were truly God's presence in a moment of need.

Certainly community, as a general experience of belonging and commitment, is an essential element of any understanding of church. People frequently evaluate parish life on the quality of community. Judging whether the parish is "alive" or "dead" is often based solely on whether or not people discover community there. Through small communities many people are discovering the value of community. Today, as many varieties of small communities develop around the world, they offer the promise of new vitality for the church and give added impulse for people to live gospel values.

HISTORICAL OVERVIEW

We will begin by reviewing the value of small communities through a historical approach. This overview will be a confirmation to those who are already convinced of their value and a consideration for reflection for those who may be wondering whether the time has come for small communities to become a mainstream part of parish life. We will then explore some of the sociological factors that shape our contemporary society as well as the challenges that these factors present for our church in the post-modern world.[1]

Small Communities in the Early Christian Tradition

As we look at the experience of the early church, we see that Jesus formed his disciples and sent them forth. After the Pentecost experience the community of disciples shared the Good News as they traveled—preaching, baptizing, and gathering people together in small communities, meeting in homes. There they retold the life, death, and Resurrection of Jesus and reflected on its meaning. It was the household church that provided the basic structure of early Christian communities.

These Christians prayed together, broke bread as they were taught by the Lord through his disciples, and shared their lives and sustenance. As they grew in their understanding of the personal and social implications of their faith in Jesus, they supported one another by faithfully living it out in the midst of a pagan environment. Without doubt it was the communitarian character of the early church "that determined the extraordinary expansion of Christianity into the socially fragmented Greco-Roman world."[2]

In the fourth century, under Constantine the Great, Christians regained freedom of worship and the Christian church became legal. Huge pagan temples were replaced by churches. Masses of people embraced Christianity and filled the new church buildings. The small communities came out of their house churches and joined the large masses of people for worship. The persecutions were over. It was no longer dangerous to be a Christian; it was now easier and even "fashionable" to profess the Christian faith.

Yet even after the peace of Constantine, the church did not abruptly change from small communities to large congregations. In some places, the small community experience continued to be an integral part of the life of the church. For instance episcopal households of the fourth century drew their inspiration from the idea of the communal life portrayed in the Acts of the Apostles (2:42) and the ascetic ideal of the desert fathers and mothers. In many of the households of bishops, people gathered as small communities for liturgical prayer and works of charity.

Max Delespesse, author of *The Church Community: Leaven and Life-Style,* speaks of the formation of communities alongside the ordinary church. Two or three decades before the Edict of Milan in 313—through which Christianity became the accepted religion of the Roman Empire— and especially after the edict, some Christians who wanted to rediscover the "apostolic life" and the primitive community formed into groups. These cenobites or monks, "not finding their place any longer in a departmentalized and in a certain way secularized Church, went out into the desert (in general this wasn't too far because they worked for the poor and they had to pay taxes) to form communities there."[3] The monastic experience, which received the approval of the bishops and the faithful, integrated community support with prayer and mission. Monasticism in the east and the west proved to be a source of vitality for the church even though it gave rise to the idea that spirituality could not easily be lived in ordinary "secular" life.

Small Communities in the Middle Ages

Small communities of lay women who lived an austere lifestyle developed in the Low Countries during the twelfth and thirteenth centuries. These women, called Beguines, took no vows, had no common rule, no general religious superior, but gave themselves to works of charity, to prayer, and to devotional exercises. Some reported mystical experiences. Although most of them lived together, they were free to retain private property and were able to leave at any time. The Beghards, associations of lay men, lived similar lifestyles. Unlike the Beguines they held no property in common, but relied upon the common purse.

History bears witness to a wide variety of religious communities, orders, and congregations founded by charismatic leaders. These leaders attracted others both because of the spirituality they professed and the apostolic works in which they were involved. Members of these groups lived in solitude or in small communities. They cared for the sick and the poor, educated youth, and committed themselves to a wide variety of social services. Some of these congregations remained local communities; others reached out in missionary zeal to people in distant lands.

Differing from religious communities yet having a communal dimension were guilds and sodalities. During the Middle Ages, guilds flourished to support merchants and craftspeople. By applying Christian principles to the life of laborers and artisans these guilds had a significant influence on society. In addition to settling matters of employment, the guilds took care of workers when ill, attended funerals of deceased members, and helped support widows and orphans. Although not pious confraternities that were subject to the assent of the local bishop, guilds were definitely Catholic in character and received their inspiration from the church.[4]

Religious guilds, too, were organized for the promotion of social work, collective almsgiving and instruction.[5] These guilds, made up of all classes of people, were forerunners of groups later organized for Catholic Action, and were, indeed, foundational to the small Christian communities that would follow.

Sodalities

Various kinds of sodalities were established throughout the centuries under church authority for the promotion of some work of devotion, charity, public worship, or outreach. Usually these sodalities were associations of lay people who met to perform pious exercises, followed a set of principles or rules, and submitted to the spiritual direction of a leader.

Sodalities of Our Lady established in Rome in 1563 proposed a Christian way of life through a particular program of spiritual formation. The sodality "tried to unify the sacramental nature of the Christian at prayer and the Christian in action. Its characteristic mark has been service of the church under the patronage of our Lady and the direction of the hierarchy."[6]

Sodalities, throughout the years they flourished, brought together people involved in the same occupations, e.g., small groups of sailors, fishermen, teachers, doctors, business people, lawyers, who met to apply their sodality principles and way of life to their particular social and professional circumstances. Young adult sodalities were formed in high schools and colleges. Their members channeled their apostolic endeavors into areas of local need.

After the Second Vatican Council the National Federation of Sodalities, founded in the United States in 1957, sought to guide sodalities in the mature Christian thought and action enjoined on them by the council. The *Notre Dame Study of Catholic Parish Life* reports that devotions to the Blessed Virgin Mary, altar societies, and sodalities are especially important sources of vitality for some parishes even today.[7]

Catholic Action Groups

In the twentieth century, under the broad heading of Catholic Action, several movements developed with a strong community base. Prominent among these were the Young Christian Workers (YCW), Young Christian Students (YCS), and the Christian Family Movement (CFM).

Founded by Joseph Cardinal Cardijn in Belgium in 1925, the YCW served to enable young workers to re-Christianize their own lives, their working and social environments and those with whom they worked. This movement took root in the United States as Young Christian Students (YCS), which aimed to Christianize the school environment and to enlist Catholic students in apostolic action.[8]

The Christian Family Movement (CFM), founded in 1947, sought to restore family life to Christ and create small communities that would influence their parishes and the wider society.[9] Today the expressed vision of CFM is to improve the quality of family life by reaching out to others.[10]

Each of the above-mentioned groups adopted the inquiry approach with the observe, judge, and act methodology that St. Thomas Aquinas used for arriving at prudent action.[11] These Catholic Action groups and similar groups developed lay leadership and helped to transform our church and our society. They were, and wherever they flourish today are, in fact, small Christian communities.

In the past, Catholic Action was sometimes seen as an expression of the apostolate in which the laity extended the work of the hierarchy. Small Christian communities that are emerging today (including those previously mentioned, e.g., CFM groups) are an expression of the church in which the laity assume their rightful role in the mission of Jesus.

Contemporary Society

In the last several decades, throughout the world more than 100,000 small Christian communities have come into being.[12] In the United States these small Christian communities have taken the form of Scripture study groups, support groups, prayer groups, ministerial communities, and other ongoing Christian communities.

In their book *Dangerous Memories,* theologian Bernard Lee and social scientist Michael Cowan examine the movement of small communities of faith emerging throughout the world, but especially in the United States.[13] They also provide an excellent overview of how intentional Christian communities have developed in different cultural settings. In Latin America where the basic Christian community exists principally among the poor and the oppressed members of the Catholic population, there is a strong concern for social justice. These basic church communities, which are supported by the Latin American bishops, received great confirmation at the Medellín (1968) and Puebla (1979) Conferences held in Colombia and Mexico, respectively. Africa's small Christian communities, initiated by the hierarchy, "correspond with the growing need being experienced by African Christians to express their own values of community, harmony, and solidarity in the context of their Christian faith."[14]

These small communities have their own characteristics and expressions based upon the various histories, cultures, and church traditions in their countries or areas of origin. Similarly these groups are called by a variety of names. For example, in Africa some of the terms used are "small Christian communities" (SCCs), "living ecclesial communities," and "neighborhood gospel groups." In Latin America groups are called "base ecclesial communities" (BECs) or "comunidades eclesiales de base."

Most sociologists and pastoral leaders agree that the Latin American form of small Christian communities cannot easily be transferred to the

American scene. Small communities developing in the United States are taking on their own unique characteristics. The U.S. bishops gave formal approval to a document *Communion and Mission* to urge the development of church communities among Hispanics.

RENEW has provided a strong impetus for the development of small Christian communities for the church in the United States. In a preliminary report on the development of small Christian communities in the United States, a research team has identified RENEW as "the single most important factor in the broad based move to establish small Christian communities within parishes."[15] The report, prepared by Professor William D'Antonio of the Catholic University of America, was issued by Loyola University's Institute for Ministry, New Orleans. RENEW, which emphasizes the development of small Christian communities, has been part of the parish life of at least 20,000 parishes in the past 24 years.

As part of the Small Christian Communities Research project, a survey was conducted in eight dioceses representing eight major sub-regions of the country. The detailed findings are found in Bernard M. Lee's book, *The Catholic Experience of Small Christian Communities*. The survey estimates "the existence, minimally of 37,000 small Christian communities in the continental United States, with a membership of over a million (including adults and children)."[16] "Some of these are post-RENEW groups, and some unknown number perhaps current RENEW groups," according to D'Antonio, principal researcher and research coordinator.[17] The same survey reveals "that about one-in-twenty regular church-attending Catholics belongs to some kind of small Christian community . . . and the church allegiance of SCC Catholics is significantly stronger than that of Catholics who are not members of SCCs."[18]

In these changing historical and cultural times, RENEW has been recognized as the "chief stimulant in the growth of SCCs" in the United States.[19] Through God's gracious action, may small Christian communities serve the continuity of the church in times of suffering and affliction, being signs of fidelity in times of crisis, and agents of spiritual renewal and courageous action during times of cultural change and upheaval.

SOCIOLOGICAL OVERVIEW

Sociologists acknowledge that we live in an age of unprecedented change. As long-range social forces converge, people's ways of feeling, thinking and acting change. In reality a cultural shift occurs. Bernard Longeran says that "Social and cultural changes are, at root, changes in meanings that are grasped and accepted." He goes on to say that "changes in the control of meaning mark off the great epochs of human history."[20] As we study the history of society over the centuries, it becomes even more evident that these changes in meanings shake the very ground of society's value system. Cultural historians have noted that the period of the 1960s with its intense, rapid ferment was a time of such cultural transformation. A new age dawned with changing values, meanings, and symbols.

Sociological Factors Shape Our Society

This age has brought with it an explosion of knowledge, systems of mass communication that instantly bring us in contact with almost any part of the planet, advancement in all forms of technology, a growth in materialism and consumerism, the quest for freedom from oppressive governments, dislocations of people from many countries, social instability, and countless other sweeping changes. In addition, questions affecting our ecological systems, economy, health, peace, etc., continue to confront us.

Today many forces that influence our ways of thinking, feeling, and acting are far from being supportive of Christian values. Changes in society—such as the unraveling of close-knit neighborhoods (i.e., neighborhoods that were once homogeneous, ethnically and denominationally), increased mobility of people, changing family structures, and the struggle for equality among races and sexes—have helped to create the need for greater support to live the Christian life. The pressures of consumerism and privatism that affect families, neighborhoods and parishes attract people toward a lifestyle that reflects little of the gospel message. One need only listen to the prevailing voices of materialism and consumerism to assess some of the forces at work in shaping our ways of feeling, thinking, and acting.

Since these forces are frequently not supportive of Christian life, today's society appears to be very much like the society before the time of Constantine. The early Christians had to reject the values of their society and often suffered ridicule, persecution, and even death as they remained faithful to the way of Jesus. In certain parts of our world it is becoming increasingly clear that to live as Jesus did—to help the poor, the alienated, those treated unjustly, and to question why people are poor—is often to invoke the wrath of the powerful. Those who truly try to live the Christian life put themselves in the position of being persecuted today as in the early church.

Observers of our times try to analyze what is happening as a result of high technology and a host of dehumanizing factors. The Secretariat for Promoting Christian Unity noted that "A breakdown of traditional social structures, cultural patterns, and traditional sets of values, caused by industrialization, urbanization, migration, rapid development of communication systems, all-rational technocratic systems, etc., leave many individuals confused, uprooted, insecure, and, therefore, vulnerable."[21]

An analysis of the responses to a questionnaire distributed by this Secretariat reveals further symptoms of society's problems. Many people feel anxious about themselves and the future. They suffer a loss of direction, lack of participation in decision making, lack of real answers to their questions. They experience fear because of various forms of violence, terrorism, conflict, hostility, fear of ecological disaster, war, and nuclear holocaust.

Many feel frustrated, rootless, homeless, lonely, lost in anonymity, alienated. They are disillusioned with technological society, the military, church laws and practices, and government politics.

In summary, all these symptoms represent forms of alienation. And the needs and aspirations experienced are so many forms of a search for presence to oneself, to others, to God.[22]

Small Groups Respond to Needs

Because of these needs, 40 percent of (or 75 million) adults in the United States come together in some form of small groups.[23] They may be neighborhood associations, Alcoholics Anonymous groups, or Bible study groups.

The identity of the groups varies, but for many of them the need to belong in a more intimate way is constant. The need to know and to be known and the need to care and to be cared for are essential to human life.

A sense of belonging is often achieved in parochial life through involvement in parish worship, ministries, and activities. This sense of belonging is sustained over longer periods of time through small Christian communities. Personal experience and recent studies bear witness to the fact that when these needs for belonging, being recognized and cared about are not met in our parishes, parishioners seek to fulfill these needs elsewhere. Some join small fundamentalist communities, evangelical communities or sects where they experience this sense of belonging, support, and basic security. Once they have made friends and have people who care about them, spend time with them, and miss them when they are absent, then they have that sense of belonging. The need to belong, to relate, and to care applies to parish life as much as to any other segment of society.

Besides offering the richness of sacramental life and of Catholic tradition, parish life has the additional capacity to respond to these needs through the development of small Christian communities where a greater sense of belonging can be felt, where people who know one another can better care for one another. In addition those who are searching for a fuller faith life and a greater sense of the transcendent God find support, insight, and encouragement in these small community relationships.

Positive trends in the religious life of the American Catholic today that have been outlined by George Gallup, Jr., can be very encouraging for the parish. These are 1) "A renewed search for depth in our spiritual lives, arising out of disenchantment with materialism as well as concern for the many problems affecting our society," and 2) "a renewed search for deeper relationships arising out of loneliness and a feeling of isolation. This search is seen in the growth of self-help groups and in the uptrend in Bible study and prayer fellowship groups. People are increasingly making the discovery that faith grows best in the presence of faith."[24]

PARISH POTENTIAL FOR SMALL COMMUNITIES

Many pastoral leaders have testified to the fact of an increased percentage of people seeking to be part of small communities.[25] And since the American parish already has many small groups or communities as part of its structure in the form of support groups, ministry groups, etc., the underpinnings for developing small Christian communities are already present. The potential for small Christian communities is in our parishes. It needs only to be activated by dedicated pastoral leaders.

Although the preceding socio-historical overview has admittedly been brief and far from comprehensive, it nevertheless gives evidence that small communities—which have always been a part of the church—have surely exerted their influence in the church. It also points to the value that parish-based small communities can have for our present and future church. This value will continue to be developed as we turn in Chapter 2 to some theological and pastoral approaches that support the development of small communities.

† † † † † REFLECTION AND FAITH-SHARING QUESTIONS

Reflect on Acts 2:42–47 and 4:32–37.

1. What do I find most inspiring and/or challenging in these descriptions of early Christian life? What other Scripture passages speak to me of Christian community?
2. Through the centuries small Christian communities have developed in response to the spiritual and social needs of those desiring to live their faith more deeply. We live in a time of tremendous change and challenge. What are some of the realities in our church or culture today that contribute to people wanting to form small communities of faith?
3. Read again the passages from the Acts of the Apostles. In what ways does this picture of Christian life reflect our parish? What would help to make this picture come alive in our parish?

2. Theological and Pastoral Approaches

Ansgar Holmberg, CST

It is amazing to realize how small Christian communities are developing all over the world. One of the prime reasons for this growth is the increasing recognition and acceptance by Christian laity of their vocation and mission in the world today.

Contrast contemporary experience with an incident that took place in 1867.

> Msgr. George Talbot, an adviser to Pius IX, wrote to Henry Manning, Archbishop of Westminster. In that letter Talbot asked both an important question and gave a provocative response, "What is the province of the laity? To hunt, to shoot, to entertain. These matters they understand but to meddle with ecclesiastical affairs they have no right at all...."[1]

No doubt this incident is not representative of the total thinking of his time; nevertheless it gives some insight into the thought of one prominent nineteenth-century church leader. Talbot's reply is a far cry from the way the Second Vatican Council described the role of the laity as participating in the priestly, prophetic, and kingly mission of Jesus (*LG* 34, 35, 36).

> It is clear that the participation by the lay faithful in this threefold mission of Christ derives from their being members of the Church, which is his Body. In other words, it derives *from the communion of the church.* Therefore, this mission must be lived, and realized *in communion* and *for the increase of communion itself.*[2]

Small communities are a means for Christians to live the mission more fully through communion with other Christians. Support for the value of small Christian communities is found in three principles that were highlighted during the Second Vatican Council: (1) the communitarian nature of the church, (2) renewed focus on the Word of God, and (3) a greater understanding of the social mission of the church. Each of these principles will be briefly explored in relationship to small communities together with some pastoral challenges and approaches for implementing these communities.

THE COMMUNITARIAN NATURE OF THE CHURCH

Contemporary society places great emphasis on individualism. Scientific and technological advancements have isolated both families and individuals. In this individualistic culture the concept of community may be a very welcome one indeed.

We are called to community in various aspects of our lives, for example: family, the community in which we worship, the community in which we live, the global community, the communion of saints. Our consciousness has also been awakened to the community of nature as a primordial community. As we increasingly recognize the fragility of the ecosystems of the earth, we are called to realize more profoundly the communitarian nature of the church and the church's relationship to all of life.

A basic theme of the Second Vatican Council is the church as communion or people of God. The church, bound together by the indwelling of the Holy Spirit, strives to live the prayer of Jesus "so that they may be one, as we are one" (Jn 17:22). God dwells in community. The three persons of the Blessed Trinity are one God. The fullness of their union of infinite love is beyond our understanding. Jesus implied a similarity between the union of the three divine persons and the union of God's children when he prayed that prayer of unity at the last supper.

"In effect, this unity bestowed by the Holy Spirit does not merely consist in the gathering of people as a collection of individuals. It is a unity constituted by the bonds of the profession of faith, the sacraments and hierarchical communion. The faithful are *one* because, in the Spirit, they are in *communion* with the Son and, in him, share in his *communion* with the Father.... For the Catholic Church, then, the *communion* of Christians is none other than the manifestation in them of the grace by which God makes them sharers in his own *communion,* which is his eternal life" (John Paul II, May 1995, *Ut unum sint* 9).

Just as God shares his life, so human beings cannot find themselves fully except through a sincere gift of themselves. It is through self-giving, therefore, that communion with God and others is established. Sacred Scripture teaches that the love of God cannot be separated from the love of neighbor (*GS* 24).

The Second Vatican Council repeatedly emphasized this communitarian character of the church in its many dimensions. The various relationships of ecclesial communion include the following:

- individual members to God
- the whole ecclesial community to God
- each member to every other member
- each particular church to the universal church
- pastors and communities to their local bishops
- the bishops with the successor of Peter
- the universal church to the whole human race

Because the communitarian character of the church is partially immersed in mystery, it is impossible to grasp fully the significance of the concept of *communion*. Yet the call to live in communion is integral to human beings and to the church itself.

The community of the Trinity is not only the model of community but the source of grace, strength, faith, hope, and love that sustains and nurtures Christians in community. John Paul II in his address to the U.S. bishops (September 17, 1987) declared that the notion of *communion* was "at the heart of the church's self-understanding." This communion is "primarily a sharing through grace in the life of the Father given us through Christ and in the Holy Spirit." The church as a communion "is realized through the sacramental union with Christ and through organic participation in all that constitutes the divine and human reality of the church, the body of Christ which spans the centuries and is sent into the world to embrace all people without distinction."[3]

Community Expressed in Christian Initiation

The Christian community expresses its communitarian nature in diverse ways, but particularly through its worship. As the sacramental rites of the church were studied and reformulated following Vatican II, the communal nature of virtually every sacrament was stressed. The catechumenate was restored through the Rite of Christian Initiation of Adults (RCIA). This rite heralds a process for the spiritual journey of those inquiring into the faith, while also providing a paradigm of ongoing conversion for those already baptized. The catechumenate itself presupposes the presence of a vibrant faith community. The rite challenges the local parish to be witness to Christian community not only to those inquiring but also to those embracing the Catholic faith.

The small community is the ideal life-giving environment for the process of Christian initiation. Inquirers and those seeking entrance into our faith can do so, not in isolation, but within a community of believers. Some parishes have small Christian communities that welcome into their midst those inquiring about the faith. As part of their ministry, they are prepared to respond to inquirers and encourage them in their faith journey. Individual small communities can help the inquirers, candidates, catechumens and newly baptized or confirmed go through the various steps and stages of the Rite of Christian Initiation of Adults or whole small communities can help in each of these steps. Small communities have the capacity, therefore, to support every step of the catechumen's journey. They thus enable the realization of the major aims of the Rite of Christian Initiation of Adults: evangelization, catechesis, spiritual enlightenment, initiation, deepening of the neophyte's sacramental life, and continuing conversion. In the Nigerian dioceses of Kano, Idah, and Ibadan, small Christian communities support catechumens who annually enter the church by the hundreds. They have discovered that the most feasible way to engage the large numbers is through small faith-sharing communities that continue to support the neophytes well beyond their initiation into the church. This process might well relieve the anxieties of one U.S. bishop, who, reflecting upon the catechumenate, remarked, "We know that people are coming in the front door, but is anyone watching the back door?" (For further development on the Rite of Christian Initiation of Adults and small communities see Chapter 13.)

Leaders Speak of the Significance of Community

Various theologians and pastoral leaders have noted how Christians are coming to a new awareness of the communitarian nature of the church and are seeking to express this more concretely in family life and small communities.

The American bishops in their document *Called and Gifted for the Third Millennium* speak of the growth of small Christian communities as a "new and promising development."

> Small Church communities not only foster the faith of individuals, they are living cells which build up the body of Christ. They are to be signs and instruments of unity. As basic units of the parish, they serve to increase the corporate life and mission of the parish by sharing in its life, generously, with their talents and support.[4]

Small Church communities reinforce the communitarian nature of the church according to *Communion and Mission: A Guide for Bishops and Pastoral Agents on Small Church Communities.*

The essence of church life in the Christian community is to become one with the Trinity through communion with one another. Living in community is to live in communion with the triune God. God is present where there is authentic communion. A life of communion and love with our brothers and sisters is the path to divine life.[5]

The Vatican Secretariat for Christian Unity has identified a host of depersonalizing structures, forms of alienation, needs and aspirations that are seemingly not being met in the mainline churches. These factors seem to indicate why some people are joining sects and religious movements. To counteract such a trend, the Secretariat suggests positive pastoral approaches for spiritual and ecclesial renewal. First and foremost is a developing sense of community. The Secretariat's document that addresses these challenges lists a wide variety of small communities that could be part of the parish community system: caring communities of lively faith, hope, and love where people feel warmth, acceptance, understanding, reconciliation, fellowship; celebrating and praying communities; missionary communities that are outgoing and witnessing; supportive communities for those who have special problems.[6]

When bishops and pastors and other pastoral leaders urge the development of parish-based small Christian communities, they recognize the value that small communities have in building up the parish, the larger church, and the wider society. When small communities are connected to the parish under the guidance of the pastors and bishops they have the capacity to enliven the church in its worship and in its mission of proclaiming the reign of God.

RENEWED FOCUS ON THE WORD OF GOD

Too often in the past "Catholicism tended to become the church of law and sacraments rather than the church of the gospel and the Word. Catholics too often neglected the spiritual riches contained in the Bible. Emphasizing the precepts of the church they allowed the proclamation of the good news to fall into some neglect."[7]

The impact of the Second Vatican Council together with the scriptural studies encouraged by Pius XII focused renewed attention on the Word of God.

- In 1943 Pope Pius XII encouraged the church to promote biblical study and renewal in his document *Divino Afflante Spiritu.*
- The Vatican II document, *Dogmatic Constitution on Divine Revelation* (*Dei Verbum*) strongly recommended the use of Scripture by all Catholics. "Easy access to sacred Scripture," it stated, "should be provided for all the Christian faithful" (*DV* 22). It also clearly stated that the magisterium, the living and teaching office of the church, has the task of giving an authentic interpretation of the Word of God, whether in its written form of Scripture or in the form of tradition (*DV* 10).
- In addition, the council urged frequent reading of the Scriptures accompanied by prayer (*DV* 25): "Just as the life of the Church grows through persistent participation in the eucharistic mystery, so we may hope for a new surge of spiritual vitality from intensified veneration for God's word, which 'lasts forever'" (*DV* 26). Praying or studying the Scriptures can help Christians come to new realizations about their own lives in light of the Word of God. Doing all of this in a community of believers can enliven faith as Christians discover together the truth that God chooses to reveal.
- The *Dogmatic Constitution on the Church* (*Lumen gentium*) spoke of church as a people made one with the unity of the Father, Son, and Holy Spirit. The text used predominantly scriptural images in describing this reality (temple, body, people). As the faithful began to be in touch with their Christian roots through Scripture study and sharing, they discovered, many for the first time, a fresh view of church as the early Christians experienced it.
- Many came to realize through their reflection on Scripture, their studying the social teachings of the church and their reading the signs of the times that the church's mission was not exclusively a "religious one, aimed at preparing individuals through faith, worship and right behavior to attain eternal life."[8] It sought as well right

relationships, justice, and human liberation through the Spirit of Jesus.

- Paul VI expanded this understanding of salvation in *On Evangelization in the Modern World (Evangelii Nuntiandi)* to include the intra-historical liberation of all people, on personal, interpersonal, and social levels.

Scriptures Form and Motivate

When the centrality of the Scriptures is emphasized in the ongoing formation of small communities, a gospel vision emerges and becomes the motivating life force for small community members. An example of how the centrality of the Scriptures helps to form people is revealed in Monique's story.

> A member of the San Egidio community in Rome for more than ten years, Monique commented on the value of the community for her. "Before I became a member of this community," she said, "I never knew the gospels, I never knew I could help the poor. Since I became a member I learned to love the gospels, to know and love Jesus, and how to help the poor." Monique works part time as a researcher and spends several hours each day teaching poor children. The gospels became the motivating life force for Monique and many others in her community.

Small communities, then, offer their members the possibility—under the guidance of the pastor and other pastoral leaders—of paying attention to the Word of God in a new way so as to apply gospel values in creating a better society. Thus when small community members participate in the liberation of people—whether that be on a personal, interpersonal, or social level—they become active witnesses to the Word of God. They participate in the evangelizing mission of the church; in truth, they participate in evangelizing the culture itself.

Let us look more closely at some aspects of the social mission of the church and how small communities can support parishioners as they become aware of and respond to the social mission of the church today.

THE SOCIAL MISSION OF THE CHURCH

For more than one hundred years the social mission of the church has been highlighted, beginning with the encyclicals of Pope Leo XIII and Pope Pius XI. In the practical order, these messages are reaching people on an everyday level. The fact that the U.S. bishops made statements in highly sensitive areas such as nuclear disarmament and economics exemplifies the church's belief that the gospel message must be connected to real issues.

Let us simply highlight some of the statements relating to the social mission of the church since Vatican II and then show how the parish—through small communities—can help people connect these statements to the real issues of life.

- John XXIII and Vatican II stated that the work of peace and justice is a requirement of the church's mission to carry on the ministry of Jesus. Both saw the social mission of the church as an implementation of the gospel.
- The *Pastoral Constitution on the Church in the Modern World* (*Gaudium et spes*) developed Catholic social teaching begun by Leo XIII and Pius XI. This work considered extraordinarily broad spheres of interest: the dignity of human persons, the proper development of culture, socio-economic life, the life of the political community, the fostering of peace, and the promotion of a community of nations.
- Paul VI gave added impetus to the social ministry of the church in his encyclical *On the Development of Peoples* (1967).
- The bishops of the church in the synod document on *Justice in the World* (1971) boldly asserted that the struggle for social justice and the transformation of society were constitutive elements of preaching the gospel.
- Sensitive to the council's mandate to discern the signs of the times in light of the gospel (*GS* 4), the popes and episcopal conferences have increasingly spoken on matters of public policy. "The preferential option for the poor" that was first expressed by the Latin American bishops has become a part of the consciousness of many Christians around the world.

- Pope John Paul II, in his encyclical letter *On Social Concern of the Church* (*Sollicitudo rei socialis*), calls all women and men—and especially leaders—to a profound transformation in their accustomed ways of thinking and acting.

Thus one would hope that all those who, to some degree or other, are responsible for ensuring a "more human life" for their fellow human beings, whether or not they are inspired by religious faith, will become fully aware of the urgent need to change the spiritual attitudes that define each individual's relationship with self, with neighbor, with even the remotest human communities and with nature itself; and all of this in view of higher values such as the *common good* or, to quote the felicitous expression of the encyclical *Populorum Progressio,* the full development "of the whole individual and of all people."[9]

Small Communities Highlight Social Mission

Since the full acceptance of the social implications of Christianity requires faith and personal conversion, opportunities that help people to deepen faith and be open to conversion are necessary.

The parish needs to provide an environment for ongoing conversion to this "constitutive dimension" of the gospel spoken of by the bishops:

Actions on behalf of justice and participation in the transformation of the world fully appear to us as a constitutive dimension of the preaching of the Gospel, or, in other words, of the Church's mission for the redemption of the human race and its liberation from every oppressive situation.[10]

Parishioners need to continually study the social teachings of the church so that they may be challenged by their message. In this way they can encourage one another to look at the hard questions of their lives and lifestyles in light of the church's social teachings and the gospel.

One of the most acceptable and effective ways of meeting people where they are and then helping them to grow is to provide parish-based, supportive small communities. It is here that people can study social issues and the social teachings of the church, where they can speak honestly to one another, where they can pray over these social concerns issues.

Believers in the gospel message are called to be counter-cultural in many ways, e.g., by striving to live a more simple lifestyle, by choosing and supporting appropriate entertainment, by trying to avoid violent language and actions, etc. By being authentic and truthful, they can call others to be counter-cultural. Where bonds of caring and trust are established among people in small communities, it is much easier to be honest about one's life and lifestyles and to speak freely about unjust systems and structures.

Small Christian communities can provide opportunities for parishioners to be open to conversion and to reflect upon how their lifestyle may impact upon others. Through study, reflection and discussion on the social teachings of the church, small community participants can apply the message and meaning of these teachings to their lives and society. Through mutual support and sensitive challenging, they can be encouraged to act on this message. The small community setting then offers a place for them to return in order to reflect upon their action. In summary, small Christian communities can support and empower parishioners as they become aware of and respond to the challenging social mission of the church today.

In order to facilitate small Christian communities' prayer, study, reflection, and action on the social mission of the church, RENEW International has initiated the IMPACT Series that aims to connect faith to a wide range of human and world issues. Among the topics included are interracial harmony, hunger, nonviolence, strengthening family life, the world of work, civic responsibility, and ecology.

Indeed the social teachings of the church and renewed attention to the Word of God have broadened our understanding of the mission of Jesus and, therefore, of the church. That mission is proclaiming in word and deed the reign of God, that is, God's redeeming and liberating action, reconciling and freeing humankind through the presence of the Spirit of Jesus.

RENEW PROMPTS GROWTH OF SMALL GROUPS

Many creative pastoral approaches have been developed since Vatican II to bring life to the mission of Jesus. Notable among these are RENEW and RENEW 2000, and RENEW: Spiritual Renewal for the 21st Century, processes designed to deepen the spirituality of the entire parish. One vital component of the RENEW process is small-group faith sharing in parish life. Rev. Philip J. Murnion, director of the National Pastoral Life Center, while indicating the many benefits that RENEW has made to the parish and diocesan church, highlights the small group experience. He states

> The value of RENEW seems to be that it touches on critical issues (personal faith, family, liturgy, social justice), provides for both parish-wide focus and small group reflection, offers training for everyone taking any leadership position and provides helpful material with many options. The small group experience has been the strongest feature, attracting about 40,000 people in Newark's parishes, some few thousand of whom had been uninvolved in church life. Imagine 40,000 people discussing justice!
>
> The participating parish is left at the end of the three-year program with newly trained leaders, new structures (small groups) and a renewed sense among the people of being a community of faith and church.[11]

This Newark experience of RENEW has been repeated in more than 130 dioceses in the United States and another 130 worldwide. The experience of these dioceses participating in RENEW revealed common interest in small groups. Diocesan and parish evaluations consistently register highest satisfaction and success with the parish small-group experience. More than five million people in over 13,000 parishes have already participated in RENEW small groups. It is significant for today's church that so many people are opting for this experience. The evaluations of these participants reveal emerging pastoral approaches that are meaningful for our church today. The knowledge gained from this widespread experience of renewal in many countries moves us to speak of the value of small communities. It also impels us to greater pastoral responsibility in fostering a responsible course of action for the continued development of small faith communities as a regular ongoing part of parish life.

SUMMARY

Thus far, we have looked at some of the socio-historical aspects of the growth of small communities in Chapter 1 and some of the theological and pastoral approaches that have occurred since Vatican II in this present chapter. Viewed together, these aspects and challenges offer many insights for the renewal of our church today.

We have seen that the increased development of small Christian communities can be a valuable, effective response to the needs of our day. Christians need one another to bond together in mutual love and support of gospel living. The Spirit of God is bringing about just such connections all over the world; small groups of people are coming together to share faith and life in small communities. These experiences allow individuals to come to know and love God more deeply and know one another's struggles and joys as they share and pray together. They find it easier to cope with an often confusing existence when their questions, anxieties, and burdens of life are shared with other believers. Scripture comes alive as the Word speaks to their lives.

In small communities, people are free to speak about Jesus and about their faith. They gain courage to share their faith stories and witness to what the Spirit has done in their lives. Thus they are evangelized. In reaching out to serve a needy world, they themselves become evangelizers proclaiming the good news to others. Through this cyclical process they learn more about the faith they profess. For "social action . . . cannot be completed without evangelization. Evangelization conversely will always have a certain impact upon social structures."[12]

The emergence of small Christian communities affirms clearly the vitality of the Catholic Church to adapt and to renew itself. Experience bears witness to the fact that in and through small communities people grow in living authentic Christian lives. In order to demonstrate the value of small communities one story has been chosen. This true story illustrates how participation in a small faith community changed the life of one couple and how that couple has changed the lives of many others and helped to transform one segment of society.

Mary and John's Story

Mary and John have been in small communities for most of their married life. They were leader couple for the Christian Family Movement (CFM) in their parish in Chicago and then later in Ridgewood, New Jersey. They were also leaders in charismatic renewal groups. The couple were faithful Catholics, but they knew they were called to more. Mary and John had lived in an affluent suburb of northern New Jersey. As parents of five children, they reached a point where four of their five children were independent—the fifth was a senior in college.

Mary and John had a history of some social concern involvements. While living in the south they tutored in a literacy program for adults. In their parish they had active leadership positions on the social concerns committee, and participated in "Bread for the World" and other activities. Motivated by these activities and especially sparked by their small group experience in RENEW, Mary and John realized they were called to live their faith by making a fuller commitment to the values of the gospel.

John, managing a sales firm of 500, had highly developed organizational skills. He requested a part-time sabbatical from his company so that he could devote more time to his justice involvements. A particular attraction was the diocesan office that concentrated on developing parish social concerns efforts. John realized his skills could be used in the efforts of the office to build a network of people throughout the diocese who would facilitate parish social concerns committees. John volunteered his two-day-a-week sabbatical to this work. Mary became a volunteer facilitator. Commitment and conviction grew. Eventually Mary and John arrived at a monumental decision. They were ready to scale down their lifestyle and deepen their social involvement. John went to work for the social concerns office with a drastic cut in salary. They moved into an integrated urban neighborhood.

For the next four years, John and Mary worked on helping urban and suburban parishes reflect on the Scriptures and social justice, educated them on issues and organization, and empowered them to address social needs and injustices. Their efforts and lives were sustained by the small communities, which enabled them to do all of this.

John's contacts made him increasingly aware of the disastrous effects of unemployment among the urban poor. Again, John recognized how he could utilize his skills. Through Mary's support and ongoing reflection, prayer, and assessment with others, John opened an employment agency in Newark, New Jersey, one of the poorest cities in the nation. For eight years John and Mary offered hope as they helped thousands of urban job seekers find employment each year.

John and Mary's story and the preceding cursory examination of the socio-historical, theological, and pastoral aspects of small communities reveal many values that small communities help to develop. The common thread woven throughout these values is spirituality. In pastoral terms the greatest values of small Christian communities are the interior growth that takes place in them and the outreach or missionary work that that growth inspires. In today's society, small communities present a wonderful opportunity to address the spiritual hungers of people and challenge them to live fully the gospel. It is particularly because of these values that we encourage and promote small Christian communities with such vigor. The following chapter will further explore in realistic pastoral terms spirituality, the cornerstone of small Christian communities.

---

† † † † † REFLECTION AND FAITH-SHARING QUESTIONS

Reflect on John 17:18-23.

1. How have I felt God call me to some form of church ministry or social action?
2. In what area am I most challenged to live out the social teachings of the church?
3. What gospel stories do I remember best because they have touched my heart?
4. Who has touched me most by their carrying out the social mission of the church?
5. When have I had a personal experience of membership in a community?

3. Spirituality: The Cornerstone of Small Christian Communities

Ansgar Holmberg csj

There is little doubt that throughout the world today there is great interest in small communities. That is not to say that the enthusiasm for small communities means they will come about easily. Marriage is an age-old institution, quite universally accepted, and yet happy marriages are achieved only with great effort. Like marriage, small communities involve the inter-relationship of people. We have strong human desires for unity and love. On the other hand, we have the human foibles of jealousy, competition, and insecurity that tend to make real community something for which we must strive.

St. Paul recognized our human nature in many of his letters.

As God's chosen ones, holy and beloved, clothe yourselves with compassion, kindness, humility, meekness, and patience. Bear with one another and, if anyone has a complaint against another, forgive each other; just as the Lord has forgiven you, so you also must forgive. Above all, clothe yourselves with love, which binds everything together in perfect harmony. And let the peace of Christ rule in your hearts, to which indeed you were called in the one body (Col 3:12–15).

A faith-filled Christian is a person of great hope. We believe that by God's gracious action in our lives we are able to overcome our human weaknesses to the point of strong relational bonds and real community. Therefore in our quest to develop small Christian communities, we wish to acknowledge a dependency on God's grace and the primacy of spiritual development to achieve this desired goal. Precisely for this reason, we consider basic spiritual realities upon which our small community efforts must be founded.

An interesting juxtaposition is seen in that a well-balanced spirituality is necessary to achieve community, while efforts to build small communities result in a well-balanced spirituality. A strong emphasis of the spiritual and a quest for deeper union with God are necessary to arrive at true Christian community. At the same time, efforts made in developing small Christian communities offer a unique opportunity for the church in helping many more people to grow spiritually and achieve holiness.

Our focus on spirituality will keep in mind these dual aims: the development of small communities with a solid spiritual base and small communities as a means of great spiritual enrichment for the body of the church.

HOLINESS

What does it mean to be holy? To be holy is to be like God, to live in conformity to God's life and will, to have heart and mind and will in harmony with God. This is the meaning of the passage: "For I am the LORD your God; sanctify yourselves therefore, and be holy, for I am holy" (Lev 11:44). "The call of every Christian to a life of holiness is a call to live one's life, in whatever situation one finds oneself, according to the spirit of Christ."[1]

Paul's second letter to Timothy reveals God's intention in this call.

> God "saved us and called us with a holy calling, not according to our works but according to his own purpose and grace. This grace was given to us in Christ Jesus before the ages began, but it has now been revealed through the appearing of our Savior Christ Jesus" (2 Tim 1:9–10).

All Are Called to Holiness

Vatican Council II issued a strong call to holiness for all the baptized: "All the faithful of Christ of whatever rank or status are called to the fullness of the Christian life and to the perfection of charity" (*LG* 40). The vocation to holiness then is the vocation to perfection in love. Jesus himself has told us we must be made perfect as God is perfect (Mt 5:48). "All of Christ's followers, therefore, are invited and bound to pursue holiness and the perfect fulfillment of their proper state" (*LG* 42).

Our call to holiness is not only an individual call, but a call to be part of the Christian community seeking holiness. All that is said, therefore, with regard to living out this call applies both to individuals in their own personal lives and to their participation in the various communities to which they belong.

Practically speaking, how is this universal call to holiness conveyed? How do large numbers of people experience that they are personally called to be holy? How is this call to holiness effectively translated in the lives of "grassroots" parishioners? Many are finding that this happens best in smaller more personal settings where people can reflect on the life of faith together. Small Christian communities provide an effective way for inviting large numbers of parishioners to understand and to experience the grace of holiness in their own lives. In this way, they better enable the church to realize more fully a universal call to holiness.

A Way of Seeking Holiness

Spirituality is a stance out of which a person lives and acts and prays. It is a way of expressing one's relationship to God, to others, to the whole of creation, including one's relationship to oneself. Spirituality can be defined as the efforts of a person to recognize, acknowledge, and respond to God's loving action in one's life.

Christian spirituality encompasses each of the above-mentioned aspects but stresses a relationship with the three persons of the Trinity and embodies all that Christianity teaches.

God then is the central focus of a spiritual life. For Christians the spiritual life focuses on God as revealed in the person of Jesus Christ. Acceptance of and commitment to Jesus Christ then are at the heart of Christian spirituality. Being open to God's grace, being in dialogue and communion with God through Jesus, and responding to God's grace and Word through the action of our lives are all part of a Christian spirituality.

INTEGRATED SPIRITUALITY

Today there is greater emphasis on an integrated or holistic Christian spirituality. It is based on the life of our Trinitarian God who dwells in community and indwells each of us. It invites us to a more personal intimate union with Jesus Christ.

"Spiritual progress tends toward ever a more personal, intimate union with Christ. This union is called 'mystical' because it participates in the mystery of Christ through the sacraments—'the holy mysteries'—and, in him, in the mystery of the Holy Trinity."[2]

The lives of the saints and the teachings of the church indicate clearly to us that developing an intimate personal relationship with Jesus is the heart of Christian spirituality.

A Special Intimacy with Jesus—The Paschal Mystery

Because Jesus became incarnate, the inherent basis of Christian spirituality is an entering into and living of the Paschal Mystery—the life, death, and Resurrection of Jesus. Baptism incorporates us into the community of the church; therefore we are involved in a communal spirituality that embraces the whole tradition of the church and is especially nurtured through its sacramental life. In baptism, we die with Christ and rise again to newness of life in him. The other sacraments nourish and strengthen our relationship with Christ. We strive to live and love as Jesus did and to incarnate the Spirit of Jesus in our lives.

Through his sufferings and death, Christ saved us from sin and set us free (Col 1:14). Through his total self-giving, Christ invites us to repentance and resurrection to be freed from the slavery of personal and social sin and to rise to new life with him. Christ challenges us to enter completely into his life, suffering, death, and Resurrection so that we may experience the power flowing from his Resurrection.

Paul's response to this invitation reveals his own understanding of the Paschal Mystery:

> . . . to know Christ and the power of his resurrection and the sharing of his sufferings by becoming like him in his death, if somehow I may attain the resurrection from the dead (Phil 3:10-11).

Entering into the Paschal Mystery calls us to a special intimacy with Jesus and invites us to share that same marvelous intimacy that he shares with the Father (Jn 14:23). One condition for sharing that intimacy and demonstrating our love is obeying the commandments (Jn 14:15). On the one hand, we cannot keep the commandments and moral teachings of Jesus as spelled out and applied over time by the church except through the saving power of God. On the other hand, we cannot fully experience the saving power of God without really living the moral life to which God calls us. Recognizing this paradox is critical for understanding Christian spirituality.

Jesus changed the whole course of human history. He freed us from enslavement to sin; he taught us the paradox of gaining life through death. "Unless a grain of wheat falls into the earth and dies, it remains just a single grain" (Jn 12:24). But if it seemingly dies, it bears new life and much fruit. The surrendering of ourselves to Jesus is absolutely essential if our lives are to bear fruit.

Small Communities and the Paschal Mystery

Small communities are uniquely suited to help people reflect on the Paschal Mystery and to incorporate aspects of this mystery into their lives. The sharing in Jesus' life, suffering, death, and Resurrection can take many forms. Let us consider several of these in relationship to small communities.

In small communities, people are able to look at their lives as if looking in a mirror. They can speak of their values and their approaches to life in light of the gospel with other people of good will who are seeking to live Christian lives. Frequently in these circumstances people are reached more profoundly than through either a teaching or a homily because they come to a self-awareness of the discrepancies between their own lives and what the gospel calls for. This need not apply only to inconsistencies in areas of personal morality, but also in areas of social morality, e.g., issues of racism or prejudice. Perhaps only in the gentle but conscientious approach used in a small-group setting, will people allow themselves to be confronted with such issues.

The small Christian community is admirably designed to help people reflect on the mysteries of Jesus' life. As people reflect, share, make application to their own lives, and believe deeply in what Jesus did in his life, they come to a richer appreciation and realization of the power of the cross and the meaning of his mission.

Small communities ideally help people to live in the power of the Spirit by choosing freedom and liberation from sin. As they die to their sinfulness and live in ever greater fidelity to the commandments and moral teachings, they come nearer to experiencing the fullness of the power of the Spirit.

Jesus' total self-giving is not a point simply to be taught. It must become a part of our lived experience. The gospel message and our shared response to the gospel in small communities challenge us likewise to die to ourselves, to surrender ourselves completely, and to commit ourselves without reservation to Jesus and his way of life. This commitment affects every aspect of our lives and calls us to greater responsibility in the works of charity and justice.

This total commitment also opens us to the power and gifts of the Holy Spirit. In community we discover and discern how to use the gifts of the Holy Spirit in meeting the needs of society. If we live the Christ-life, just as Jesus did, we can change the course of human history.

Created Whole and Holy

Jesus often tells us that we are created in the image of God, whole and holy. He calls us to see our lives as whole and holy. We seek wholeness and holiness in every aspect of our lives: physical, mental, emotional, spiritual, intellectual, and relational.

Being whole means accepting and loving ourselves unconditionally as we have been accepted and loved by God. As we integrate all aspects of our lives, we discover God in the ordinary as well as in the extraordinary and sacramental moments of our lives.

Our prayer, too, is less compartmentalized. We bring to prayer the very real parts of our lives—be they messy or good.

As persons who strive to live in the holiness of God, we embrace all aspects of God's life and work: creation, redemption, sanctification. We share in God's work by being creative with our gifts, by reconciling and healing, and by reverencing all of God's people and all of creation as holy. It is within our families and communities and within our work and leisure that we both discover God and express our creativity with God.

Relationships and the Reign of God

Throughout his life Jesus proclaimed the reign of God, described its characteristics in the parables he told, and gave witness to the inbreaking of God's reign through his miracles. As we meet and grow through small faith-sharing communities, the relational aspects of the reign of God are more easily recognized in our lives. Jesus showed us that a radically new relationship is possible between God and humans and among human beings themselves. It is a relationship of integrity, wholeness, and freedom from fear and anxiety. It is a relationship of justice and peace. It is a reconciled people living in harmony. It is the reign of God that touches all of life.

Conversion of Mind and Heart

Following Jesus in the power of the Spirit requires a conversion of heart and mind. Something marvelous and spontaneous happens when we totally surrender ourselves to the will of God and openly call upon the Holy Spirit for direction. It is similar to the "Fiat" of Mary. From that first "yes," the course of the human family is and will be forever changed. Imitating Mary's "Fiat" in our own lives gives us what John Paul II refers to, in his Apostolic Letter *As the Third Millennium Draws Near,* "as the joy of conversion." As we live in this spontaneous joy, everything speaks of God.

This matter of conversion, starting within ourselves and affecting the totality of our lives and relationships, is the basis for anything that could be said about small Christian communities. Conversion is the heart of the matter of all that could be said throughout these pages.

Desiring an integrated spirituality, we seek to make our attitudes, our values, our behavior to be in accord with the call and the teaching of Jesus Christ. We gain strength to live this way through prayer, the sacramental life, and our commitment to community life.

The ever present reality of human sinfulness will demand the ongoing conversion of each of us and prevents a full experience of the reign of God until the end of time. Yet as we, who are empowered by the Spirit, struggle for integrity, compassion, and reconciliation, the reign of God will increasingly be experienced here and now in our personal lives, in community, and in the wider society. It appears that this kind of integrated spirituality is what the prophet Micah spoke of when he told us to act justly, love tenderly and walk humbly with God (Mic 6:8). Jesus built on Micah's teaching and called us to embody the Good News in all dimensions of our lives when he gave us the beatitudes as a way of life and urged us to love the least of our sisters and brothers.

Marked by a Sense of Mission

Christian spirituality is always marked by the sense of mission and the spirit of mission that Jesus embodied. This missionary dimension of spirituality embraces the areas of family, work, the economic and political order, ecumenism, and the ecological and social elements of our lives. Vatican II helped to broaden the understanding of Jesus' mission of proclaiming God's reign. Given the council's emphasis on scriptural foundations and on God's revelation in the events of everyday life, we are encouraged to relate our faith to the events and realities of life in a more integrated way.

Inner and Outer Life

Small communities should expand our horizons. Our quest to know and discover our God more intimately should bring us into the depths of the interior life. Discoveries in contemplation and a deeper union with God are breakthroughs that our restless modern spirits badly need. On the other hand, a clearer understanding of the mission of Jesus and the movement of the Holy Spirit in our hearts should propel us beyond the bonds of cultural Christianity into exciting new levels of outreach and ministry in our lives.

Growth inwardly and outwardly is the greatest challenge facing small Christian communities. It is imperative and absolutely necessary if small Christian communities are to become an acknowledged, valuable, and integral part of church life. Groups of people turned in on themselves and living in a comfort zone of self-concern do not deserve the name "community." The very nature of Christian community demands the outward thrust of mission.

Church documentation supports the vision of spirituality found in small communities. The *Dogmatic Constitution on the Church* encourages all the people of God to work in harmonious community. The *Pastoral Constitution on the Church in the Modern World* is very possibly the church's clearest teaching on the integration of all life and holistic spiritual responsibility. The post-conciliar document on the *Rite of Christian Initiation of Adults* challenges all Christians to see life as a continuing journey and conversion as a lifelong challenge. All of these documents find rich expression in the life and activities of small communities. Thus the spiritual vision of small communities is well rooted in the teaching of the church.

APPROACHES TO AN INTEGRATED SPIRITUALITY

Keeping in mind the interplay between well-formed small communities and the development of a healthy spirituality within the larger church through small communities, we will further explore some approaches to integrated spirituality. These include moving away from the privatization of spirituality and a concern over dualism, the healthy effects on a parish of a dynamic spiritual life cycle, and storytelling (faith sharing) in relation to small communities. We will conclude this section with a story and then relate how small communities can help people achieve the integrated experience of God that they seek.

From Privatization of Spirituality to Mission

Spirituality calls us to a mission that is broader than simply ministry or service within the parish. Joe Holland, a contemporary thinker who specializes in the relationship between theology and social theory, says that the Catholic laity are presently being formed by a privatized spirituality that does not allow them to connect their creative spiritual energy with public life.

> Privatization of spirituality means that spiritual consciousness is confined to the sphere of intimacy—self, family, friends, parish. It does not extend to the sphere of non-intimacy, that is to the public and technologically institutional structures of culture, politics, and economics. This is a typically American phenomenon, inevitably found in the American Catholic experience.[3]

Other observers of contemporary society corroborate this fact.[4] In essence they acknowledge that public life is one area that the Catholic laity find it most difficult both to relate their spiritual life and to draw nourishment for their spiritual life. Although the desire to reach out to secular society is present, laity frequently lack certainty about what this means or how they are to accomplish it.

Jesuit theologian Avery Dulles states that U.S. Catholic lay people still have an "immense" way to go to make their mark on society. In addition, he says, once-thriving Catholic apostolic groups seem to have been replaced since the 1960s by "more inward-looking organizations."[5]

John Paul II's *Apostolic Exhortation on the Laity* speaks of the need to address the continuing lack of impact on society from the Christian message. He seems hopeful when he speaks of "a new era of group endeavors of the lay faithful." Although these lay groups are very diverse from one another in various aspects,

> they all come together in an all-inclusive and profound convergence when viewed from the perspective of their common purpose, that is, the responsible participation of all of them in the church's mission of carrying forth the Gospel of Christ, the source of hope for humanity and the renewal of society.[6]

He elaborates how those who participate in movements, small groups, or communities can have a great impact on the transformation of society.

Catholic spirituality can be neither a flight from the world nor simply interior renewal. It must move beyond merely interior attitudes in order to break out of the prison of privatization and find expression in some aspect of transforming the world.

Dualism and Spirituality

The privatization of spirituality has been partially caused by the concept of dualism that has shaped some of our thinking and action. Perhaps at this juncture a brief consideration of the role of dualism in our past history will shed more light upon our consideration of spirituality.

To some extent, our concept of church, and consequently our concept of spirituality, has been influenced by the ancient dichotomy drawn between spirit and matter. Hellenistic thinking of the third and fourth centuries, which embraced a philosophy of Neoplatonism, adopted a two-world view of life. Body and soul were seen in great tension and basically at war with each other. The soul struggled throughout life to break through, to soar to the heavens, to live the superior life of the spirit. The spirituality arising from this basic dualism of body and spirit is characterized by flight from the body and the world.

A dualistic approach to spirituality can be seen in people who believe they are spiritual because they receive communion weekly yet whose business practices are questionable. When confronted about a particular unjust practice they may simply respond, "That's the way business is!" They fail to connect spirituality to daily events of life.

Today there is much movement away from this dualistic approach espoused for centuries and toward a one-world view of reality.

> In modern thought, there has been a shift towards a one-world view. There are two ways to get a one-world view. The first is to deny everything that used to be denominated as supernatural; then only one kind of reality is left. The second approach to a one-world view is to think of God and history as naturally related, naturally interconnected, mutually involved, and of temporal reality and human history as theater for the drama of redemption.[7]

The Vatican II document *Pastoral Constitution on the Church in the Modern World* fosters this one-world view when it speaks of church and the world as mutually related (*GS* 40). Yet because we have been conditioned through the years—through our culture, thinking, literature, and language—it is not always easy to move away from dualistic concepts. Being with others in small communities can help us integrate a one-world view into our way of thinking.

A DYNAMIC LIFE CYCLE

How can the one-world view of the *Pastoral Constitution on the Church in the Modern World* be effectively experienced in parish life? How can community be part of a dynamic life cycle for parishioners that will provide opportunities for spiritual growth? How does the weekly cycle affect the way people live? We propose a three-phase cycle.

1. Parishioners strive to live by Christian principles and values throughout the whole week, not just on Sundays.
2. Parishioners gather weekly in their respective small Christian communities. There they break open and reflect on the Word of God, and connect the Word with life. As people think through the implications of the Word and are strengthened by the community and the Scriptures, they come to new insight and resolutions about their lives. Growth in appreciation of the Scriptures in small communities during the week prepares the members to be more attentive and receptive to the Word as it is proclaimed at the Sunday liturgy. This preparation helps parishioners to listen more attentively to the homily that is intended to relate the Word of God to our lives.

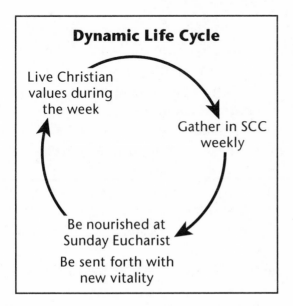

Dynamic Life Cycle

Live Christian values during the week

Gather in SCC weekly

Be nourished at Sunday Eucharist

Be sent forth with new vitality

3. Those in small communities then take all of the aspects of life that have been reflected on in their small community and bring it to the parish eucharistic celebration. There they are reminded that they are part of a universal church community where they intercede for one another. As they offer their lives at the sacrifice of the Mass they enter into union with the Lord who is made present in the eucharistic banquet. They are strengthened for mission and are sent forth to live that mission wherever they are called—in their family, their community, the larger church, the workplace, and the social arena.

The third part of the cycle, the eucharistic celebration, is essential because "The liturgy is the summit toward which the activity of the Church is directed; at the same time it is the fountain from which all its power flows" (*SC* 10).

Small community members grow in holiness through living out this weekly cycle of reflecting on their experience in the light of God's Word and bringing all of this to the eucharistic assembly. The renewed faith and the sense of mission that they have found through their small community experience enrich the larger community. The joy of the gospel finds its highest expression in the Eucharist. It is there that we celebrate what God has done for us in Christ Jesus.

All of us can help to enliven worship with the richness of our faith that has been strengthened in our small communities. All the members of the parish community gather around the altar of sacrifice. The priest presides for the parish family as the congregation worships the Triune God, who sanctifies them by Word and sacrament. We are both nourished and sent forth to nourish others through the celebration of the Eucharist. The eucharistic celebration truly has the capacity to shape and transform the entire community in all its beliefs and endeavors. It goes without saying then that the Eucharist also helps to shape and transform small Christian communities. Hence, the Sunday parish celebration of the Eucharist is the most significant gathering place for small Christian communities!

When this dynamic life cycle becomes part of people's lives the potential for spiritual growth increases. The liturgical renewal following Vatican II, which has made all liturgical rites more expressive, finds a rich pastoral complement in a small community's reflection on the Paschal Mystery. The small community members strengthen the larger gathering by their developing sense of commitment and mission. Their reflection on events of Jesus' death and Resurrection enables them to enter more fully into the rites. Through both reflection in small communities and participation in liturgical celebrations then, participants are drawn more closely into union with Christ and share more fully in the reality of the salvation offered through him. In turn, the rites speak more clearly to them and enable them to enter into the mysteries with deeper faith and to celebrate more wholeheartedly. An ongoing cycle occurs where faith is strengthened, lived out, and celebrated. Lent, Easter, Pentecost come alive!

STORYTELLING

Embracing the reign of God, facing the challenge of conversion, and launching out on our spiritual journeys are frequently made possible through the storytelling that small communities so beautifully foster.

When persons share faith stories and their parish respects and values these stories, both the individual and the parish community grow deeper in their faith life. In the large parish, there is often nowhere to tell the story of our faith journeys. Yet contemporary awareness has rediscovered the value and power of telling our stories and listening to others to interpret the meaning of our lives.

As we look at the concept of story in relationship to small Christian communities, we note certain elements:

- The gospels are narratives, the actual stories of Jesus as remembered by members of the early Christian communities. Every time small communities read the gospel they are reviewing the story of Jesus, reflecting on how it intersects with their lives.
- When we share our faith stories we are telling how God is acting in our lives. In the telling we may hear, perhaps for the first time, how

God is moving in our lives. It is often in the telling itself that we experience the Spirit's presence. This helps others see and believe in the God who is really at work in us.

- As we hear others talk about their lives we realize how God is present and acting in their lives.
- Not only do we hear the narrative of Jesus' life but we start to apply the Word to our lives today.
- As we listen to one another we have a sense of the Spirit acting in the community.

In all of these aspects we are trusting in Jesus' words, "For where two or three are gathered in my name, I am there among them" (Mt 18:20). We trust that Jesus is present and his story is being retold and applied to our lives. We might call this an immanent experience of God. Yet in the sharing of Scripture and life there is also a profound search for God—for the answer to the question, "Who is God?" The search for God that takes place in small Christian communities can lead to an experience of the transcendent God who dwells in mystery.

Storytelling Is Faith Sharing

Telling our faith stories or faith sharing, then, is being aware of or recalling a time, a life event, a situation, a word, a moment of grace when God touched our lives, challenged us, or spoke to us. God speaks to us in various ways: through the silence of our hearts, through the Word of God, through the sacraments, especially the Eucharist, through the presence, words or actions of another, or through nature.

Why do we share faith?

We share faith in order to

- recognize and take ownership of how God is acting in our lives
- reveal to others how God is at work in our lives, our world
- welcome and encourage the faith of others
- witness to divine mystery

- build up another
- lead us to conversion of heart

Faith sharing helps us to make connections with others and allows us to see and hear how sacred our lives are and how precious all life is. Our spirits are touched by someone else's story and this builds up our faith, hope and/or love.

What Does Faith Sharing Require?

Since God leads each of us on our spiritual journey, faith sharing requires that we be open to the presence of God in our lives and in others' lives. We are challenged to see with new eyes, to hear with new ears, to feel with a new heart, to be touched in the depths of our being by a God who is love and who wants to reach us in diverse ways, to permeate every fiber of our being.

Faith sharing is enhanced by revealing how a particular word of Scripture speaks to us at this particular time in our lives. Sometimes being in touch with an aspect of God's creation—another person, the ocean, the wind, the trees, the mountains—gives us an experience of God or draws us to reflect upon God's grandeur, beauty, majesty, diversity.

The Emmaus Story as Paradigm for SCCs

Here is a brief paraphrase of the Emmaus story (Lk 24:13–35), a favorite Scripture story for small community members.

Two disciples walking along the road to Emmaus sharing a life experience (storytelling) were joined by a "stranger." The stranger chides them, "Oh how foolish you are," and starts to unfold the meaning of the Scriptures beginning with Moses and the prophets. In the telling, the disciples are captivated by this stranger and invite him to share a meal. As they eat supper, they recognize Jesus in the breaking of bread. But he vanishes. They remember! They recall: "Were not our hearts burning within us while he was talking to us on the road, while he was opening the Scriptures to us?" They get up immediately and return to Jerusalem to tell the Good News—a new story of God with them. They go back to the larger community to share the marvelous events that had happened to them in their small community.

Parallel dynamics occur in small communities. In sharing a life experience, in telling our faith stories, we are joined by Jesus present in the community and in the Word. The meaning of our faith lives unfolds as we break open the Scriptures with others in small community. These events are then celebrated when we gather with the larger community at Sunday Eucharist.

We recognize the presence of God in our midst. We dialogue and pray and our hearts are changed—never to be the same again. And because we cannot contain the new story of God acting in our lives, we reach out and give witness to our families and the wider community. We have a sense of being on mission! The God story seeks release and must be told in and through us!

The New Zealand Story

Many people are searching for meaning in their lives. They seek God and desire to be holy. They desire an integration of faith in their daily lives.

Consider the following story that illustrates this point:

Father Tom was working with RENEW in New Zealand. In flying from one island to another he was expectantly awaiting the beautiful view of Mount Cook. A flight attendant began to speak with him and in the course of conversation said, "I used to be Catholic myself—now I belong to a non-denominational, fundamentalist group." He then related how his seven sisters and brothers, who had all gone to Catholic schools, had also left the church.

The inquisitive young man asked the reason for the priest's travels. Realizing time was of the essence, Father Tom outlined five key aspects of the RENEW work he was engaged in. He shared that through the small communities RENEW promoted, people came to know Jesus personally. They reflected upon Scripture and came to a deeper appreciation of the Word of God. They were finding it easier to pray and to share prayer with others. Through small communities people felt a sense of belonging and mutual support. Finally, in these communities they were able to connect their faith to their daily life. When the flight attendant heard this he exclaimed, "It's too bad we didn't have this a long time ago. I'd still be a Roman Catholic myself."

The flight attendant's response is all too typical. On the six continents in which we have worked we meet people who are looking for more than an intellectual understanding of their faith. They are looking for the place where they can best experience God. The Catholic Church offers a rich means for spiritual growth and of experiencing God through the sacraments, especially the Eucharist, and through teaching and guidance in the tradition of our Catholic heritage. Complementing these can be the ways of experiencing God that so attracted the young flight attendant

- strong emphasis on Scripture
- personal relationship with Jesus
- deeper prayer life
- connecting faith to life
- and a more intimate sense of community

Small Christian communities wonderfully promote and bolster each of these practices.

No matter how many times the flight attendant's story is told, people nod in agreement. The experience of countless families seems to verify the reality of this story. These five above-mentioned aspects contained in RENEW resonate with their deepest heart wishes. Perhaps the small communities forming all over the world are the Spirit's way of showing us how to help people experience God more fully, how to be holy, how to live a more integrated spirituality.

In our existential society, parish life can be strengthened by offering a strong experience of God through small Christian communities. Integrating the richness of the Catholic tradition with small Christian communities offers a long-term path to spiritual growth for parishioners. It is precisely because God's presence and power can be dynamically experienced in small communities that we promote these communities with such enthusiasm in this book.

CONTEMPORARY EXPRESSIONS OF SPIRITUALITY

Different social and historical situations call for different expressions of spirituality, and Christians today are experiencing new forms of prayer and action. In small communities participants have the opportunity to study and reflect upon these. In so doing, some of their own understandings may be challenged and broadened.

Expressions of spirituality today reflect people's needs as well as their developing levels of awareness. Included among these expressions are the recognition of the connections between each person's relationship with the Trinity, with other persons, and with all creation. Made in the image of God, we have the unique gift of being open to personal relationships, open to God. It is our personal awareness of ourselves that enables us to relate to other human beings and to God in a personal way.

Pope John Paul II helps us to see that the call by God to respect and reverence the earth is a strong teaching of our faith. "It is the *ecological question*—ranging from the preservation of the natural habitats of the different species of animals and of other forms of life to 'human ecology' properly speaking—which finds in the Bible clear and strong ethical direction, leading to a solution which respects the great good of life, of every life."[8]

With this new awareness we might choose a simpler lifestyle. We might have a better sense of collective responsibility to the planet and the human community. We do well to keep in mind John Paul II's hope that we will change our "spiritual attitudes that define each individual's relationship with self, with neighbor, with even the remotest human communities and with nature itself."[9]

We attempt to cooperate with God's creative providence in our world as we understand our response through contemporary expressions of spirituality and through ecological, social, political, ecumenical and ecclesial concerns and activities. The more we strive to cooperate with God, the less temptation there will be to privatize our spirituality. Otherwise, our church, our earth, our society will be impoverished. It appears that the task of pastoral leaders is to help parishioners to discover the revelation of God in family, work, leisure, in areas of social responsibility, in all of creation.

BEYOND A PRIVATIZED SPIRITUALITY

The type of holistic spirituality that small Christian communities are capable of nurturing has a clear ecclesial dimension. In his Post-Synodal Apostolic Exhortation, *The Lay Members of Christ's Faithful People*, Pope John Paul II quotes the Synod Fathers who say that local ecclesial authorities ought to foster "small basic or so-called 'living' communities, where the faithful can communicate the Word of God and express it in service and love to one another; these communities are true expressions of ecclesial communion and centers of evangelization, in communion with their pastors" (*Christifideles Laici*, 26). The spirituality of small Christian communities is integrally connected to all facets of life from the domestic church to the larger church, from the marketplace to the broader society.

Because community intrinsically includes mission, small communities move beyond a self-nurturing social type of group. Mission is never an addendum but is well integrated into the life of the community members.

Through involvement in small Christian communities people have the experience of a healing, reconciling, evangelizing, challenging community and thus are helped to envision the potential for such a communal dynamic in the wider society. Moved by the Spirit, small Christian communities reflect on the Scriptures and come to understand the breadth of the applications of God's Word. When people authentically share the Scriptures, they see the implications not only for their personal lives but for the wider society as well. Therefore, they are led out of a privatized spirituality into a spirituality which embraces all of creation.

Through small communities parishioners can challenge each other to die to self and be co-creators with God as they struggle to build economic, political, and social systems that uphold the dignity of all human beings. They can express their creativity as they become more in touch with the evolutionary study of our universe, particularly our earth, and work to make it and keep it ecologically safe for ourselves and our children. They can be reconcilers and healers in bringing the wisdom, justice, and love of God into play in every area of their lives. In all of this, they can discover and experience God in their relationships, in their worship and work, in all of creation!

PASTORAL QUESTIONS

Two significant questions arise. First, is this not the Catholic moment for the church to actively promote evangelization and mission in small communities within the context of church life? This deserves careful thought given the points of value for small Christian communities from historical, sociological, theological, and pastoral considerations (mentioned in the previous chapters) and from the fact that people around the world are turning to small communities.

Second, cannot the church seize this moment and offer leadership and motivation for parishioners to gather in small Christian communities, thus meeting many of their spiritual and human needs? By promoting small communities the church has a tremendous opportunity of offering the fullness of the spiritual life to its people who in turn can offer that life through evangelization to the whole living community.

Small Christian communities are an outstanding means of spiritual renewal and evangelization. These goals must always be kept primary if they are to achieve their full potential. Moreover small communities are promoted in this book as part of the very mainstream of the Catholic Church. We propose that small communities be at the heart of church life, that they become an integral, ongoing part of parish life. With the renewal of the church and the new evangelization as pastoral priorities, the healthy development of parish-based small communities is suggested as a means of that renewal and evangelization.

In the following chapter we propose a challenging pastoral direction: "The Parish as a Community of Communities."

† † † † † REFLECTION AND FAITH-SHARING QUESTIONS

Reflect on Colossians 3:1-17, an extension of the opening passage in this chapter.

1. What does holiness mean to me? What does spirituality mean to me?
2. How has my participation in a small community helped me to reflect on the mysteries of Jesus' life?
3. Conversion is at the heart of the spiritual life. What are some ways I have continued to experience conversion?
4. What could I do that would help me to have a deeper conversion to the Lord?
5. How have I experienced the "dynamic life cycle" (as described on pages 47-48) in fuller ways since making a commitment to a small Christian community?

PART II

The Pastoral Direction and Its Implementation

4. Proposing a Pastoral Direction: The Parish as a Community of Communities

Marion C. Honors, CSJ

The recurring theme of the parish "becoming a dynamic community of communities" has been highlighted by the Synod of the Laity, the U.S. Catholic bishops, and many others. This concept of "the parish as a community of communities" provides a pastoral direction for parish life today and in the years to come—a direction that can strengthen our faith as we live in a secular society and call us forth from the climate of privatized religion. In his wisdom the late Joseph Cardinal Bernardin said:

In the U.S., many of our parishes are quite large and, consequently, may exhibit anonymity more than community. In such settings, it is often difficult for effective evangelization to take place. A possible solution is to restructure the parish as a community of communities. In such a vision and structure, Catholics gather in small groups determined by neighborhood, family, needs, interests, or a common ministry in order to pray, read Scripture and share.

Authentic community is vital to effective evangelization. It nurtures believers. If Catholics experience community on a smaller scale, they may form and experience more of a community when they gather for parish liturgies on the weekend.[1]

What Cardinal Bernardin said about the importance of small communities for evangelization also applies to other aspects of parish life.

Restructuring the parish as a community of communities develops authentic community and nurtures believers, thus infusing all of parish life with new vitality.

John Paul II, in his encyclical on missionary activity, highlights the value of small faith-sharing communities. Although written with "young" churches in mind, the immense potential for all parishes is evident.

> A rapidly growing phenomenon in the young churches . . . is that of "ecclesial basic communities" which are proving to be good centers for Christian formation and missionary outreach. These communities decentralize and organize the parish community, to which they always remain united. They take root in less privileged and rural areas, and become a leaven of Christian life, of care for the poor and neglected, and of commitment to the transformation of society. Within them, the individual Christian experiences community and therefore senses that he or she is playing an active role and is encouraged to share in the common task. Thus, these communities become a means of evangelization and of the initial proclamation of the Gospel and a source of new ministries. At the same time, by being imbued with Christ's love, they also show how divisions, tribalism and racism can be overcome.[2]

WHAT IS A PASTORAL DIRECTION?

Any pastoral direction flows from a long-term, ideal vision that inspires and motivates people to strive for its realization. A pastoral direction clarifies the vision by giving a sense of direction and energizes those carrying it out by giving a sense of purpose. It does not define the total picture but gives a desired goal toward which to move. The pastoral direction must be suitable for those for whom it is intended and ideally come into being through a collaborative process.

We apply this term *pastoral direction* to the implementation of the vision of the parish as a community of many small communities. The proposed pastoral direction is a long-term line of action, an ideal to move toward. Years of working at it will bring us closer to the goal. It has the capacity to energize, to give life to parishioners and staff alike, and to give an added sense of purpose to the parish. When a parish chooses this pastoral direction, it does not realistically expect that every parishioner will be involved in a small community.

While not every parishioner will participate in a small community, the pastoral direction will serve everyone. Ultimately the richness of faith lived in the small community setting will spread to every aspect of parish life and beyond.

Although we do not expect to see the complete fulfillment of the vision, the ideal gives great energy and hope as we strive for it. Hopefully, when this small Christian community pastoral direction is adopted in parishes and dioceses, it will come into being through a collaborative process and express mutuality in relationships.

FOSTERING A COMMUNITARIAN STYLE OF PARISH LIFE

Small Christian communities are rooted in the history of the church. The parish as a community of many small faith-communities is a way of reclaiming our roots. Small Christian communities are part of our Christian tradition. The parish embraces many communities and offers the opportunity to all parishioners to connect life and faith on a regular basis through a small community experience and, thus, to lead all to be actively involved in interior spiritual renewal and the mission of Jesus.

The U.S. bishops have said that "the parish is, for most Catholics, the single most important part of the church. This is where for them the mission of Christ continues. This is where they publicly express faith, joining with others to give proof of their communion with God and with one another."[3]

The parish, then, is the focus of this pastoral direction. This pastoral direction suggests that the parish, the community of believers who gather to celebrate their faith, can be spiritually renewed in faith through the experience of small communities. Through such ongoing renewal the mission of Christ can be fostered and sustained with a deepening sense of commitment and indeed enthusiasm.

A VARIETY OF SMALL COMMUNITIES

The proposed pastoral direction fosters a style of parish life with a great variety of small communities. Therefore, we shall not attempt to suggest only one model or one concrete definition of small communities. We are referring neither to covenanted communities nor to in-depth communities where people live under one dwelling. We shall address only parish-based communities of mobile people.

The pastoral direction is not a parish activity or program. It does not imply that everything in the parish changes. Nor does it imply a pastoral burden of totally rearranging the parish into newly created communities. Various types of small groups and communities may already exist in a parish. Probably small parish meetings range from groups that come together for a specific purpose, to communities reflecting a broader concern for shared faith life through prayer, dialogue, mutual support, and community action. Some of the small parish meetings already manifest deepening bonds of faith and affirmation. Modification of their style of meeting toward a more communal style will be enriching for all involved in these groups.

More than one type of small community or one approach to implementing this pastoral plan is needed. Flexibility is essential in meeting the pastoral circumstances of a wide variety of parishes. Therefore, from the many possible means of achieving the end, we propose three general approaches as guideposts:

1. **Seasonal small groups** that provide parishioners the opportunity to meet periodically during the year to grow in their faith life.
2. **Ministerial communities** that provide those parishioners involved in specific ministries the environment needed for spiritual growth and support in order to grow effectively in their ministries.
3. **Small Christian communities** that provide parishioners the opportunity to meet on a regular basis for the purpose of calling one another to grow in openness to the gospel, transforming every area of their lives.

In our discussion (here and in the following chapters) of seasonal small groups, ministerial communities, and small Christian communities, we will try to highlight what is unique about each type of group or community and show why small Christian communities are an ideal to work toward.

- **Seasonal small groups** are purposely called "groups" because the style of meeting is not totally communal. The degree of commitment in sharing is not as great as in small Christian communities. Bonds of friendship and support are not as strong as one would find in small Christian communities where people come to know one another more profoundly. Yet great good comes from seasonal small groups. They provide a splendid opportunity for spiritual growth. Often those participating in seasonal groups begin to understand what community is and experience a willingness to be open to community.

- **Ministerial communities** help to move participants beyond the experience of a "group" toward experiencing some of the basic elements of community—prayer, sharing, learning, mission, and mutual support— while still placing their emphasis on a particular ministry. Those adopting the pastoral direction would encourage all parish small groups, committees, ministries, societies, and organizations to adopt a more communal approach in their meetings.

    Let us heed the words of the U.S. Bishops, "Every parish meeting can begin with the reading of the upcoming Sunday's Gospel, followed by a time of reflection and faith sharing."[4]

    The common purpose of seasonal small groups and ministerial communities is growth in the faith life of their members. In addition, ministerial communities focus on the one "assigned" or favorite ministry. Constant challenge to growth, in the fuller sense of what it means to be a small Christian community, needs to be offered to these various groups. A balance needs to be achieved, therefore, in helping people to take ownership of and feel good about the commitments they have made in seasonal groups and ministerial communities, while at the same time challenging them to see the deeper gospel ways and call of the small Christian community.

Three Types of Small Communities

	SEASONAL SMALL GROUPS	MINISTERIAL COMMUNITIES	SMALL CHRISTIAN COMMUNITIES
Definition	A face-to-face gathering of six to twelve people who meet for a short period (four to six weeks) for the common purpose of growing in their faith life.	A face-to-face gathering of approximately five to twelve people who meet on a regular basis with the common purpose of growing in their faith life and supporting one another in a particular outreach or ministry.	A face-to-face gathering of six to twelve people who invest time with one another for the common purpose of applying gospel values to every aspect of their lives.
Basic Purpose	To provide people an opportunity to share faith and a supportive environment where spiritual growth can take place during the various seasons.	To provide those parishioners involved in ministries the communal environment needed for support and spiritual growth.	To create an environment where people can grow in openness to the gospel, transforming every area of their lives.
Time Commitment	Usually six weeks, during the autumn, Lent, or Easter season; four weeks during Advent.	Frequently two years, renewable after evaluation and/or discernment.	Initially, three years, renewable after evaluation and discernment. Or the community may choose to divide, with each part taking in new members and starting new communities.
Challenge	To move beyond the comfort level, to accept risk, and to move toward action and ministry. In other words, to move to deeper levels of sharing, prayer, learning, mutual support, and mission.	To deepen their sense of community, to develop in their specific ministry and to begin to understand the ministerial implications of all areas of their lives.	To become increasingly wholehearted in their basic commitment to the movement of the Spirit within them.

- **Small Christian communities** include the elements found in seasonal small groups and ministerial communities, but move beyond the limitation of one specific ministry or a particular function. They are aimed at a more integral and all-embracing experience of the gospel way of life. Many small communities stay intact for years.

The accompanying chart summarizes the main aspects of the three types of groupings discussed in this chapter. It will serve as a good reference in understanding the differences among the three groups as well as the progression from seasonal groups to small Christian communities.

HOW TO IMPLEMENT THE THREE APPROACHES

Since every parish is unique, each will adopt its own way of implementing the vision of the parish as a community of many small communities. The successful implementation of this vision depends on two factors: (1) utilizing a combination of approaches, and (2) developing the Core Community that designs a precise parish plan and works it through to full implementation.

From one perspective the three groupings—seasonal small groups, ministerial communities, and small Christian communities—show a sense of progression toward the fullness of community, the third of which, small Christian communities, shows a more complete understanding of Christian community. Some parishes, in implementing the pastoral direction, would even follow this order: first developing seasonal groups; then approaching ministerial groups to adopt a more communal style; and, finally, promoting and establishing small Christian communities. Other parishes might start with all three approaches at the same time or within the same year. It is not suggested that any one approach by itself will necessarily develop the parish as a community of many small communities; however, the use of a combination of these three approaches will move a parish toward the fulfillment of its goal of implementing the pastoral direction.

Each parish will benefit from studying these three approaches and setting realistic goals based on the particular needs of the parish. Vatican

II clearly states that "efforts . . . must be made to encourage a sense of community within the parish" (*SC* 42). In describing the role of the pastor in forming a genuine Christian community, the council also speaks of the community spirit embracing "not only the local church but the universal church." "The local community should not only promote the care of its own faithful, but, filled with the missionary zeal, it should also prepare the way to Christ for all" (*PO* 6).

Seasonal small groups are a good beginning. As already existing groups take on a more communal style and, in some instances, truly develop into small communities, they will become part of the ongoing lifestyle and structure of the parish. They will contribute to a more spiritually alive church and help parishioners to think and act more readily out of gospel values. Small Christian communities have the capacity to form and empower Christians in all areas of their lives for mission in a world crying out for the Good News. Can we not echo and heed Cardinal Bernardin's words?

> Let us create faith communities in the Catholic tradition where the active, the inactive, the unchurched, the young, the middle-aged, and the old will find life-transforming experiences of Jesus, prayer, Scripture, and community.[5]

It is just such small faith communities that are the heart of the proposed pastoral direction!

SMALL CHRISTIAN COMMUNITIES: A SIGN OF GOD'S REIGN

In the remainder of this chapter we will highlight some of the ways that small basic communities are a sign of God's reign as they influence personal lives, transform parish life, and impact on the world in a positive way. These are among the reasons we believe they ought to receive serious consideration as a pastoral direction for parishes.

Centrality of Eucharist

Vatican II notes that "No Christian community . . . can be built up unless it has its basis and center in the celebration of the most Holy Eucharist"

(*PO* 6). The pastoral direction of the parish as a community of communities supports the centrality of the Eucharist that builds up the larger community. Small communities in the parish provide people the opportunity to deepen faith, thus enriching the Sunday liturgy. Small communities create a balance of Word and worship and, through both, lead people to works of charity, mutual help, missionary activity, and different forms of Christian witness.

When small community members participate in Sunday Eucharist they bring with them the richness of their faith lives that they have expressed in action. Nourished by the Word and Eucharist, they hear the commission again to live and proclaim the gospel to others.

Spiritual Growth and Renewal

Parish-based small communities foster spiritual formation and growth in the lives of so many parishioners. Small Christian communities set a climate that is very favorable and helpful to individuals and to the parish community in experiencing spiritual renewal and a deeper relationship with God. Through the small community it appears that the grace of God touches lives in authentic and life-forming ways; people are drawn to Christ and to the vibrant living of the gospel.

As small communities become rooted in the parish a powerhouse of spiritual renewal is built. Not only will small communities help parishioners but they will also serve to help the entire parish to experience spiritual growth and renewal.

Adult Faith Formation

The U.S. Bishops speak of the value of small communities in their Pastoral Plan for Adult Faith Formation in the United States, "Small communities are powerful vehicles for adult faith formation, providing opportunities for learning, prayer, mutual support, and the shared experience of Christian living and service to Church and society." They "have offered guidelines for authentic small faith community development in *Called and Gifted for the Third Millennium* and in *Communion and Mission*."[6]

To support adult faith formation RENEW International has developed a four-part *Catechism* Series for small communities entitled, *Why Catholic? Journey through the Catechism* as well as many other resources.

Evangelization

> Embracing all the activity of the parish is a basic vocation and commitment to evangelization. This means not only calling active believers to ever deeper faith, but also bringing the message of Christ to alienated Catholics, inviting people to join in the church's belief and worship, and making the Gospel real by applying it to the issues and conditions of our lives. The witness to the Gospel of Jesus acquires power from the continual reflection on faith and its demands to which parishioners devote themselves. Although the parish undertakes special efforts to bring the Gospel of Christ to those not active in the church community, it realizes that the most effective instrument of evangelization is the parish's visible hospitality, its vitality, and its own faithfulness to Christ.[7]

We believe that this call to evangelization can best be responded to through small Christian communities. If parishes were a community of communities they would be structured to do the work of evangelization. Parishes would not need an evangelization committee, a passing event such as a rally, or a periodic evangelization program. Instead they would constantly have people in small communities sharing faith, speaking about gospel values, and gaining courage from their small community to share with the inactive or the unchurched outside the community.

Small communities also provide an ideal welcoming place. Those inquiring about the faith or looking to find a way home discover new friends in the warm and informal setting of small communities.

Small Christian communities are known for their hospitality. Usually a friendly and gracious environment is developed there and offered to all who come. Thus small communities live the first step of evangelization, hospitality, by being places of warm welcome.

In effect, as small community members understand that evangelization is intrinsic to their being Catholic Christians, parishes will be on their way to being evangelizing parishes. Small communities are a training place for that evangelization process. No matter what their main focus (liturgy preparation, social concerns, etc.) each is about the work of evangelization. Christian community calls each person to the basic responsibility of evangelization. Leaders of small communities can be prepared to see that this call is constantly being issued.

In small communities people can trust others enough to think through the evangelization implications of the gospel and apply these to their world. Consider the following story:

> Joe, a rising New York executive, was a member of a small community. Holding a position of responsibility in his corporation, he was influential with other corporate managers. For a long time he was a rather quiet member of his group. Finally, after two years of praying and sharing with his small community, he gained the courage to go into work and challenge an unjust corporate policy. Joe could not have risked his career without the loving support of his community. No matter what the outcome at work, Joe knew he had his community to return to for love, support, and encouragement to live the gospel values he believed in.

The pastoral direction of the parish as a community of communities provides a means by which evangelization can be part of the fabric of parish life through the ongoing action of more permanent small communities. As these communities grow in number, the parish will arrive at a most practical, concrete way to engage every parishioner in the work of evangelization. (Chapter 13 will treat the topic of evangelization and small Christian communities in greater detail.)

Ministry Is Enriched

Today many people are involved in ministry without a good support base. Some experience burnout because they are constantly giving of themselves without receiving support in their spiritual life or ministry.

As small ministering communities develop, many diverse needs can be addressed. Peer ministry can take place within small communities. Individual members of the small ministering community itself can reach out to one another in loving service. And because Christians are not called simply to be involved in church ministries, small communities offer special support for people to live their family and life commitments and to dedicate themselves to their work in the world. In our society a structure is needed in order to help people to remain faithful while prompting them to action.

Unity

The development of small communities throughout the parish has the potential to give marvelous new life and creative energy to every ministry and every aspect of parish life. Their spiritual richness and focus on the mission of Jesus can be a unifying force in the parish.

> The mission of the parish is significantly enriched when it provides the people an opportunity to meet in smaller groups in which they can speak and better understand the meaning of their faith, and, by doing so, strengthen their commitment and celebrate their unity in Christ.[8]

Mission

The pastoral direction supports people in their faith journey and missionary work. The *Decree on the Church's Missionary Activity* (*Ad Gentes*), which calls the work of evangelization the fundamental task of the people of God, invites all to undertake a profound interior renewal so that they may play their part in the missionary work of the church (*AG* 35). Small Christian communities have the capacity to prompt and sustain that profound interior renewal. They are of themselves places where the faithful are evangelized and formed as evangelizers to spread the gospel and participate in the transformation of the world.

Small Christian communities, therefore, exist not for themselves alone, but to enable parishioners to participate more concretely in the mission of Jesus. In small communities, people have the opportunity to observe various dimensions of the mission of Jesus, decide what aspect of the mission they can best participate in (based on their gifts and the needs or situations that arise), and then act on these decisions. If all small communities are formed for mission, evangelization, and justice and see these as intrinsic to their faith, what a marvelous transformation we would see in the church and the world. The reign of God would be proclaimed anew.

More Effective Leadership

A parish with many well-trained small community leaders will have a broader base of solid leadership. The efforts of the parish staff in forming these leaders are multiplied as the leaders, in turn, minister to those in their small communities.

Networking of small communities provides an excellent system for communication. Messages from the pastor, as well as urgent needs within the community, can be communicated quickly and effectively through the leaders of small communities.

This chapter calls for thinking big about something small. It calls for thinking in a big way about how the parish can be affected by the dynamism of many small Christian communities. Let us encourage imagination and creativity in this transformation!

GARY'S STORY

One individual whose life was touched by a small Christian community was able to expand his vision, to think big, and to influence many, particularly in the area of the development of lay leadership. This man was Gary. At the age of twelve Gary received the only formal religious formation he would have in his lifetime. For two weeks Gary was instructed in the catechism and then received the sacraments of Eucharist and confirmation.

When Gary first moved to his parish, he attended Mass because of the staunch Catholic faith of his wife Monica. One of the parish priests invited Monica and Gary to participate in a small sharing group. As the young couple continued to meet with this small group, Gary's faith deepened and his gift for cutting through to the essentials became more and more apparent.

The following year Monica and Gary were encouraged to start a CFM group. They became the leader couple, responsible for visiting and inviting others to be part of their group and, later, leaders of all the CFM parish groups.

When the parish council was to be initiated, Gary became coordinator of a committee to prepare for it. For eighteen months this group of parishioners met with the pastor and staff to plan how to involve every spectrum of the parish in the formation of the council. As part of the preparation, people developed and wrote study materials based on the documents of Vatican II. Using his gift for writing, Gary contributed immensely to this project.

Gary had a wonderful way of challenging people. When 300 signed up for small groups in preparation for initiating the council, Gary said, "That's not enough. Don't you think we should have gotten 500?" Gary said this not for the sake of numbers, but so that many more would have the experience of praying and learning through small groups. The challenge was met! Not 500 but 600 people were signed up to be part of the small-group reflection process. The small groups in the parish of which Gary and Monica were members had a great deal to do with the birth of RENEW. The roots of RENEW were planted and sprouted forth from this parish thirty years ago. Gary's challenge to think big is really part of the RENEW story.

Gary continued to be a leader. Extremely popular, exceedingly fair, he won the admiration of all. Gary was elected president of the parish council. He and Monica represented diocesan CFM groups on the Family Life Apostolate Board. Showing interest when the diocese was developing its pastoral council, Gary served on the planning committee and later was elected its first chairperson. Later, with a new archbishop, he served four more years as chairperson of the diocesan pastoral council. Gary continued to give untiringly of his service when called forth in many other capacities.

Gary had been formed by small communities when he studied and researched the documents of Vatican II. Respected by all, Gary was elected to the Regional Advisory Council and then the National Advisory Council for the National Conference of Catholic Bishops. From his humble beginnings Gary attained the highest elected office of the laity representing 60 million Catholics as chairperson of the Bishops' National Advisory Council.

In this capacity he was one of the advisors to the bishops in their writing of the pastoral *Economic Justice for All.* In seeking advisors, the bishops also contacted major firms to give their reaction to the pastorals. In an unusual turn of events, one of the firms contacted by the bishops' committee asked Gary to write its response. Gary was not only advising the bishops, but also advising those from whom the bishops were seeking advice. Who knows how far-reaching the influence of this one person was? In this instance Gary's spiritual and religious formation came from various small Christian communities and from Monica and their six children, his primary Christian community.

When Gary died of cancer his small community wanted to remember him in a special way. They wrote letters to all of Gary's friends and associates and invited them to contribute to a memorial fund in Gary's name. More than $7,000 was collected. The original intention of the community was to support Gary's youngest son, Tom, who was giving a year of service as a Georgetown student volunteer to the people of Samanco, Peru. The overwhelming response enabled the group to subsidize several students.

When Tom returned he wrote a letter to all who contributed. After recalling colorful memories of his amazing year with the young and the old, Tom closed his letter with these words:

> This brings me to the purpose of this letter, which is to thank you who believed enough in this program to support it. You did so for my father, which made the experience even more special for me. My father was someone who would have understood this program as you, his friends, have. I look at the long list of people who have contributed and I feel ashamed because I don't recognize all of the names. There are some I remember hearing only as a small boy, and others that I know very well, but I am struck by the mutual commitment to a shared community that goes far beyond the limits of this parish; a community that stretches around the world and beyond.

The small community of Monica and Gary, Dolores and Joe, Peggy and Art, Marilyn and Dan, in life and in death, continues to touch the world with their love.

LOOKING AHEAD

The following three chapters on seasonal small groups, ministerial communities, and small Christian communities will further expand our understanding of each while showing their interrelatedness. The variety shown here suggests the possibility of different combinations and a multiplicity of developmental approaches that could be used by a parish according to its circumstances. This variety and flexibility may offer more concretely realistic approaches than one uniform means to achieve this pastoral direction.

Many people will continue to progress through the three approaches presented here. The various ways that people are engaged in seasonal small groups, extensively described in Chapter 5, obviously apply also to ministerial communities and small Christian communities. One approach builds on the other.

Forming a precise parish plan depends principally upon two understandings: 1) the three basic approaches to small community formation and 2) the work of a parish Core Community for small community development. Chapters 5, 6, and 7 elaborate on each of the three approaches. Chapter 8 offers guidance for the creation and ongoing work of a parish Core Community. This Core Community is commissioned with the responsibility of small community development within the parish. Its tasks are clearly delineated. As the parish Core Community creatively plans for implementing small communities and offers clear guidance on small communities, the parish as "a community of many small communities" gradually becomes a reality.

††††† REFLECTION AND FAITH-SHARING QUESTIONS

Reflect on either John 15:1-10 or 1 Corinthians 12:4-27 and on the words (from *Redemptoris Missio*) of Pope John Paul II on page 62.

1. Is there a greater sense of community and outreach in our parish since members have shared faith in small communities? In what ways?
2. What is the connection between small communities and evangelization; and between small communities and the "care for the poor and neglected"?
3. How can small communities in our parish be a means to evangelize?
4. What steps have we taken or can we take to make our parish "a community of communities"?
5. How can I contribute to our parish's plan for evangelization?

5. Seasonal Small Groups

If the parish goal is to bring a large number of parishioners to experience community, then extensive efforts to introduce people to seasonal small groups must be made—both for their intrinsic value and for the implementation of a new pastoral direction. The methods suggested here for implementing seasonal small groups do not, therefore, stand in isolation but are very much part of the larger picture of forming the parish as a community of many small communities. All of the concrete means suggested here to involve parishioners in seasonal small groups are not only valuable in developing these groups, but can also be used as the foundation for forming ministerial communities and small Christian communities. Providing opportunities for all parishioners to have a small group experience is part of a massive approach toward the parish becoming a community of small communities.

Seasonal small groups serve a dual purpose. First, the groups, in themselves, offer a wonderful opportunity for spiritual growth for large numbers of people. Second, from the perspective of developing the parish as a community of many small communities, seasonal small groups offer initial steps in forming ministerial communities and small Christian communities. For example, seasonal small groups introduce people, perhaps for the first time, to the rich experience of faith sharing and give a taste of the possibilities open to them in ministerial or small Christian communities. Careful planning and implementation of seasonal small groups can reap a harvest of ongoing parish small communities in the future.

Ansgar Holmberg, CSJ

- **Definition** A seasonal small group is a face-to-face gathering of approximately six to twelve people who meet for a short period (four to six weeks) for the common purpose of growing in their faith life.

- **Purpose** Seasonal small groups provide parishioners—for a limited time—both an opportunity to share faith and a supportive environment in which spiritual growth can take place.

- **Time Commitment** The time commitment of a seasonal group is usually a six-week period in autumn, in Lent, or in the Easter season, and a four-week period during Advent. Lent is probably the best starting point because many parishioners are looking for a special way to prepare for the feast of the Resurrection and the Easter season. Therefore, the Lenten season often seems to be the time when people are most willing to commit themselves to sharing in a small group. This experience can be repeated with new commitments made each time a group meets.

- **Value** Providing seasonal opportunities may, in fact, be the best and least threatening way to give people a taste of a group that touches on small community. Many continue to meet in their small groups seasonally for years during autumn and during Lent. Bonds of friendship are strengthened, and they continue to support one another even during the times they are not meeting. For others, the seasonal experience furthers the desire to develop the communal experience in a deeper or more ongoing way. The members of the group may decide to focus on a particular ministry needed in the parish or larger community, and become a ministerial community, or they may decide to meet as a small Christian community in a regular way throughout the year, either weekly, every two weeks, or monthly.

- **Challenge for Seasonal Small Groups** The challenge for those who are in seasonal small groups is to move beyond the comfort level, to accept risk, and to move toward action and ministry. In other words, they are challenged to move to deeper levels of sharing, prayer, learning, mutual support, and mission.

PLANNING FOR SEASONAL SMALL GROUPS

In order to implement a small group experience for the entire parish, planning must begin about three months before the actual small group meetings are to be held. If a Core Community is in place, it takes responsibility for implementing seasonal small groups. In those parishes with no Core Community, the parish staff and/or parish pastoral council need to form a "small group committee" which would be responsible for implementing this process. (This committee may very well become a Core Community in time; therefore, for our purposes here we will use the term "Core Community.")

It is best if those who participate in this ministry do so in a communal and, therefore, supportive style. In moving toward the fullness of the vision of the parish as a community of communities, it is important to model the communal style in every way possible.

Such a "Core" is composed of approximately six to twelve parishioners who are able and willing to take responsibility for promoting and implementing the various aspects of seasonal small groups. One person serves as coordinator and also as a contact with parish staff, parish pastoral council, and small group leaders.

The following pages outline the responsibilities of such a Core Community and guide them in a step-by-step process to implement seasonal small groups in their parish.

The responsibilities fall into thirteen areas

1. Establish a Time Line
2. Select and Train Invitational Ministers
3. Publicize and Communicate
4. Select Materials
5. Conduct Personal and Home Visits
6. Designate and Conduct Sign-Up Sunday
7. Prayer Commitment Sunday
8. Leadership Training
9. Telephone Campaign
10. Determine Groups

11. Small Group Evaluation
12. Follow-Up Celebration
13. Evaluate the Core Community's Work

At its first meeting the members of the Core Community discuss the preceding responsibilities and each member assumes responsibility for some area(s). A time line is established and future meeting dates are scheduled. A check list is given at the end of this chapter to assist the work of the committee. (See Sample A at end of chapter.)

The thirteen areas of responsibility are described below.

1. Establish a Time Line

Establish a time line including dates for the following:

(a) Core Community Meets	Three months before small groups begin.
(b) Small Group Experience	Autumn—First week of October for six weeks. Lent—Week of Ash Wednesday through week before Holy Week.
(c) Select & Train Invitational Ministry Team	Begin 10-11 weeks prior to Sign-Up Sunday.
(d) Publicity and Communication	At least four weeks prior to Sign-Up Sunday.
(e) Select Materials	Four weeks prior to Sign-Up Sunday.
(f) Select Small Group Leaders	Four weeks prior to Sign-Up Sunday.
(g) Conduct Personal and Home Visits	Begin six weeks prior to small group gathering.
(h) Sign-Up Sunday	Two or three weeks prior to first week of small groups.
(i) Prayer Commitment Sunday	One week prior to beginning date for small groups.
(j) Leadership Training	Prior to or between Sign-Up Sunday and beginning date for small groups.

(k) Telephone Campaign   Week following Sign-Up Sunday.

(l) Follow-Up Celebration   Soon after last week of small groups.

2. Select and Train Invitational Ministers

The importance of inviting parishioners—especially young adults, single and married—is key to involving people in seasonal small groups. Therefore, it is necessary to select and train parishioners who will be part of the Invitational Ministry. Several members of the Core Community can work specifically with this ministry and recruit and train others to be involved. Some Invitational Ministers are involved in personal and home visits, while others are part of the telephone campaign. (See Chapter 9 for more on the Invitational Ministry.)

3. Publicize and Communicate

Quality publicity and communication for the forthcoming small group effort is essential to parishioners' response to the invitation to join a seasonal small group. Parishioners with publishing or advertising expertise can be called upon to assist in this effort. In addition to a parish-wide invitation, existing groups such as school faculty, catechists, or single parent group members may be invited to meet for a small group experience for a period of time.

The following tasks to be accomplished—together with a time line—are suggested to achieve maximum visibility while publicizing the event.

Publicity and Communication Time Line

Bulletin announcements   Each week for four weeks prior to Sign-Up
                                                 Sunday.

Pulpit announcements   Each week for three to four weeks prior to
                                                 Sign-Up Sunday.

Flyers, banners, letters to families   During the three or four weeks prior to
                                                 Sign-Up Sunday.

Notice in a variety of local papers, including shoppers' newspapers; announcement on local radio and TV stations	Two weeks before Sign-Up Sunday.
Communication with parish staff and pastoral council	Prior to and throughout process.
Communication with leaders of every committee, organization, ministry and group in the parish	Immediately after first small group committee meeting.

4. Select Materials

The Core Community is responsible for guiding the selection of the small group material. Booklets that incorporate five elements of Christian community (prayer, sharing, mutual support, learning, mission) are very helpful in the development of small groups. The Core Community is initially responsible for deciding what small group material is to be used. As the small groups continue meeting, they may wish to select their own materials with the guidance of the Core Community. The materials can be purchased by the parish and used by various small groups, or purchased by the small group members themselves.

RENEW International has a wide variety of materials in both English and Spanish for seasonal small groups, especially for use during Advent and Lent. In addition, materials on the Sunday readings, reflections on the *Catechism of the Catholic Church,* as well as a whole array of IMPACT booklets on family life, the world of work, nonviolence, civic responsibility, hunger, mysticism, etc., are all available through RENEW International.

5. Conduct Personal and Home Visits

The Invitational Ministry team makes personal and home visits to targeted parishioners, such as newly arrived parishioners, parents whose children are to be baptized, and parents of first communicants. They also may organize gatherings (i.e., cafe evenings, parties in people's homes, etc.) in order to invite people to be part of a small group. In the process they share their own commitment, enthusiasm, and hopes for what can happen in a small group. (See Chapter 9, Invitational Ministry, for detailed information.)

6. Designate and Conduct Sign-Up Sunday

Designating one Sunday as "Sign-Up Sunday" is a very effective means to invite parishioners to be part of seasonal small groups. As indicated in the time line, Sign-Up Sunday is held two or three weeks before the small groups are scheduled to begin. The responsibilities for those working with this aspect include the following:

- select a speaker for Sign-Up Sunday
- select and prepare persons to assist on Sign-Up Sunday
- design, distribute, and collect sign-up cards
- involve other parish groups in this effort

(For a complete explanation of how to prepare for and conduct Sign-Up Sunday, see Chapter 9, Invitational Ministry.)

7. Prayer Commitment Sunday

Prayer Commitment Sunday gives everyone an opportunity to be part of the ongoing spiritual renewal of the parish by participating in a prayer network. A prayer network is simply a group of people who are bonded together by their commitment to pray for the renewal of the parish during the seasons when small groups are held. The prayer network has the role of ensuring a strong prayer base for all small group activity.

The invitation to participate is given on Prayer Commitment Sunday, one week prior to the date for small groups to begin. Both the celebrant and a member of the small group coordinating committee may issue the invitation.

No matter what one's obligations or schedule might be, all are able to be part of a massive prayer effort for the renewal of the parish. Announcements in the parish bulletin and at the Sunday liturgy one week prior to Prayer Commitment Sunday will alert people and prepare them to make a serious prayer commitment. On Prayer Commitment Sunday commitment cards and pencils are available in pews or at church doors. The commitment cards need not elicit names or addresses. Sample B (at the end of this chapter) shows a prayer commitment card that may be copied or adapted for your parish. Completed cards may be collected by the ministers of hospitality or placed in baskets at the doors of the church after the financial collection.

8. Leadership Training

Leadership training takes place before Sign-Up Sunday or at least two weeks before small groups begin to meet. The time needed for training is approximately four hours, usually two evening sessions of two hours each. A Core Community member, pastor, or a diocesan staff person facilitates the training sessions. (See Chapter 10 for resource material.)

Included in the training sessions are the following:

- prayer and faith sharing, based upon the Scriptures
- discussion of how to lead a small group
- group dynamics
- reflection of the responsibilities of being a small group leader
- basic skills in using Scripture
- overview of materials to be used
- distribution of list of names, addresses, and telephone numbers of people in each leader's group (if not already done)
- distribution of materials to leaders; the leaders can deliver materials to their small group members before the first meeting
- confirmation each group has a meeting time and place that the leaders will communicate to their respective small group members (if not already done)
- explanation of small group evaluation and follow-up celebration
- basic guide for small group leaders

When leaders are given the list of people in their respective groups, they are told to visit them between Sign-Up Sunday and the actual first meeting date and give them the materials to be used. Many sign up for small groups and never go to the first meeting. Perhaps they have fears that override their genuine desire to attend. A visit may help participants overcome their fears.

When leaders visit new participants in their own home, they are doing much more than handing over materials to be used. They are bearers of hospitality, warmth, welcoming, kindness, and caring. They carry the spirit of the parish to each home. There they can establish relationships immediately and work through any difficulties their group members may have, e.g., getting someone to babysit or stay with sick or elderly family members, getting a ride to the small group meeting, etc.

When members are given in advance the materials they will use at their small group meeting, they will have time to reflect on the Scriptures and questions to be used in the first session. This may also allay any apprehensions a member may have about being in the faith-sharing group.

Many times leaders need encouragement to take the initiative to visit small group members in their own homes. It is not always easy dealing with the unknown. However, it is far better to extend oneself before the first meeting than to be disappointed later when participants do not attend.

Leaders can be supported in this effort by the Core Community. For example, leaders can meet in groups of twos to role play, introducing themselves and welcoming their small group participants; they can be urged to prayerfully prepare to meet their participants, etc.

9. Telephone Campaign

Some of the Invitational Ministry team organize and conduct the telephone campaign that takes place during the week that follows Sign-Up Sunday. This campaign assures that every parishioner who has not signed up for a small community after Sign-Up Sunday receives a personal telephone invitation. Some Core Community members are involved in selecting, training, and working with the Invitational Ministry team. (See Chapter 9 for detailed information.)

10. Determine Groups

Immediately after sign-up cards are collected, the names of those who indicated their desire to participate are arranged into groups according to their stated time preference. It is possible that while trying to accommodate each person's choice there may not be enough people to form a group at a particular time. The Core Community then has to do extra work by calling and renegotiating with them to arrive at an agreeable meeting date and time. When this has been completed, those who have been selected and trained as leaders are assigned a group.

The Core Community prepares lists for each leader with names, addresses, and telephone numbers of their group members together with the meeting time and place. If it is later discovered that a group is without a leader, a member of the group is invited to assume the role of leader. In the event this happens, there should be personal preparation of this leader.

11. Small Group Evaluation

During the last session of the small group's seasonal gathering the leader asks the members to evaluate their small group experience and to consider becoming part of an ongoing faith-sharing group. The written evaluation (see Sample C at the end of this chapter) is forwarded to the Core Community together with the names of those who wish to continue to meet in a faith-sharing group on an ongoing basis. In addition, other needs might surface, e.g., some might want a retreat day or evening and others might desire Scripture study.

12. Follow-Up Celebration

Soon after the last small group meeting, participants in all small groups come together for a celebration. This session includes prayer, a time of sharing and witnessing, a time for refreshments, and a time for looking ahead.

Someone may give a presentation challenging those who participated in small groups to become involved in a particular ministry. Persons knowledgeable about ministerial communities may be invited to share their insights, the needs of the parish, and how these needs are being met through outreach. Those who wish to sign up for a ministry or a ministerial community are encouraged to do so. Those who wish to continue with their small groups are encouraged to resume meeting. Some may choose to be part of a small Christian community. Small group materials may be on display for perusal or someone could speak about available materials.

13. Evaluate the Core Community's Work

After studying the small group evaluations and experiencing the follow-up celebration, the Core Community meets to evaluate the small group experience, their own way of being community and working together, and to discuss future plans. If the pastor or a parish staff person is not present, Core Community members need to present the evaluation and projected plans at a later date to the pastor. *This is an opportune time to explore and begin the development of a Core Community if one is not already in place.*

Other Opportunities

- Offer an evening of reflection for all small group participants during the small group sessions to encourage the groups and to show their unity with the parish.
- Hold a meeting with small group leaders during the sessions and/or after the follow-up celebration to discuss their experiences. This time would also enable the Core Community to affirm the ministry of the leaders as well as to discover the strengths and the areas to be strengthened either now or in future training sessions of small group leaders. If this meeting is held after the small group sessions, those interested in being small group leaders could express their availability and willingness to serve in the future. In addition, they could name members of their small groups who have the potential for being small group leaders in the future.
- Set up a special evening to explore further how groups could move into ministry.

MULTIPLY SMALL GROUPS

Small groups that continue to meet can split or multiply in diverse ways. Examples given below can be encouraged or adopted.

- Every small group leader finds an assistant within the group to share the leadership. The assistant leader is encouraged during a period of training to bring friends and prospects to the group he or she is in. After a period of time, e.g., six months, the assistant leader and friends or newcomers spin off and form a new group. The original group leader seeks out a new assistant, and the cycle repeats itself.
- Small group members are encouraged to reach out to new people and invite them to their group. When their group reaches twelve members, they are challenged to divide and grow. Those using this model have discovered that healthy groups "give birth" to new groups.

In church work we like to count numbers. A caution is in order here. An overemphasis on the multiplication of groups could lead to a certain amount of superficiality in the quality of these groups, especially in the area of mission.

CONCLUSION

As valuable as the experience of seasonal small groups may be, they fall far short of the real potential for growth that small communities offer. Challenge participants to move beyond the personal benefits of group faith sharing and connect this experience to their ministry in the parish or in other areas of their lives. Invite them to reflect on the implications of ministering in all of life's situations.

Our next chapter will explore the concept of ministerial communities and give some practical helps in developing them.

✝ ✝ ✝ ✝ ✝ REFLECTION AND FAITH-SHARING QUESTIONS

Reflect on Ephesians 3:14-21 and 1 John 4:7-16.

1. The passage from Ephesians reminds us of the many ways we can benefit from participation in a small community—especially a deeper relationship with Jesus Christ. How did my first experience of being in a small faith-sharing group affect my relationship with Christ? When I meet apprehension among those I invite to join small communities, how do I respond?
2. Are we as a Core Community faithful to our responsibilities? Do we share responsibility? On what do we need to work?

SAMPLE A

Seasonal Small Group Experience Check List

Core Community

List names and telephone numbers of Core Community members on the back.

Dates for Core Community meetings

Dates for parish-wide small group meetings

1. *Publicity*

   • what has to be done_____

   _____

   • by whom _____

   • when_____

2. *Sign-Up Sunday*

   • date _____

   • what has to be done_____

   _____

   • by whom _____

3. *Selection of Materials*

   • what has to be done_____

   _____

   • by whom _____

   • when_____

4. *Select and Train Invitational Ministers*

   • when _____

   • where _____

   • by whom _____

5. *Conduct Personal and Home Visits*

   • when _____

   • where _____

   • by whom _____

6. *Determining Groups*

   • when _____

   • where _____

   • by whom _____

7. *Leadership Training*

   • what has to be done _____

   _____

   • by whom _____

   • when _____

   • where _____

8. *Prayer Commitment Sunday*

   • date _____

   • what has to be done _____

   _____

   • by whom _____

9. *Telephone Campaign*

- when _____

- where _____

- by whom _____

10. *Follow-Up Celebration*

- what has to be done _____

  _____

- by whom _____

- when _____

- where _____

11. *Evaluation of People in Groups*

- how _____

- when _____

- where _____

12. *Total Evaluation*

- how _____

- when _____

- where _____

SAMPLE B

Prayer Commitment Card

In order to ask God's blessings on our parish efforts at spiritual renewal, I promise the following:

- Attend one weekday Mass
- Offer one day of fasting and prayer
- Prayerfully read the Scripture readings for the following Sunday
- Read and pray with the Scriptures 15 minutes each day
- Say the rosary once a week or each day
- Spend time before the Blessed Sacrament
- Pray the following prayer each day

Prayer to the Holy Spirit

Come, Holy Spirit, fill the hearts of the faithful. Enkindle the parish community of _____ with the fire of your love. Send forth your Spirit and we shall be created and you shall renew the face of the earth. Amen

SAMPLE C

Seasonal Small Group Evaluation

(1) What were the strengths of your small group experience?

(2) How do you feel the small group experience can be improved?

(3) Of the *five elements of community* named below, which was most operative in your small group? Circle the appropriate one.

PRAYER   SHARING   MISSION   SUPPORT   LEARNING

(4) Which of the five elements did you feel needs to be more developed in your small group? Circle the appropriate one.

PRAYER   SHARING   MISSION   SUPPORT   LEARNING

(As a result of meeting in a seasonal small group, some parishioners express the desire to continue to meet on a regular basis either with the same group or with another group of people. We call those groups that meet regularly for the purpose of applying gospel values to every aspect of their lives small Christian communities.)

(5) Would you like to meet regularly in a small Christian community? If so, circle the appropriate frequency.

WEEKLY   ONCE EVERY TWO WEEKS   MONTHLY

(6) Other comments

_____

Your Name

6. Ministerial Communities

Megan Holmberg, CSJ

The parish does not exist for itself but for the mission of Christ. People are called forth to minister to one another in the parish community as well as to those around them where they live and work. With these two truths in mind, we may very well ask, "How can we best enable people to minister?"

As mentioned earlier, small communities are being experienced as a means of deepening the spiritual life for many people today that prompts them to express their faith in action. The same principles that support small Christian community development can easily be applied to every parish group or ministry. In other words, the elements of community building—sharing, mutual support, prayer, mission, and learning—can gradually be incorporated into every parish gathering or meeting. When groups consistently strive to include these elements in their meeting we say they are developing a communal style of meeting. When the value of a communal style as a base for ministry is clearly seen, then the development of all new ministries would likewise follow the model and be ministerial communities.

FROM COMMITTEE TO COMMUNITY

A close examination of the parish reveals a wide range of already existing parish groups, committees, organizations, societies, and ministries.

Many of these groups, though small in number and specific in purpose, are not communities. They are frequently groups or committees of people who come together more for a function than as a way of life. The parishioners in these committees are often highly motivated and are extremely hard working. Unfortunately, some committee meetings are so task oriented they lack a sense of community.

Since a comparatively large number of people are involved in parish committees or ministries, the parish could easily begin to develop in a more communal direction by encouraging a greater sense of community in committees, ministry groups, parish staffs, peace and justice ministers, parish pastoral councils, Holy Name Societies, etc.

Why Move from Committee to Community?

- Many people who are committed to ministry also desire to grow personally and receive the support that comes from Christian community in order to continue their ministry effectively. Effective ministry includes awareness of the church's role in the world and the need to serve its mission.
- The ministries themselves will be more effective since they will flow from people who know the life and power that come from Christian community. The ministers will bring that life and energy to their ministry efforts.
- More people are willing to respond to the call to minister and continue in that call if they know they will not simply be involved in a task, but will have opportunities to grow spiritually.
- Many who engage in a prayerful, communal style of ministry experience that the task that needs to be accomplished not only is completed more quickly but also is accomplished in a spirit of greater joy and peace.

Parishioners, once having adopted the pastoral direction of the parish as a community of communities, realize the benefit of having all groups in the parish move toward community. Therefore, they encourage basic elements of community building—sharing, learning, mission, mutual support, and prayer—to be gradually incorporated into all parish committees concerned with ministerial service. A phrase that is being heard more and more is "An end of committee in the Catholic Church and a beginning of community."

• **Definition** A ministerial community is a face-to-face gathering of approximately five to twelve people who meet on a regular basis with the common purpose of growing together in their faith life and supporting one another in a particular outreach or ministry.

• **Purpose** The purpose of ministerial communities is to provide those parishioners involved in ministries the communal environment needed for support and spiritual growth. An effective parish goal is to have all ministries in the parish come from a base of small community. If this goal is adopted, then each ministry group should clarify and agree as to how its members will live out each of the five elements of prayer, sharing, learning, mission, and mutual support.

• **Time Commitment** Ideally there would be a stated length of time for each person in the ministerial community. Frequently this time is at least two years but could be renewed after evaluation or discernment. Often when people clearly state the length of time they are willing to be part of a ministerial community, there is greater commitment both to the ministry and to spiritual growth in the community.

• **Living the Five Elements** As they strive to be a community, members of ministerial groups incorporate the five elements of community more fully into their gatherings. As they strive to grow spiritually, they spend quality time in personal prayer as well as in communal prayer during their meetings. They seek to learn more about their faith and the skills needed for ministry. They support one another as fully as possible in their lives and ministries. They are more at ease in sharing their faith. And lastly, they make a more conscious effort in their ministry to dedicate themselves to the mission of Jesus. (Each of these five elements will be seen even more fully in small Christian communities in which parishioners make a commitment to meet regularly and to grow together as a small faith community.)

• **Challenge for Ministerial Communities** The challenge for those in ministerial communities is to deepen their sense of community, to develop the understanding, knowledge, and skills needed in their specific ministry, and to begin to understand the ministerial implications of all areas of their lives.

• **Value** Ministerial communities have great value in themselves. A poignant story of conversion is told by a Milwaukee priest who encouraged faith sharing at parish pastoral council meetings.

> I was working with a parish that was starting a new parish pastoral council. As part of prayer formation I urged the council to spend twenty minutes in prayer and reflection during each meeting. Paul, the parish custodian, felt that this was "too much time to spend on prayer and not enough on action." Reluctantly he agreed to go along with the suggestion, but said he would not take a turn preparing the prayer. Several months later at an agenda meeting he changed his mind. It was now his responsibility to choose a reading for the next meeting.
>
> When it came time for the prayer, Paul read the story of Martha and Mary. We were feeling he was kind of putting us in our place. But when it came time for Paul to share his reflection, he surprised them when he said, "I have always been a Martha. This is the first time I was asked to be a Mary and I really like it." Later Paul recounted, "My wife told me that since I came on the council there was a difference in how I responded at home."[1]

How often do we neglect the opportunity to help people to grow spiritually? The suggestion that prayer be given priority time during council meetings led to a conversion of heart for at least one person, Paul, and his story has since touched many hearts.

Ministerial communities can also help people move toward small Christian communities. This special category of ministerial community does not imply that the other two approaches neglect ministry. Rather the development of ministerial communities is meant to focus on what already exists in abundance in most parishes, that is, all kinds of ministerial activity and committees. Parishes have put much creative energy into developing ministries, e.g., social concerns ministries, liturgy ministries, ministries to the separated and divorced, ministries to the bereaved, etc. By helping these ministries move toward being ministerial communities, parishioners can begin to see the vision taking form without the overwhelming prospect of dismantling all the good that has already been accomplished or starting a whole new creation.

HOW DO MINISTERIAL COMMUNITIES DEVELOP?

How do we encourage ministry groups within a parish to develop a more communal lifestyle? Significant to the development of ministerial communities are Core Community members and pastoral staffs who are convinced of the value of giving all those who minister an opportunity to grow spiritually through their ministry groups or committees. Once Core Community and staff members have themselves experienced a communal style of working, they will speak more authentically and convincingly to others and be better able to motivate them to incorporate into their meetings and lives the five elements of community.

The concepts of invitation and motivation are key factors in the development of ministerial communities. The groups or committees that can be approached include current parish committees/ministries, other small sharing groups, special interest groups, and short-term ministries. In addition, when the parish starts new ministries, they can begin immediately by using the five elements of community.

Parish Committees or Ministries

Some parishes may wish to implement the pastoral direction in a gradual manner by identifying and working with one or more current parish committees that seem ready to implement this approach. Other parishes may begin by taking a broader approach and inviting all those involved in parish committees or ministries to an evening of reflection.

First, let us look at how one would approach a parish committee. Members of the Core Community may speak to the chairperson of the group simply about incorporating into their meeting a time of prayer and a period of Scripture sharing. In this way the parish is gradually bringing about a new style of parish activity. The members are encouraged to accept the fact that God will bless their work if they are more prayerful. A period of twenty minutes to a half hour at each meeting will contribute immensely to a greater prayerfulness in the group. A simple process could be used. The group would choose a Scripture passage. After reading it and allowing some time for reflection, the members would share what it means to them. The group can look at the implications of the reading in light of the circumstances coming up during the week. They can make applications for their particular ministry and then take some time for prayer together. As a group adopts this style it usually approaches its task in a spirit of faith and with a greater sense of support from one another.

Second, let us look at the possibility of holding an evening of reflection for all parishioners involved in ministries or committees. After the invitation has been sent out and responses received, the Core Community can arrange for those involved in the same ministry to sit together, preferably at round tables.

The agenda would include the following elements:

- welcome
- a time of prayer and faith sharing
- an explanation of the elements of community building
- a reflection process to help participants examine their present ministries in light of the five elements of community
- a time for each ministerial group to strategize how it can grow in each of these elements
- a time for interested groups to make a commitment to develop a more communal style of meeting

Either at this time or when ministry groups set goals and objectives for their mission or outreach, they can evaluate how well they are incorporating the five elements of Christian community. This process can help determine which areas of community growth need strengthening. For example, committee or ministry groups that focus on social concerns, public relations, or finances may choose more time for prayer and sharing. Committees or ministry groups that focus on prayer, spiritual life, or worship may already spend time in prayer and sharing Scripture, so they may decide to spend more time on learning or outreach.

Other Small Sharing Groups

In addition to ministerial communities, there may be other groups, such as small faith-sharing groups or Bible-study groups in the parish that have met for several years. They, too, can be approached and told about the benefits of incorporating the elements of community into their gatherings. Obviously, they will already be using one or more of these elements.

New Ministries

Some groups may recognize that they as a group are called to ministry. They may have seen the need in their parish for a particular ministry, e.g., to the bereaved, to the elderly, to youth, to the homeless. They can approach the pastor and parish pastoral council about their ideas for beginning a particular ministry. After receiving approval, they, too, can begin to incorporate into their meetings any of the elements not already present in order to provide the strength of community for their own lives and for their new ministry.

When a parish starts new ministries, the Core Community can encourage those who will be working in these ministries to form ministerial communities from the beginning and not simply task-oriented committees. By integrating the five elements into their meetings, these groups will be ministerial communities from their inception.

Several examples are given below. They simply show how new ministries may come into existence either by forming small communities for a specific ministerial outreach or by inviting existing small groups to assume a more communal style and a particular ministry.

Hospital Visitation

A small community could be formed to visit a hospital or nursing home in the name of the parish. The support, spiritual nourishment, and ongoing learning that people receive from their meeting as a small community can give greater vitality to hospital/nursing home visits. This process can also help to make the volunteers more pastorally sensitive.

Hospitality

A small community could assume the ministry of hospitality. This ministry is multidimensional. For example, ministers of hospitality enrich the community experience of Sunday Eucharist by welcoming the people who gather. In addition, they assume the role of reaching out by personal visitation to all new members in the name of the parish community. Their own involvement in a small community will help them to experience hospitality and strengthen them for reaching out to others. At the time of their visits they may present new parishioners with a booklet or brochure outlining all the services and opportunities of parish life, invite them to join a small group to meet other people, or simply be available to answer questions. By linking new as well as long-term members of the parish, ministers of hospitality continue to foster the spirit of unity within the larger community.

Social Concerns

A small community may take on a ministry of direct service, e.g., collecting food or clothing for the needy, cooking meals for soup kitchens, or sheltering the homeless in church facilities or their own homes.

In addition to specific social concerns ministries in which people are involved in direct service to others, small ministerial communities could be involved in action for systemic change. They may also pray about and study contemporary issues and church teachings and be advocates for those who are homeless, needy, or oppressed.

The Elderly and Homebound

A small community might decide that more attention and care need to be given to the elderly and the homebound. They might explore "Meals on Wheels," home visitation, shopping, transportation, and the companionship needs of these parishioners. They would meet periodically to pray, to share ideas, and to support one another. During the liturgical seasons of Advent and Lent, they could lead a small sharing group in the home of one of the homebound or elderly.

Family Life

Many are concerned about the future of family life. A small community that prays and shares together could volunteer to work in building up family life in specific areas, such as preparing couples for marriage, assisting those who are separated or divorced, teaching natural family planning, or promoting better communication between parents and children.

Visiting Parents of Children (School)

A small community could visit and encourage parents of school children to take a more active interest in the parish and outline the various ways this could happen. The parents themselves could be asked to form a small group and explore the ministry of parenting. Visits by members of the small group could encourage parents of school children to explore church-related activities.

Special Interest Groups

Special interest groups, for example, prayer groups, Pax Christi groups, Cursillo groups, Marriage Encounter groups, teachers, adult catechetical classes and catechumens, meet regularly because of a common interest or experience. Although the particular focus of these groups differs, their development as small communities is similar to that of ministry groups within the parish. While maintaining their unique focus (prayer, study, married life, a particular outreach, etc.) they could reach agreement as to how each of the five elements of community would be integrated into their style of meeting or ministry.

Ministerial communities are ideally suited for teachers and catechists who recognize that the spark of religious living is ignited by the gift of faith. Learning assists religious faith, as St. Paul attests: "Keep on doing the things that you have learned and received and heard and seen in me, and the God of peace will be with you" (Phil 4:9). In the sharing of faith among teachers and catechists the fire of the Holy Spirit engenders new life. Faith is caught more than it is taught. Imagine the glorious impact upon students if teachers and catechists across the land centered their lives upon a loving and active relationship with Christ!

The reason for citing the above examples is obviously not simply to mention ministries, more fully explained elsewhere, but rather to consider the enriched possibilities of these ministries coming from a strong communal base.

Short-Term Ministries

Some ministries, for example, the ministry to the separated and divorced people in the church, are short-term ministries. People remain a part of these ministries while dealing with the trauma of transition from married life to single life. Although the term is short for those in need of ministry, there is usually an ongoing ministerial group in the parish that schedules, organizes, and offers hospitality for them. The separated and divorced could find in a small supportive setting others with whom they can share their hurts and struggles. In realizing that others have gone through similar traumas they often find courage and healing and resolve to begin their lives in a new way.

Other ministries within the parish, for example, the ministry to the bereaved will also benefit from a small group experience. Those who have suffered the loss of a loved one—spouse, parent, child, relative, or friend—often feel isolated and need time and support to deal with their loss. Those involved in ministry to the bereaved can invite those who have recently lost loved ones to gather in a small group setting. Here, through prayer and sharing, peer ministry again takes place as memories are recalled and tears are shed as part of the grieving and healing process. Elizabeth Collier, in her book, *Grieving the Death of a Loved One,* offers a marvelous tool for such a ministry (available from RENEW International, 888-433-3221).

ADDITIONAL BENEFITS OF MINISTERIAL COMMUNITIES

Many ministerial communities in the parish would contribute tremendously to the parish and beyond. Some benefits have already been stated; still others are revealed below.

- All ministries, committees, and organizations would be more prayerful and imbued with the spirit of Jesus and his mission as envisioned by the church. Prayer and Scripture sharing would encourage an openness to the Holy Spirit in all parish deliberations. Parishioners formed through ministerial communities often come forward to assume leadership roles within the parish, in the larger church, and in society.

- If a parish strove to be a community of many small communities, worship would be enlivened by the depth of faith of all those participating. Liturgical ministers could gather in their respective ministry groupings to plan and evaluate their ministries. At the same time, they would also pray and support one another. Ministers of the Word, celebrants, eucharistic ministers, ministers of hospitality, the music director and choir or folk group, altar servers—all would feel a greater sense of community and communicate this to the worshiping congregation.

- While family constitutes the most fundamental unit of church according to Vatican II, its very life would be strengthened in a variety of ways through support received in small communities. Parents trying to live and teach Christian values in their families would be strengthened in their endeavor when supported by others in peer ministry living the same values. Children, too, would benefit from small community support. Children suffering the loss of a parent through separation, divorce, or death or who have always been part of a single-parent family benefit from the communal relations of their single parent. Yet many find a place to talk about their loss and receive support in small groups, e.g., in a program such as "Rainbows for All God's Children." (Call your diocesan Family Life

Ministry for information.) The small community can become extended family for them.

- Children experiencing catechesis in a small community setting often feel freer to pray, to question and to discuss their faith. Often a small community for children takes on a particular outreach (in the same way an adult group does) such as visiting the sick or making favors for nursing homes, running errands, or raking leaves for homebound persons.

- More than periodic reunions are needed to follow through with teenage or young adult weekend retreat experiences. If small communities were implemented to complement these experiences, young people would be helped to live out what they learned and experienced in an ongoing, supportive atmosphere. Often young people return from these weekends full of enthusiasm, having made or renewed their commitment to Christ. Support is needed to sustain this commitment, and peer support is most influential for youth. A sound pastoral approach is to strengthen this conversion experience within small community follow-through and in periodic reunions of the larger group.

- High school and college students alike would find support in a small community where they could talk through something they heard in class, a moral issue, their vocation, etc. Young people growing up in this style of church have the potential for greater appreciation and ownership of faith. They would more easily feel a sense of belonging and most probably would remain a vital part of our parish communities.

- Sick and aged people in their own homes, nursing homes, and hospitals would no longer say: "I used to be a parishioner in 'Hope Springs' parish." They would still be parishioners. They would know it, feel it, and experience it as ministers to the sick, homebound and elderly visited, prayed and shared with them. Some of their needs would be met by their friends in ministerial communities. They would no longer worry about who would drive them to stores or doctors' offices, help with meals, or accompany them to the communal anointing of the sick. They could call upon their ministerial community friends as an extension of their family.

- No longer would the unknown or forgotten parishioner have no one present at his or her Mass of Christian burial, or, worse, be buried without any liturgical service. In a parish of small communities, hopefully, everyone would either be a part of a community or would be touched by the loving outreach of ministerial community members. No one would be unknown or forgotten! Community is as important today as it was in the time of Jesus' own ministry. No one is meant to be alone.

SUMMARY

All committees or ministry groups that strive for balance in incorporating into their meetings five elements of community building are growing more in Christian community themselves and are contributing to the development of the parish as a community of communities. When this approach of the pastoral direction is implemented, it enables many parishioners to be involved in ministry and, therefore, many more people to be ministered to both within and beyond the parish.

In Chapter 7 we will consider the basic commitment of those who belong to Christian communities, a detailed description of five elements of community, and some concrete helps for implementing small Christian communities in the parish.

✝✝✝✝✝ REFLECTION AND FAITH-SHARING QUESTIONS

Reflect on Luke 10:38–42, the basis of a personal testimony in the opening pages of this chapter.

1. Am I a "Martha" (constantly "doing," a "good worker") or a "Mary" (reflective, "good listener")?
2. Anxiety and lack of faith, not doing enough or trying to do too much, can put us "off balance." How does Jesus challenge me to achieve a balance in my life?
   • If I need to develop the "Martha" in me, what step can I take?
   • If I need to develop the "Mary" in me, what step can I take?
3. Considering the ministry/ministries in which I am involved in my parish, how can I help move the group toward a period of faith sharing with Scripture as part of our meetings?
4. How can I personally or we as a Core Community continue to challenge and support parish ministers to develop as ministerial communities?

7. Small Christian Communities

Those parishes that adopt the pastoral direction of the parish as a community of communities realize the tremendous potential for spiritual growth and evangelization that small Christian communities afford. Therefore they make the opportunity to belong to a small Christian community as much a normative part of parish life as religious education, sacramental preparation, and other parish experiences. Although seasonal small groups and ministerial communities offer countless opportunities for parishioners, it is ongoing small Christian communities that present an ideal to work toward. For it is in ongoing small Christian communities that people are especially helped to know and relate to one another, reflect on their life of faith in the company of others, and strive to apply the gospel to daily life.

Anegan Holmberg, csj

GOD BUILDS COMMUNITY

Those involved in small Christian communities often realize that although they make a sincere effort to share community, it is actually God who calls people to community and God who builds community. In fact, community itself is

> first and foremost a gift of the Holy Spirit, not built upon mutual compatibility, shared affection or common interests, but upon having received the same divine breath, having been given a heart set aflame by the same divine fire and having been embraced by the same divine love. It is God-within who brings us into communion with each other and makes us one.[1]

The parish, however, can nurture community and help to create the environment in which community happens.

• **Definition** A small Christian community is a face-to-face gathering of six to twelve people who invest time with one another for the common purpose of applying gospel values to every aspect of their lives.

These communities go beyond the limitation inherent in ministerial communities (that usually focus on particular ministries) and try to open members to see all of life as the field for ministry. They move beyond a means of function to assume a style of relationship that speaks clearly about community. Moreover, whereas ministerial communities are usually just breaking into the experience of a communal style, small Christian communities, as they grow, explore greater depths of community.

The particular type of small community that we shall be referring to as small Christian communities has particular characteristics that most completely embody what ministerial and seasonal small groups aspire to and have achieved to a degree.

• **Purpose** The basic purpose of small Christian communities is to create an environment in which people can grow in openness to the gospel, transforming every area of their lives and enhancing their commitment to live the mission of Jesus. Members must initially have some under-standing of this purpose in order to call forth one another in their spirit-ual growth. Through regular gatherings the full implications of being a small Christian community become increasingly apparent and challenging.

• **Time Commitment** Those involved in small Christian communities commit themselves to meet on a regular basis: weekly, every two weeks, or monthly. Ideally individuals initially agree upon a long-term com-mitment such as a three-year period. This length of time allows them to develop the richness of community. Periodically they reconsider whether they want to continue as a community.

• **Challenge for Small Christian Communities** The challenge for those in small Christian communities is to become increasingly whole-hearted or unconditional in their commitment to the movement of God's Spirit within themselves, within one another, and within the world. They seek total openness to God's grace moving them to holistic spiritual growth.

Those in small Christian communities and those working to develop and nurture them are guided and challenged by the characteristics of authentic small Christian communities as described by the U.S. bishops:

- obedience to the Word of God
- common prayer
- a commitment of time for building personal relationships
- meaningful participation in the life of the local parish
- some form of apostolic mission to the wider society
- an adherence to the Catholic faith
- an explicit relationship of communion with the church[2]

• **Value** Pastorally speaking, if small Christian communities were imple-mented in our parishes, they could make a significant change in our world. Small Christian communities help parishioners take their call to holiness seriously and try to be more open to the Spirit of God working in them—

especially through their prayer and sacramental lives. They likewise enable people to start living out their faith more fully in the family, in the neighborhood, in the global marketplace.

Can you imagine what would happen if everyone who came to a parish were invited to be a part of a small community? What a sense of belonging people would feel! How people would be challenged to grow and really get to know Jesus better! People who came to know ten or twelve people in small communities would really care for and support one another in their daily lives, and in times of crisis or sorrow or celebration. People would learn together and make a difference in their families, in their workplaces, in society.

An example of a small Christian community making a difference in their city comes from Hartford, Connecticut.

> One small Christian community which heard about the opening of a store in their town that would sell pornographic materials quickly mobilized their parish through other small communities. They successfully protested its coming. The store never opened.

• **An Ideal To Work Toward** Why are small Christian communities an ideal to work toward? The mission of Jesus relates to every aspect of our lives—our work and ministry, our relationships in family and community, and our leisure times. If people lived the gospel fully in all concrete aspects of their lives, both their lives and society would change.

Small Christian communities help people to find time and space to pray and to think through a variety of life issues: family, neighborhood, community, parish, business, society, ecology, politics, economics, etc. Small Christian communities help people to

- reflect on the actual events of their lives in light of Scripture
- pray through their experiences
- see contradictions between their actions and their values
- think through a Christian response
- move to appropriate action

The communal style of meeting is a welcome relief from a totally task-oriented, busy, alienated, and even lonely life experienced by so many in our society today. The very way a small Christian community comes together already achieves much of its purpose. This communal style is in itself a way for the reign of God to be realized in our midst.

Those who join ongoing small Christian communities use the community experience to integrate a deep spirituality into every aspect of their lives rather than to center on a specific ministry. This spirituality finds expression in a basic commitment to God that we will briefly explore.

COMMITMENT OF SMALL CHRISTIAN COMMUNITY MEMBERS

Small Christian community members make a basic commitment to nurture faithfully a deeper relationship with God. People become part of small Christian communities for various reasons. Some enter into these communities with a clear understanding of the commitment. More often, they begin with general good will and a basic understanding that the small community is going to call them to a deeper spirituality and a more loving care for people. Gradually, through participation in the small Christian community, they come to realize, appreciate, and accept the very full commitment that is called for in these communities. When those in small Christian communities are faithful to this commitment, the Spirit of God will be active in their lives and they will be prayerful, in good relationship with others, and committed to a better world.

Donal Dorr in his book *Spirituality and Justice* writes convincingly of the need for a balanced spirituality based on Micah 6:8. He speaks of three major spheres of spirituality: the personal, the interpersonal, and the public. Simply outlined, he makes the following correlation.

Walk humbly with your God—personal relationship with God
Love tenderly—the interpersonal aspect
Act justly—the area of public life[3]

This correlation is an excellent way to remember the threefold commitment to which Christians are called. The basic commitment of being faithful to the Spirit of God in our lives is expressed in a personal relationship to God, a relationship with one another, and a relationship with the larger community (from the parish to the world). Together these three expressions indicate a commitment to spiritual growth and point toward a balanced spirituality. In a very real way, these expressions are three aspects of the conversion process. Our spirituality must be rooted not just in one or two of these aspects, but in all three.

Although each expression of this commitment is integrally related to the others, it is appropriate to take each expression separately and examine its many facets.

Faithfulness to God

In small Christian communities, people are called to seek God above all else and make the effort to grow in a personal, loving relationship with God. Since God ultimately is the source of community, it follows that people in small Christian communities are called to be deeply in touch with that source if they are going to become a community where the power of the Spirit is more fully alive. Put simply, am I able to say that I have a personal relationship with Jesus? Is that evident to others by the way I live my life? When I awake in the morning, how long is it before I consciously think of God? How often do I reflect on God's presence during the course of the day and how much does that relationship influence my decisions and actions?

Small Christian communities can help members express their commitment to God in a variety of ways. Through these communities members encourage one another to live in God's presence and develop their relationship with God. They challenge one another to see God in all people and live out that awareness, especially in relationship to the seemingly less attractive, to the poor, to the oppressed and marginalized. They urge one another to find many other ways of expressing their faithfulness to God: by setting aside a specific amount of time each day for personal prayer and Scripture reading, by developing a mature Catholic life through sound learning and reading, and by embracing an integrated spirituality.

Faithfulness to One Another

When parishioners agree to be part of a small Christian community, they also agree to support the other members in living gospel values. This support is not just for crisis times but is often necessary on a daily basis. Small Christian communities call for a deep sense of mutual support so that people, in caring for each other, will grow in their ability to sense and rejoice in another's happiness and accomplishments as well as to detect any depression or frayed emotions.

Those in small Christian communities try to enable another to speak about a difficult experience so as to uncover its root cause. Such personal caring will help people whose jobs are in jeopardy by helping them to find new employment, will help parents who are experiencing difficulties in raising children, will reach out in times of sickness and grief and times of celebration.

Commitment

When small community members are committed to one another they will do extraordinary things. They will spend hours or days with a sick person in a member's family; they will help a community member to move or to build a home; they will adjust their own plans and schedules to join in a spontaneous celebration of an unanticipated joy. Because lasting spiritual relationships are formed in small communities, members begin to look upon one another as family. If perchance someone in the community dies and there are no close relatives, the members of the community might even have such a sense of responsibility that they would offer to assume responsibility for raising the children who were left.

In Milwaukee, Cle and Bob became the parents of a twelve-year-old girl and her sixteen-year-old brother thanks to a concern nurtured by RENEW. Bob was the attorney for a forty-three-year-old woman stricken with cancer. He was aware that the woman, long separated from her husband, wanted her brother to care for her children. However, as the woman's condition became critical, the brother became distressed. Near the end of the woman's life, he confided to her, "I can't take the children. I have three of my own to raise." Bob and Cle thought to themselves, "What do we do? This is no time to hesitate." Immediately they assured the woman they wouldn't let anything happen to her children. And that's how they became parents of a second family.

Openness

Community demands openness to people as they really are, not as we would like to see them. In the early honeymoon stage of community, people tend to idealize one another. As they continue to meet, they begin to know one another's faults and shortcomings as well as the good qualities. The real challenge is to remain open and patient with one another as irritating qualities surface.

When someone's aggressiveness or anger shows, friends need to be able to listen not only to the words spoken but also to the whole person (for example, voice inflection, body posture, facial expression) and then respond appropriately. Through active listening and loving responses members help, encourage, and effectively challenge one another. When members are truly committed to one another, trust, love, and honesty can eventually carry them beyond their difficulties and/or self-centeredness to new and deeper levels of relationship.

Forgiveness

When looking at the qualities that community calls forth, it becomes evident that forgiveness is often the most difficult of all. It is easy to support one another when all is going well. The test of Christian community is the willingness to forgive and overcome deep hurts, and the willingness to be forgiven. Christian community is called to be the "forgiving community of the forgiven." Forgiveness does not let hurts grow. When members of a small Christian community are committed to one another they need to review regularly how they relate to one another.

An amazing story of forgiveness and redemption wrought through the intervention of a RENEW faith-sharing community took place in the Diocese of Madurai, India. The incident took place in a rural village.

In a moment of frenzied fury occasioned by a family feud, Arul killed the wife of his elder brother Vincent and was sentenced to prison. Vincent vowed to seek out Arul on his release and kill him in revenge. With him he carried the knife he intended to use.

In the meantime, a RENEW faith-sharing community sought out Vincent to help him deal with his loss. He eventually joined the community.

On the day of Arul's release from prison, members of the community decided to meet him and bring him to a meeting at which forgiveness was the chosen theme and his brother would be present.

The brothers ignored each other at the start but in the midst of the meeting, Arul fell on his knees, asked for forgiveness and cried out, "Oh God, my sin is too great to be forgiven; please take my life in reparation for my sin."

On hearing this, Vincent leaped toward his brother, throwing off those who tried to restrain him. But instead of assaulting Arul, Vincent embraced him and the two wept copiously for 15 minutes. Members of the faith-sharing community, overwhelmed by the reconciliation, wept with them and joined in praising God. Today the brothers are ardent members of the RENEW small community and live in peace and harmony.

Accountability

Accountability to one another is a pivotal quality of small community members and has very practical implications. Among them is the responsibility of coming to meetings prepared. One aspect of preparation is praying during the week so that one brings the richness of God's Spirit to the meeting. If any neglect preparation frequently, they are called to their responsibilities by the others in a gentle, encouraging way. Members can be challenged while still affirming their goodness. To encourage and to challenge one another are not merely good things to do; such actions are at the heart of authentic Christian community.

Faithfulness to the Larger Community

Within this expression of the commitment to the larger community are two areas: the broader one of the world, the more focused one of the parish. Each will be considered in turn.

Parishioners often do not extend themselves beyond the parochial community, but rather confine their outreach to parish interests, activities, ministries. We will begin by reflecting on our commitment to the world first, in order to highlight the responsibilities of small Christian community members to reach out beyond the parish.

Commitment to the World

Commitment to the world means that small Christian community members strive to live and proclaim the gospel in every area of their lives. This brings the gospel into the family, the neighborhood, the marketplace, into areas of community life and politics, and eventually into every aspect of society—local, national, international!

Commitment to the world also means that small Christian community members have as much awareness about what is going on in distant places as they do about what is going on in their own area or country. Our interest in problems in our own neighborhood, city or town is often related to wider national and international problems. Through reflection and analysis members of small communities can become more knowledgeable about these linkages and about the basic unity of the human family.

Being committed to the world also means struggling to realize that all people are sisters and brothers. It means remembering them at prayer times, learning what can be done to address unjust structures, and acting to make this world a better place.

Commitment to the Parish

The small Christian community's mission to the larger community includes being part of the parish and part of the larger Catholic community. When small Christian communities do reach out in these areas they avoid the danger of becoming a closed group. When small Christian communities have a sense of mission there is less chance that they will be seen as elitist or separatist or in their own little church. Part of that mission is to be in service to the larger parish, the diocesan church, and the wider Catholic community.

The parish Sunday liturgical celebration is where all the people in small Christian communities come together with the other parishioners. Here it is extremely important that small community members reach out to other parishioners with a sense of hospitality. Hopefully, people will be able to say, "Look at these people in small Christian communities—see how they love one another and how they love us. Something wonderful must happen when they are together." Small Christian community members can provide a beautiful welcome for the alienated, the stranger, the newcomer, the visitor.

Members of small Christian communities need a wide vision to see where gospel values can be applied. From that vision, they can discern where to put their efforts and where to advocate that others in the parish or in the larger community use their gifts.

In effect, small Christian communities call people to respond to life-issues because the gospel, which has taken root in their hearts and minds, seeks expression. It creates in them an interest in making a better society and fostering the reign of God among us!

ESSENTIAL ELEMENTS OF COMMUNITY

In developing small Christian communities we emphasize five essential signs of communal life: sharing, learning, mutual support, mission, and prayer. These elements express a spirituality that acknowledges complete dependence upon God for the creation of community. The use of these elements also helps to assure the growth of vital community while providing a structured format for meetings.

These elements are certainly not all-inclusive, nor do they attempt to fully define small Christian communities. They are listed not as static qualities; they are intended to convey a sense of movement. The dynamic of small Christian communities is living, ever-growing and always deepening.

1. Sharing

Sharing means talking freely about God and about life experiences and reflecting on these in the light of Scripture and tradition.

In an atmosphere of trust, members share the meaning of faith and the Scriptures and reflect on how that faith and the Scriptures relate to their life experiences. Often this sharing results in more profound insight and in strengthening the belief of others in the small community. As the realities of people's lives are brought forth they are measured against the Word of God that becomes a two-edged sword demanding new hearts, attitudes and actions.

Personal sharing of faith empowers, challenges, and helps to transform lives. If people want to be in community, they have to be willing to share. Their commitment to one another implies a sense of openness. They make a conscious effort to build up the trust level within the community. Sharing in small communities encourages others to speak and often motivates people to change some aspect of their lives. In this setting people are often challenged to be totally responsive to the Lord. The role of the leader is key to helping people be open to meaningful communication, although all are responsible for drawing others into sharing Scripture, faith, prayer, and life experience.

In small Christian communities, people develop attitudes that carry over into every aspect of life. As these communities become life-sharing communities, lasting spiritual relationships are formed.

Consider the following example.

Monica was deeply saddened at the news that her friend Dolores had several inoperable, malignant tumors. Reminiscing about their past, Monica recalled how their being part of a small Christian community for 25 years helped them cut through all the superficialities of life and get to the heart of the matter—Jesus. Monica's words, "We aren't just friends, we are spiritual sisters," show the powerful and profound relationships developed in small Christian communities.

2. Learning

*Because small Christian communities are part of the wider church they
are called to an ever fuller knowledge and understanding of the gospel,
of the Catholic Church and its teaching on faith and morals, and of the
relationship of that teaching to the circumstances and issues of their
members' lives.*

The term *learning* is deliberately used to connote a broad sense of
learning. It includes catechesis, i.e., religious instruction for those already
baptized; skills, e.g., communication and leadership skills; learning about
the faith, gifts, and needs of others in the small community; learning about
the parish, local, national, and international situations; learning simple
methods of social analysis, etc.

The truly Catholic life of faith recognizes faith as a gift of God that
comes, at the same time, from the faith life of others. Through Scripture
and tradition, as they have been kept alive and applied by the church community and its teaching authority over the centuries, faith is nourished
and matures. Small community members are aided in their journey by the
teaching of the church that offers an authoritative guide as they search
the Scriptures.

Small Christian communities have the responsibility of being knowledgeable about their faith. Catechesis can take place in and through small
communities. For example, materials can be used that cover the foundational importance of Scripture, the nature of the church, the significance
of the sacraments, the primacy of Eucharist, and the basic call to holiness
and mission. The very nature of small communities also calls for members to have a clear understanding of their role and connectedness with
the larger parish, diocese, and universal church.

Through catechesis, small community members become more aware
of how God is revealed in the world, in Scripture, in the church, and in
their own personal lives. As Christian people journey together to maturity in faith, learning also provides the means for discovering and developing gifts, discerning how gifts are to be used for others, and recognizing

the diversity of roles that God has given, so that the body of Christ may grow to full stature. Commitment to learning acknowledges that the Christian is a seeker after truth and awakens the learner to the reality that one can never exhaust all there is to discover of the wonders of God, life, and the universe.

Because of the discipline and time required, practical ways to learn are needed. If a small Christian community member hears a lecture on prayer, takes a course on Scripture or theology, reads a good book, listens to a tape, attends a workshop, or participates in a retreat, and then shares some of the information experienced, the whole group will grow in knowledge. Some small communities decide to read an article pertinent to their life of faith and discuss it together. Others invite a speaker to the small community or to the parish to address an area of interest. Some parishes are discovering the importance of developing a resource library.

One of the most helpful ways for a small Christian community to grow in knowledge is to make a commitment to a long-term process of Christian formation. (Using *Why Catholic? Journey through the Catechism* [see p. 301] would be a tremendous asset to small communities in their process of Christian formation.)

3. Mutual Support

In a society in which gospel values are all too frequently ridiculed and rejected, the believer needs a community that is supportive of these values. The small Christian community encourages fidelity to the gospel and also challenges itself and its members to a more profound and authentic commitment to Christian living.

Support systems that once existed, such as the extended family, the neighborhood, and the secure job, are gone for the most part. The church has found it difficult to provide a structure that offers sufficient support. In a society that tends toward hopelessness and self-concern, Christians need the encouragement and support of others who share their belief in God.

Some parishioners who desire to grow spiritually realize they can do this best in a small community where they have the support of others. In fact, an experience of Christian community is becoming all the more necessary for the Christian who desires a deep faith life.

As individuals pray and share in their small communities the quality of the support they offer one another will grow. They come to know one another better and are more aware of both spoken and unspoken messages.

This support can be expressed in the form of mutual correction. When people truly want to grow, they are open to receive suggestions or corrections from others. They also gain courage to speak the truth in love as they offer their suggestions or corrections to others.

Mutual support flows very naturally out of prayer and sharing in a small community. It expresses itself in friendship, commitment, caring, and service. It is a response to Christ's call to love our neighbor as ourselves. Mutual support speaks to our human longing to be loved, encouraged, needed, respected, and challenged.

An Irish woman unknowingly encouraged and challenged the members of her RENEW small community.

> Anne Marie from County Mayo pledged that her action response for the coming week would be to write a letter of reconciliation to her brother to whom she hadn't spoken in years. No one else in the group made a response or offered to share a personal action for the week.
>
> As Anne Marie walked home confronting herself on her family disclosure, she felt disturbed and dissatisfied. She felt she had made a fool of herself. Each day she would say to herself, "I'll do it tomorrow," but she failed to do so.
>
> The following week, when the community gathered, Anne Marie was amazed when three individuals told their personal stories of reconciliation, all inspired by Anne Marie's outpouring. Anne Marie was deeply touched by the power of the Spirit working through her. She freely confessed her failure to carry out her proposed action but did it that very day.

Mutual support can be the simple expression of letting a person know someone is only a telephone call away; it can be a promise to remember someone in prayer; it can be more concrete in helping a person with studies or work or ministry. Mutual support may even be offering financial assistance to a community member in need. The kind of support needed in any given situation will become evident through the prayer and sharing that take place in the small community setting.

As people meet in small Christian communities they grow in their support of one another. As their trust level increases, so, too, do the situations and events, beliefs and values, dreams and hopes they share. With these sharings, people come to new realizations of how they can be more supportive. People who share community start to know they can count on one another in joyful and difficult times.

The following story illustrates the point more clearly.

> Bill, a member of a small group for some time, was troubled because his teenage daughter had run away from home and there was no indication as to where she was. He was so terribly upset, ashamed, and embarrassed that he told no one in his small community. One night Ed shared about his teenage daughter—she too had run away. Bill was totally disarmed by Ed's sharing. That sharing opened him up to a new experience and appreciation of the support of his community. The entire small community helped both men to express their feelings, comforted them, prayed with them, and promised to support them in their search for their daughters.

(Much of what could be said under "Mutual Support" was expressed earlier under "Faithfulness to One Another." Those discussing or evaluating these five elements within their small Christian communities would do well to review that section.)

4. Mission

Authentic Christian communities are, like Jesus, committed to a life of loving mission or service. As a group and through its individual members, the community will work for compassion, justice, reconciliation, and peace within the group, in the family, in the workplace, in the neighborhood, and within the wider society.

The purpose of forming a small Christian community is to help people live more like Christ. Jesus both preached and lived a message that had social implications. He said that his followers would be known by their works, by how they love one another. Jesus' own example challenges us to feed the hungry, clothe the naked, comfort the afflicted, be life-giving to others. A small Christian community's journey together includes reaching out and serving the needs of others.

Mission or outreach provides a way for people to respond to their desire to make the world a better place. Mission includes direct service to others, advocacy, and commitment to systemic change. The realm of mission includes everyday life in family, work, civic community, and parish as well as every area of human endeavor to which our lives are connected.

Small Christian communities differ from social, discussion, or study groups. Through the support received in their small Christian community, members reflect on gospel values and follow through with concrete action. They do not simply focus on service, but are conscious in their daily lives of the implications of the mission of Jesus. For example, someone may be the primary caregiver for an elderly parent and through this care may come to see how the system deals with the elderly with regard to medical benefits, housing, Social Security, etc. He or she may then choose to work toward replacing an unjust order or policy with one that gives greater opportunity to the elderly.

Someone else may be working for a corporation that is failing to pay a living wage to its workers in the third world. Challenging that person to think through this situation and work to change the unjust policy may require much prayer, study, reflection, sharing, and support. To act on such an issue may cause many repercussions. The person risks losing position, salary, status, perhaps even a part of his or her identity. Community support after the person has acted on his or her convictions may be even more necessary and valuable than the support given previously.

In addition to individual life situations, small Christian communities can study, pray, and discern how to move beyond their local situations to address the needs of the wider community and the world, particularly the needs of the poor. Not only do needs have to be addressed but also the underlying causes of those needs. An examination of a particular situation by the community may uncover unjust policies that could be addressed.

Community members support one another in this effort to uncover and act upon both personal and structural injustice. Through their reflection and prayer they gain new insights about how they can bring the gospel message to bear on their decisions.

The very flow of communal meetings leads the small community members to action decisions whereby they will carry out the work of mission. The process of sharing can start with general concern, move people to reflection on their personal experience in relationship to that concern, and then to a point of deciding "what they are going to do" about the concern. The leader and all the community members are vigilant in seeing that the community comes to a resolution of specific action. That sense of responsibility carries over to the next meeting when people report on how they carried out their intended mission action.

A beautiful example of this process took place in All Saints Parish, Puyallup, Washington.

> At a small-group meeting one participant, Shawn, who works at a Catholic Community Services family shelter in Tacoma, told of his pain in trying to help families find affordable housing. Too often he had to tell them, "Nothing is available."
>
> Moved by Shawn's account, one member suggested that the group involve itself in the problem. "I think God wants us to stop talking and start doing," said another.
>
> For the next five months the group met weekly. They researched housing needs. They wrote grant applications. They prayed for guidance.
>
> They formed a corporation called Mi Casa (My Home), requested and received non-profit status and began to search for apartment units they could purchase. They applied for a $130,000 grant from the state and solicited contributions from friends and parishioners.
>
> Eventually Mi Casa was able to purchase two six-unit apartment buildings. Mi Casa hired a sister to manage the buildings and to assist the residents with other needs and development work.
>
> All 12 units are full. Mi Casa is a success. And it started with RENEW.

Hopefully the day will soon arrive when the notion of community cannot be spoken of without the implicit understanding of mission. In the long run, small Christian communities will probably be judged more than anything else by their success (or failure) in carrying out mission.

5. Prayer

The element of prayer emphasizes the centrality of God's active presence in each small Christian community member's life and in the life of the community itself.

Prayer—both personal and communal—is emphasized here as a means of spiritual growth. One's prayer life and how one lives out the whole of life are very much related to the growth of small community.

As people open their hearts in prayer, they very often seek a deeper relationship with the triune God and with others. Prayer is an honest acknowledgment of our dependency on God's grace and of our inability to create community and carry out mission by ourselves.

As community develops people must be constantly challenged to grow in their individual prayer lives and in communal prayer. Those coming to a community meeting can only contribute from the richness of their daily lives. The community offers a wonderful opportunity to learn more about prayer and to establish an accountability to one another that encourages growth in daily prayer.

In praying together the small community consciously opens itself to God's gracious action. As the community prays together, there can be a keen sense of that presence and a greater willingness to acknowledge dependence on God and on one another. In small Christian communities, then, people come to know God more profoundly—God who is at once near and distant, loving and yet hidden in mystery. The environment and dynamic of small Christian communities provide both a transcendental and an experiential dimension for participants to discover God through prayer, sharing, and outreach: transcendental in the search for God who remains mystery; experiential in discovering Christ in the midst of two or three or more gathered in God's name (see Mt 18:20).

A wide variety of prayer forms—from quiet centering prayer to praying the Liturgy of the Hours, the official prayer of the church—are available today. Prayer can be as simple as learning to read Scripture prayerfully and reflectively, perhaps taking one passage or one line at a time, savoring each word, letting it sink into one's heart and make its home there. The daily examen can be an extremely effective way to become more conscious of the presence of God. In this practice, one invokes the Spirit to see where God has been at work in one's life and where one has failed to be present to God. It helps us to look at how we have responded to or moved away from moments of grace. The use of the examen is a very beautiful and practical way to end the day.

In a small Christian community setting, members can share the prayer forms they use. By sharing how they pray, members can teach and inspire one another to develop new styles of prayer which may lead to a greater intimacy with God. Sharing about their prayer life at meetings can encourage all to be more faithful to prayer. In the small Christian community's atmosphere of trust, people may even feel free to admit that they have not been praying—an admission that may be the starting point in developing a prayer life. (See Chapter 14 for further reflection on prayer forms.)

Some may seek spiritual direction to assist them in their spiritual journeys. In this way they are enabled to look at the totality of their lives with a person experienced and knowledgeable about the spiritual life. Often through spiritual conversation with another, the "blind spots" of one's life are brought to greater consciousness, one is in greater touch with the conversion process, and a more profound sense of God's action in one's life is gained. At their gatherings, small Christian community members can discuss the benefits of having a spiritual friend or spiritual director who shares a person's spiritual journey.

A small Christian community may occasionally bring in a guest speaker or hold a day or an evening of reflection. By so doing the members share a common experience that can be a springboard for further growth in the spiritual life. During this period of reflection they also have the opportunity to take quiet time to reflect on the quality of their life as a small Christian community.

Members can greatly benefit from spiritual reading and daily reflection on the Scriptures. They can share and exchange spiritual books that they have read and recommend books and tapes to one another. Members can also call one another to frequent participation in the sacraments of penance and Eucharist where they can encounter Christ in profound ways!

At their meetings participants are encouraged to share the commitments they have made to spiritual growth since they last met, and how faithful they were to those commitments. In this way they become accountable to one another and challenge one another to growth. Through prayer small Christian community members acknowledge that the good they accomplished is a reflection of the presence of God. They realize how directly God's action is involved in the creation of community and how deliberate must be their choice for deeper union with God for the realization of true Christian community.

In addition to the above practices, small Christian community members can prepare for their meetings by prayerful reflection upon God's action in their lives since the last meeting and by attentiveness to the Scriptures and other readings to be discussed during the session.

As each of the above elements is incorporated into the daily lives of the small Christian community members, spiritual growth will take place. The quality of small Christian community members' daily lives, how they live out their relationships, how they allow God's Spirit to operate in their everyday lives—all of these reflect how God can act in a small community setting.

DEVELOPING SMALL CHRISTIAN COMMUNITIES

Those who begin or join small Christian communities have various expectations and understandings. Some who respond to the invitation to small Christian community involvement come with a very rudimentary understanding of the commitments involved. They may start with a general willingness to see what small Christian community is about and gradually grow in *understanding the commitments* involved in being a part of a small Christian community.

Others may begin with a very clear realization and appreciation of the full concept of small Christian communities and the commitments that will be involved, and be willing to grow through this experience.

Still others, who are invited after being involved in seasonal small groups or ministerial communities, may already see the importance of the basic communal approach bearing on all aspects of their life and the need for deeper commitments and respond in a wholehearted way. The initial experience they had reveals the depth of possibilities for spiritual growth, support and mission, and motivates and challenges them to continue in a small Christian community.

Personal invitation is the most effective means of appealing to a group or individual for making a commitment to small Christian communities. The depth of communal commitment called for in small Christian communities and the serious pursuit of fulfilling the spiritual and social mission of Jesus demand an emotional and spiritual readiness and maturity. The formation of small Christian communities, therefore, calls for a certain amount of discernment on the part of the Core Community that extends invitations, as well as on the part of those seeking to join small communities.

The Core Community can encourage the development of small Christian communities in a variety of ways. Four key factors in developing small Christian communities are highlighted here.

Invite, Motivate, Witness

The first step is *personally* to extend an invitation to individuals or to groups of people who are good candidates for commitment to small Christian communities. (General invitations are more suited to seasonal small groups.) A personal invitation motivates response. When this invitation is accompanied by some form of witnessing or sharing, it is highly effective. Sharing the value and beauty of small Christian communities and pointing to reasons why people join small Christian communities are also helpful.

Seize the Moment After Seasonal Small Groups

After the seasonal small group experience, participants are invited to complete an *evaluation form* that explains the nature of small Christian communities and asks if parishioners would like to continue meeting on a regular basis in the style of a small Christian community. If there are sufficient members who discern to continue as a small Christian community, their leader can help them decide on the most convenient time and inform the Core Community. If the number who wish to continue as a small Christian community is small, the Core Community may arrange for others from other seasonal small groups to join with them.

Invite at Follow-Up Celebrations

After holding seasonal groups, a Core Community may have a *follow-up celebration,* for example a potluck supper followed by time for sharing and witnessing by small group participants. On these occasions, the Core Community can give a brief explanation of the nature of small Christian communities and provide sign-up cards for those who discern to continue meeting on a more regular basis as a small Christian community.

Issue Individual Invitations

Some small Christian communities develop as a result of an *individual's suggestion or invitation.* The person issuing the invitation may be a member of the pastoral staff, a Core Community member, or a parishioner. The invitation may be given personally to an individual parishioner or to a group of parishioners.

A pastoral leader can invite a group of parishioners together to talk about what it means to live the Christian life fully. This simple invitation may interest and intrigue people since it is a call to meet new people, to grow with others, and to influence society.

Invite New Parishioners as SCC Participants

New parishioners may want to meet new people or may come from an experience of small communities in another parish and are looking to be part of another. When they register and make this known the staff can give their names to the Core Community who will meet and place them.

Develop Leaders

A second key factor in developing small Christian communities is leadership development. Once small community leaders understand their role and responsibilities, a major part of developing small communities has begun. Through their leadership they will help members to use a structured format in their gatherings based on the five elements of community.

Gradually they will help members to understand their commitment to nurturing a deeper relationship with God. Together, the leaders and small community members can explore how faithfulness to this commitment will lead them to be more prayerful, to build a good relationship with each other, to be actively involved in the parish and to be effective in working for a better world. (See Chapters 8 and 11.)

Establish a Core Community

In order to develop small Christian communities effectively, a strong Core Community needs to be established to carry out all of its responsibilities, such as motivating and inviting parishioners, developing and pastoring small community leaders, selecting good materials, etc. (See Chapter 8 for a full development of the Core Community and for other areas of responsibility.)

Staff Support

Another important factor in developing and sustaining small Christian communities is staff support. Parishioners need to know that the pastor and staff believe in and encourage small Christian communities.

Small Christian communities need the guidance of sound pastoral leaders. As people discover or rediscover the power of the gospel, these leaders can help them understand the true and full meaning of God's Word. Guidance from the pastoral staff and the use of good resources can help strengthen the understanding of our Catholic faith and tradition.

People in small Christian communities need to receive encouragement from parish leadership. People are basically good and often need some form of encouragement to put their goodness into action. Parish leadership is in an ideal position to offer such encouragement.

Small Christian communities need to experience a sense of belonging. Members of small Christian communities should feel part of a larger believing, praying, celebrating, missionary church community. The staff can help them appreciate that they are part of a long tradition in the church and that they have a role to play in the church. "They need to be tied into the life of the whole parish and they need to be kept from becoming self-enclosed cliques. This support from outside can help groups to be open to new members, to reach beyond themselves and to take leadership in forming other groups."[4] (For additional material on priests and staff support see Chapter 11.)

SUMMARY

In these last three chapters we have looked at three related approaches that the parish can use in the process of becoming a community of small communities:

1. inviting all parishioners to participate in seasonal small groups during the fall and/or Advent and Lent;
2. encouraging all ministries to come from a base of community by developing ministerial communities;
3. providing opportunities for parishioners to be part of parish-based, ongoing small Christian communities.

In order to extend these opportunities for spiritual growth for all parishioners we recommend that a Core Community for small community development be established. In Chapter 8 we will explore this idea in detail.

ANN'S STORY

Let us close with Ann's story, as told by her friend, which captures a sacred moment in the life of one small Christian community.

Our small community had gathered in my living room as we do every week to pray, share the Scriptures, and make connections to our own lives. We quieted ourselves through sharing of spontaneous prayer, and then someone read the gospel passage for the coming week. The faith sharing started in the direction of what it means to be a lost sheep. As the sharing went on, I looked to my left and saw my dear friend Ann begin to cry. Silently. No noise. Just streams of tears cascading down her face.

I was frozen. Ann and I talk every day. I thought, "My God, what could have happened since yesterday to make this very private, down to earth, perfectly together woman react like this right now?" "Just be with her," I thought. "Let her decide whether to share." "Oh God," I prayed, "be with her and help us to be present to her." No one commented on the fact that Ann was so visibly upset, but the miracle of the moment began to unfold as everyone in the room continued to share but gave Ann every opening to talk.

It became a sensitive climate—serious conversation mixed with laughter. Ann was laughing too, and everyone was letting her set the direction of conversation. Still, she did not say what was the cause of her tears until we were ready to close the meeting with prayer and someone said, "Ann, I noticed that you were upset. Is there anything that we can do?"

"I hadn't planned on coming tonight because the day was so hard," she said, "but something made me come here. I thought I could handle it all by myself. Today I signed the divorce agreement and I saw twenty-five years of marriage go down the drain. I heard my husband say, 'I don't want to be married anymore.' We had so hoped that he would come back to us—but he's not. I feel so lost—just like that sheep in the gospel story."

As she continued to share, I was more certain than ever that healing was taking place; the dying and the rising that we remember about the death of Jesus and that we live over and over again in our own lives.

It was an honor and a privilege to share that moment with Ann, and to end the evening with prayer for her husband, for her, and for all the lost sheep of the world—for the times when each of us feels lost and for the wisdom to allow ourselves to participate in God's time to gift us with new-found life.

Ann continues to be her usual "together" self as she moves forward in her life, but says she will never forget the love that she experienced that night, and neither will we. We are all different people now.

✝✝✝✝✝ REFLECTION AND FAITH-SHARING QUESTIONS

Reflect on John 15:1–10 and Micah 6:8.

1. A time when I felt God at work in bringing about community was....
2. Small Christian communities directly connect faith to life issues, e.g., family, work, civic responsibility, etc. Why is this so important in our own lives and in the life of the church today?
3. Have our small communities moved beyond doing laudable projects to actually carrying out the full implications of the gospel message in their daily work environment, in social justice issues, etc.?
4. What advantages in terms of reflection and action do small communities offer in the above-mentioned areas?
5. Which of the five elements—prayer, sharing, mission, learning, and mutual support—need to be strengthened in my primary small community? How do these elements help us to grow spiritually?
6. In developing small Christian communities, what immediate steps would I or we take?

8. Core Community Development

The implementation of the vision of the parish as a community of many small communities is certainly a responsibility to be shared by committed people. Pastors and other pastoral staff members will probably be reluctant to embrace this direction if the full weight of its implementation rests with them. Therefore, it is recommended that a Core Community for small community development be started. In this community willing parishioners are united with pastor and staff in a spirit of collaboration.

Since a Core Community of committed, prayerful people can work wonders for a parish adopting the pastoral direction, we will offer specific guidelines for the selection of the Core Community and outline its role and responsibilities. In addition a formation process for developing a Core Community is outlined here. The parish staff will find these sessions helpful when they begin to form a Core Community. In the process of using these sessions, those chosen for the Core Community begin to experience for themselves what it means to be a small ministerial community.

Marion C. Honor, CSJ

WHAT IS A CORE COMMUNITY?

A Core Community is a group of six to twelve parishioners who come together with the pastor and/or one staff member

- to form community themselves
- to foster opportunities for developing the parish as a community of small communities
- to ensure sound development and care of these communities

CHOOSING THE RIGHT PEOPLE—
WHO ARE THEY?

Once the pastor, staff, and parish pastoral council have accepted this pastoral direction as a priority for their parish, the pastor and staff, perhaps together with some parishioners, need to choose six to twelve parishioners to serve on the Core Community. This group discerns the names of possible Core Community members, keeping in mind the following criteria:

- people who believe in and are committed to small Christian communities and who see their value and impact on the world
- people who know how to motivate others and make things happen
- people who are willing to pray and work to see that this vision is implemented
- people who are willing to grow as a community
- people who are willing to make at least a one-year commitment but preferably a three-year commitment

The means of selection ought not to be one of merely appointing people or asking for volunteers, but of truly asking the Spirit's guidance for potential members of this community. It is wise to list more names of people than are needed since not everyone may be able to respond affirmatively.

After names are surfaced an exploratory meeting will help these potential members to learn more about the Core Community. The pastor personally invites each person to this meeting and shares why each was chosen to participate.

QUALITIES OF CORE COMMUNITY MEMBERS

The following qualities also ought to be kept in mind when selecting Core Community members. Although each person may not have these qualities in the same degree, it is essential that all qualities be found in the Core Community as a whole.

Faith-filled—a firm belief in the gospel of Jesus Christ and in the value of small communities to help people live the Christian life. The faith-filled person recognizes the importance of the church's sacramental life in maintaining Christian identity.

Committed—a willingness and availability to commit time and energy to renewal and growth of the people of God through small community development. Commitment is one of the key elements of community development. The Core Community members envision their own community responsibilities as very important to a renewed church and worthy of deep personal commitment.

Relational—an ability to relate and work well with diverse parish groups, parishioners, and staff, e.g., priests, sisters, brothers, lay staff, and deacons.

Respectful—an appreciation for all those with whom they come in contact, an openness to differences of opinion.

Able to make things happen—the ability to motivate others in order to live out the goals and objectives.

Organized—the competence to accomplish the tasks related to the development of small communities.

Sensible—the ability to use good judgment and to share laughter and joy with others.

Spiritual—the ability to grow in adult Christian spirituality and to articulate their faith. Christians who are maturing spiritually ought to have an openness and respect for the diversity of ways that faith is expressed.

In essence, people of faith are needed who have relational ability, believe in this pastoral direction, desire to see it implemented in their parish, and are willing to commit themselves to work for its gradual realization.

SELECTING A COORDINATOR OF THE CORE COMMUNITY

There is great value in choosing a coordinator for the Core Community before the Core Community development begins. The person the pastor chooses as coordinator may be in another ministry. In order to serve as coordinator, he or she may need to leave the former ministry for the possible greater good of the parish. When the coordinator is in place beforehand, the group starts with clarity of leadership, stability, and a greater sense of direction and will more easily engage the interest and involvement of highly qualified people. A vague start could easily cause the loss of interest of the most valuable people. Some may fear that they may be pressured to fill the coordinator position.

As the pastor/staff and parishioners discern the Core Community members, they can also be alert to the person they believe would best coordinate the work of the Core Community. (It is best to have several names in order of preference in case the first person is unable to assume the responsibility.) The pastor then personally contacts the person chosen for the role of coordinator and encourages this person to accept this role.

If a coordinator is not selected before the process of developing a Core

Community, the Core Community members themselves could select a coordinator through a process of discernment. If this selection process is used, it is understood that the person chosen by the Core Community would be acceptable to the pastor and the staff.

ROLE OF THE CORE COMMUNITY

The role of the Core Community is to hold before the parish the vision of the parish as a community of many small communities and to work toward its implementation by fostering the development of small groups and communities in the parish. That effort must be sensitive to the ways in which the parish is already encouraging small group/community experiences. For example, if the parish has used the RENEW process, some small groups may continue to meet periodically. Other groups may have already moved toward being small Christian communities.

Ideally the parish staff and parish pastoral council will clearly articulate the pastoral direction. Yet, practically speaking, the Core Community together with the parish staff members may assume this role and propose the pastoral direction to the council for affirmation. Once the pastoral direction has been articulated and affirmed, the Core Community, together with the pastor or other pastoral staff persons, assumes primary responsibility for its implementation.

In developing the parish as a community of communities, the Core Community plans and implements seasonal small groups, fosters the incorporation of five elements of community in the various parish groups, committees, ministries, and organizations, and initiates, encourages, and supports the development of small Christian communities.

RESPONSIBILITIES OF THE CORE COMMUNITY

The responsibilities of the Core Community are explained below. As the Core Community addresses these responsibilities, the pastoral direction begins to take root and grow in the parish.

Growing Together as a Community

The members of the Core Community commit themselves not only to the ministry of small community development, but also to forming community among themselves. Thus they incorporate the five elements of community growth into their meetings and way of life. Absolutely essential among these elements is prayer. Through both personal and communal prayer, the Core Community discerns the implications of the pastoral direction for the parish.

As the members of the Core Community increasingly open themselves to being filled with the Spirit of God, they become more life-giving to others and have greater potential for building Christian community. They experience first-hand the joys and disappointments, the struggles and hopes of striving for community and are better able to understand the growth of other groups and communities.

Developing a Climate of Acceptance for the Pastoral Direction

The Core Community works to develop a climate of acceptance for the pastoral direction throughout the parish. It presents the direction to various groups in the parish. A variety of means, including speaking at Sunday liturgies or holding a parish assembly, can be employed to present the direction to the entire parish. Since the Core Community members are concerned about a style of parish, working toward total acceptance continues to be part of the ongoing ministry of the Core Community. For example, as the membership of the parish pastoral council changes through the years, the Core Community can make a presentation to the council as well as to committees and ministerial groups so that new members can understand the value of seasonal small groups, ministerial communities, and small Christian communities.

Planning and Evaluating

The Core Community begins by assessing what small groups, ministerial communities, and small communities are already in place in the parish. (See Appendix, pp. 283-89, for some helps in doing this assessment.)

The Core Community then plans by setting long-term goals. In order to set goals, the community may focus on the question: "Considering the pastoral direction, what do we want our parish to look like in five years?"

One possible goal would be to have ten percent of the parish in small communities within five years. After developing a goal or goals, the Core Community sets yearly objectives as stepping-stones toward achieving the long-term goals. Some examples of first-year objectives toward a five-year goal could include the following:

1. to hold seasonal, small groups during Lent;
2. to work with three ministerial committees that seem most receptive to growing from committee to community;
3. to initiate two new small Christian communities within six months.

The second-year objectives build on and extend the objectives of the previous year. This could include increasing the number of times for holding seasonal small groups, e.g., in both the autumn and Lent, scheduling a large group experience for all participants in ministerial communities, or doubling the number of new small Christian communities.

The Core Community ought to have a good sense of accomplishment in achieving its yearly objectives. By following a planning process the Core Community moves step by step toward implementing a new vision of parish. It is recommended that the Core Community coordinate its yearly objectives/plans with other parish ministries.

Successful planning involves evaluation. Throughout the year the Core Community evaluates the progress of parish small communities. Periodically and annually, it evaluates if and how well the objectives have been accomplished. The Core Community uses this information as it plans for the following year.

Recruiting Invitational Ministers

The Core Community can enlist the help of other parishioners called "Invitational Ministers" to broaden the base of inviting people to small communities. These Invitational Ministers make personal and home visits as well as telephone calls, and they conduct Sign-Up Sunday. The need to select extremely credible people, particularly young adults and parents who can visit parents of first communicants and other parents of school-age children, is crucial to inviting young adults to participate in small communities.

Invitational Ministers can be as creative as their imaginations allow in developing ways to invite people. They can organize gatherings, i.e., café evenings, parties in people's homes, lunches, etc., and participate in parish activities such as a potluck supper, choir practice, Girl Scouts, etc., in order to share about small communities.

They can organize the telephone campaign, assuring that every parishioner who has not signed up for a small community after Sign-Up Sunday receives a personal telephone invitation. (See Chapter 9 for a complete explanation of the "Invitational Ministry.")

Developing Leaders

The development of small community leaders may very possibly be the most important way to ensure that the pastoral direction of small communities will take root in the parish and succeed. A well-formed lay leadership is needed to guide parish-based small communities. While great strides have been taken in recent years in the formation of lay people, more emphasis can be given to the specific role of small community leadership formation.

A prime responsibility of the Core Community is to plan and coordinate training for small group/community leaders. Development of small community leaders is imperative if the small community is to be focused. The leader has the responsibility for guiding the community through the faith-sharing, prayer, and action response of the small community sessions. The leader keeps the community on the topic with charity and flexibility, gently includes hesitant members, and develops a warm, accepting, open climate and group cohesiveness.

As the pastoral direction of small communities takes root and grows, small community leaders—through their own attitude of openness, flexibility, and faith conviction—can help evangelization to flourish. Since every small community is responsible for this mission, leaders need to develop an "atmosphere of evangelization," that is, they need to encour-

---

Sharing the Faith

Small community leaders can help evangelization to flourish in three ways:

- openness
- flexibility
- faith conviction

---

age an openness on the part of all to be evangelized or reevangelized and to go forth to share their faith with others.

Leaders need to ensure that their small communities are always inclusive, always open to inviting new members and welcoming them. This will be both blessing and task for the small communities as they are enriched by the faith sharing of new members and are stretched in their reaching out to welcome and adjust to new members who are searching for God in their lives. Small community leaders can help members consciously accept the adjustments that will be necessary for new persons to be integrated into the small community.

Small community leaders set the tone and atmosphere in which others are encouraged to share faith. At each meeting ample opportunity should be offered for each member to share where he or she met Jesus during the past week in prayer, through participation in the sacraments and/or in relationships with others. The members also need time to share the occasions when they were able to evangelize, e.g., talk to another about their faith in Jesus, invite a relative, acquaintance, or friend to their small community or to another parish event or gathering.

As each small community grows, it will need to discern the time to "divide and multiply" and form into two or more new small communities. Although many will want to stay together, the spirit of evangelization may call for the formation of new communities. Understanding the stages of community growth will help the leader in this area. If a small community prayerfully decides to divide, time for celebrating the past, expressing feelings over the new life to which God is calling the community, and prayer for the future ought to be a part of the process.

When small community leaders can participate in a process in which core concepts of the Catholic faith are presented simply and clearly, they will both grow in the knowledge of their faith and come to appreciate the value of being formed in community. The participation of small community members in discussion and sharing of experience, prayer, and reflection can be a critical part of the process.

As small Christian community leaders grow in faith, the potential for prayer, learning, sharing, mutual support, and mission is boundless.

In addition, the Core Community provides continuing support for small community leaders in a variety of ways, including the following activities.

Providing Materials

The Core Community coordinates (and at times may develop) resources for small communities to use during their gatherings. Often the Core Community will have a bibliography of available resources or have sample copies from which the small community leaders may choose their materials. Some parishes may buy materials in quantity and lend them to small communities for a period of time.

Good materials are essential in enabling small Christian communities to grow. Materials that touch on various aspects of our faith, the moral and social teachings of the church, the Sunday readings, and those which open up possibilities for prayer, reflection, sharing, and action are recommended. The most important materials are not necessarily those with which people are most comfortable but those that stretch their thinking and help them to relate the gospel to all areas of their lives.

In these materials a progression of questions is important for the gradual engagement of small Christian community members. The best materials for small community members to use are those that go from objective thought to reflection on personal experience to concrete and specific action. The action may be a determination of how to grow spiritually or what to do about a problem or situation. The flow of the meeting should naturally lead to action.

Materials such as *Why Catholic? Journey through the Catechism* and the IMPACT Series skillfully interweave the key elements for small Christian community growth. IMPACT booklets, many of which use the social inquiry approach of observe, judge, and act, are designed to help people connect faith to a wide range of human concerns and issues. Participants will be led not only to prayerful reflection and fruitful sharing but also to concrete actions that positively influence human attitudes and behavior.

In addition to knowing key materials for small Christian community development, the Core Community needs to be aware of materials that will facilitate development of ministerial communities. It is important to select materials that will be non-threatening and easily used by current parish committees or ministries. *PrayerTime (Cycles A, B, C)*—by Robert Heyer, editor (RENEW International)—is a three-volume series designed specifically for ministerial communities. The purpose of these books is to foster and facilitate a prayerful and supportive environment through which all types of ministry within the parish can be enriched and empowered. (All materials cited above are available from Small Christian Community Resources, RENEW International, 1232 George St., Plainfield, NJ 07062-1717.)

When members of any conceivable committee, ministry, group, or organization in the parish spend the first 20-30 minutes using these materials, they would move in a gentle way toward the community values of which we have been speaking. Using such resources may offer the first opportunity for many in the ministry to share Scripture and spontaneous prayer in a small group setting. When a particular parish committee/ministry begins to pray in this way on a consistent basis, people become more present to themselves, to one another, and to God. Also parishioners will become more comfortable in sharing Scripture, faith, and prayer. As community develops among participants, more positive outcomes for ministry can certainly be projected.

Coordinating Activity

In many ways the Core Community coordinates the activities of the various small communities. The Core Community sponsors occasions that will bring them together for large-group experiences—weekend retreats, picnics, Christmas parties, potluck suppers, rallies, etc.—and sees that overall harmony is maintained through a good system of communication. The best form of communication is personal. It can be enhanced by e-mail, parish Web sites, bulletins, and newsletters.

Providing Pastoral Care

The ministry of pastoral care is one of the most beautiful aspects of the Core Community's work. The members foster the growth and development of all the small communities in the parish. Their ministry includes encouragement, caring, looking after, tending to, challenging, developing, and nourishing growth with leaders and small communities themselves. Because of its importance this responsibility is more fully developed in Chapter 10.

Communicating

The Core Community maintains good communication with parish staff, council, and other groups working in the area of community building and tells parishioners of its activities and efforts through appropriate channels.

Being Accountable

The Core Community is accountable to the pastoral leadership: the pastor and/or parish staff and/or the parish pastoral council. It is recommended that parishes develop whatever structure most effectively facilitates good communication. It is possible in a situation in which the pastor and parish strongly advocate the pastoral direction that the consultative bodies of the parish pastoral council and the Core Community could eventually become synonymous.

The presence and ministry of a Core Community can ensure that the vision of small communities will remain constant in the changing circumstances of a parish. For instance, if the pastor is changed, the coordinator needs to communicate with the new pastor about the ministry of the Core Community, invite his involvement, and work in close harmony with him.

Rotation of Core Community Members

When parishioners are first asked to be part of the Core Community a time commitment is usually determined. This term is usually for two or three years. In order to insure the viable continuation of the Core Community it is necessary to set up a system of rotation so that not all members of the Core Community end their ministry term at the same time. It is also wise to begin discerning after the first year those parishioners who will be invited to be part of the Core Community.

FORMATION PROCESS FOR CORE COMMUNITIES

A formation process has been developed and used successfully in the development of Core Communities. The following outline briefly describes this formation process. (The complete process is available from RENEW International.)

Session I: *A Pastoral Direction of the Parish as a Community Made Up of Many Small Communities*

Session II: *Responsibilities and Qualities of Core Community*
- rationale for small communities
- definition and need for Core Community
- responsibilities and qualities of Core Community

Session III: *Hopes and Expectations*
- tasks involved
- time commitment
- frequency of meetings
- prayer life of Core Community
- knowledge and skills to be gained

Session IV: *Developing Goals and Objectives for Core Community*
(This session usually requires two meetings or an extended meeting.)
- ministry goal and objectives
- Core Community life goal and objectives

Session V: *Discernment of Gifts*
- prayerful reflection on gifts
- obstacles to identifying gifts
- reflection on the Holy Spirit, gift-giver

Session VI: *Reflection on the Mission of Jesus*
  - the reign of God
  - the meaning of the mission
  - being "sent forth"

SUMMARY

We began this chapter with a definition of the Core Community, qualities to look for in the selection of Core Community members, and some recommendations for the selection process itself. Then we looked at the role and responsibilities of the Core Community. As these responsibilities are lived out, the development of seasonal small groups, ministerial communities, and small Christian communities will gradually take place. As these various approaches to achieving this pastoral direction are put into practice, the whole life of the parish can be affected in a positive way. (See Chapter 13.)

Of course, the task of implementing this pastoral direction is never fully accomplished. Core Communities will always be able to invite parishioners to be part of seasonal small groups because of the mobility of people and because of the varying circumstances of parishioners' lives. Some people will become available and open to this kind of invitation for a short-term small-group experience at different times in their lives.

As parishioners become involved in the various ministries of the parish, the Core Community, together with those already involved in ministry, can introduce them to a communal style of meeting. In addition, the Core Community will always find ways to support small community leaders and the small Christian communities themselves as they strive to apply the gospel to all areas of their lives.

Core Community members will fulfill their responsibilities with greater spirit and support as they continue to grow as a small Christian community. A prayerful, resourceful Core Community is crucial in bringing to life all facets of the pastoral direction.

† † † † † REFLECTION AND FAITH-SHARING QUESTIONS

Reflect on 2 Corinthians 4, which speaks of servant leadership.

1. If our parish has not yet developed a Core Community, what ideas from this chapter will help us to start one?
2. After reading the qualities of the Core Community members and calling on the Holy Spirit, what parishioners come to mind?
3. As I read the responsibilities of the Core Community, in what area do I believe I can best use my gifts?
4. How is our parish already encouraging small communities?
5. The "Core Community members will fulfill their responsibilities with . . . greater spirit and support as they . . . grow as a small Christian community themselves." What steps will our Core Community take to grow as a small Christian community?

9. Invitational Ministry

Anegan Holmberg, csj

Those involved in the Invitational Ministry hold an important key to help unlock spiritual treasures for people by inviting them to participate in small communities. Whom do we invite? EVERYONE is the key word! Yet special attention ought to be given to those who have not heard the good news, those who are alienated or "inactive" parishioners, young adults as well as teenagers.

It appears today that there is a resurgence in a longing for God and a yearning for that which the world cannot give us. This is a unique and opportune time for parishes to invite into small groups or communities anyone who is open and searching to share in God's wonderful revelation in Jesus Christ. If parishes do this, they will indeed become evangelizing parishes.

What makes it difficult for so many of us to reach out, to visit with others and invite them to share in the Good News of Jesus? Perhaps this prevailing reluctance is a problem that is basically spiritual. Are we as a church sometimes content just to be a "comfortable private club"? If we accept the gospel call to conversion and holiness of life, then we, too, want to share the good news of our lives with others. Those who will give of themselves in the Invitational Ministry are urged to seriously grow in their own spiritual awareness and commit to ongoing conversion in their own lives. When this growth is in process, the invitation to others will be imbued with the joy of conversion.

To meet the needs of people today, those inviting (evangelizers) must first discover Jesus. The proclamation of Jesus' good news must come from the excitement of a personal, deep relationship with the Lord. Jesus was compassionate and spoke of love and care for the people of his time. He knew their hurts and needs intimately. The new evangelization that

John Paul II calls for must speak in a meaningful way to the circumstances and conditions of people's lives.

Many people today are struggling with disillusionment. Disappointment quickly comes when one's goals center on success, material things, and pleasure. Although all people may at times suffer from disillusionment, younger generations have particular reasons to experience this feeling. For instance, the downsizing of corporations, a result of a new world economy and advanced technology, has placed tremendous pressure on people to excel and increased the demands of working hours required to obtain corporate security. Anxiety and insecurity are hallmarks of our time. Some young couples today are finding it increasingly difficult to buy their own home or attain the same level of affluence and success their parents experienced.

What Are People Looking for Today?

There are indications all around us that people today, and especially younger people, are seeking a deeper spirituality. Interest abounds in angels, near-death experiences, and miracles. Yet people do not always look to the church to answer their spiritual needs.

It is no secret that we are challenged by the younger Catholics today who are absent from our liturgies as well as other aspects of parish life. Yet, recent studies have revealed that the vast majority of twenty- to thirty-year-olds long for many of the same things all human beings desire. Young adults long to be appreciated and loved, to be listened to, and to be heard. They desire to experience a sense of community and deeper relationships. They need self-esteem and are concerned about human rights, increasing violence and abuse, ecological problems, struggles with addiction and loss of meaning, and hope for the future. They are looking for a way to reconnect and to experience community and faith in their everyday lives.

Small Christian communities can certainly meet some or all of these needs. If we can help people, especially young adults, realize that some of their basic needs will find expression in small groups and/or small communities perhaps we have a good entry point. We must concern ourselves with the work of ongoing spiritual renewal within the church if we are truly to foster a new evangelization. One key way for spiritual renewal to happen is through growing in faith together with others in a communal setting.

Come and See

The task of the Invitational Ministers is to reach out as Jesus did to those who are seeking and invite them to "come and see." Deep within ourselves we must have a firm belief and conviction that the answers to our deepest human needs are to be found in Jesus and his saving Good News. We are challenged to know, love, and experience Jesus in our own lives so that we can proclaim with full-hearted enthusiasm the words of Jesus: "I came that they may have life, and have it abundantly" (Jn 10:10).

Directing someone to a place or to a group of people that will welcome them warmly is a wonderful ministry. Small communities will play a major role in the building up of a welcoming community among all parishioners and strangers as well. They provide an environment of community in which people can learn to trust. If we are to be the community of Jesus in our world, we need to welcome "the stranger."

Who Are the Invitational Ministers?

The Core Community calls forth some parishioners to be part of a Invitational Ministry to invite people to small communities. This ministry is a group of eight to ten people (some of whom are members of the Core Community) who come together to grow spiritually themselves, to learn effective means of inviting, and to carry out the ministry of inviting. They recruit and prepare others to visit or call as many people as possible for the purpose of engaging others to sign up for a small group/community in the parish.

How Invitations Are Offered

Invitations are offered through Sign-Up Sunday, by personal visits, by home visits, and by telephone calls.

Selection of the Invitational Ministers

The Core Community is responsible for discerning the names of people to serve on the Invitational Ministry. They need to select people of different ages, making certain to include young adults and teenagers. In selecting they will do well to keep in mind the following kinds of people:

- people open to being evangelized themselves,
- people willing to pray and share faith,
- people who are credible and can motivate others,
- people who are willing to listen and understand the circumstances and conditions of other people's lives,
- people who are comfortable approaching others to listen and talk with them,
- people who respect others' confidentiality.

Qualities To Look For

Credibility—the ability to be seen as someone who is believable and reliable.

Enthusiasm—an ability to express with sincerity and attractiveness the message "come and see."

Sufficient Motivation—an ability to get people to sign up; in other words, not being afraid to ask a commitment of others.

Confidentiality—the ability to listen to another and respect his or her privacy.

Compassion—an ability to enter into the suffering of another with the desire to help.

Good Listener—the ability to let another know he or she has been heard and understood.

Confidence—an ability to convey a sense that participating in a small community will provide for the person exactly what he or she needs.

Responsibilities of the Invitational Ministers

The responsibilities of the Invitational Ministers fall into six main areas:

1. Pray personally and share faith together in order to grow into a community.
2. Make personal and home visits; select, recruit, train, and organize additional people to help make home and personal visits as well as telephone calls.
3. Organize gatherings (i.e., café evenings, parties in people's homes) in order to help people meet a few other parishioners. Once they are comfortable in knowing others, invite them to be part of a small community.
4. Organize and conduct Sign-Up Sunday.
5. Organize the telephone campaign, assuring that every parishioner who has not signed up for a small community after Sign-Up Sunday receives a personal telephone invitation.
6. Provide the following materials for all who are offering invitations:
   - blank sign-up cards
   - referral cards for pastoral needs to the pastoral staff
   - a listing of parish services (from the pastor and pastoral staff)
   - envelopes to address after the visit
   - a way to record their visits and the responses they receive.

Important Activities for the Invitational Ministers

As the Invitational Ministers assume their responsibilities the following activities are suggested:

- Pray for the guidance of the Holy Spirit. An important element for those planning for and doing the Invitational Ministry is prayer support. Take at least one half hour each time you gather for prayer and faith sharing. Assure that prayer is at the center of all your efforts.

Pray for one another when you are making visits as well as for the person(s) being visited.

- Assure, when possible, that visitors go out in two's.
- "Check in" with those doing the visiting on a regular basis to provide support and perhaps even some suggestions.
- Become familiar with the materials to be used.
- Collaborate with the Core Community to decide exactly what kind of publicity you will need to inform the parish that personal visits will be made. (For example, letters from the pastor, bulletin inserts, brochures, flyers, information booklet on the parish itself, etc.)
- Following a formation period, gather for further planning and possibly choose and prepare others to share in the Invitational Ministry.
- Visit a specific number of persons and then attend a reflection session after the first week of visits.
- After prayerful reflection on initial visits, continue with assigned visits.

Selecting and Recruiting Others To Help with the Personal Visits and Telephone Calls

The selection of others to help with the visits and telephone calls is extremely critical for this ministry. Obviously if the parish is going to try to reach out to young adults and those who may be alienated, young, credible, enthusiastic visitors and callers are needed.

The Invitational Ministers will be making visits as well as organizing the invitational efforts. It is advisable to focus on friends who may not be overly involved in the parish. Maybe some of them in need of stronger spiritual connections in their lives would like to be a part of inviting others. It is so important to build a strong, committed group of people to help offer the invitations.

The Invitational Ministers can brainstorm names of possible visitors with parish staff members. The school principal and/or the director of religious education as well as the coordinator of the Christian initiation team may well know the names of people who can sufficiently motivate others and get things done. It is also wise to look for some people who are not currently involved in the parish.

Once the Invitational Ministers have decided whom to ask to help with the visiting, a personal invitation is offered to them. Through sharing their own commitment, enthusiasm, and hopes, those involved in this ministry offer many people a way to enliven their faith life and find greater meaning in their lives. As those making telephone calls and visits begin to personally invite people, they will become more comfortable with personal visits and will discover how much more effective these contacts are than letters or phone calls.

Training and Preparing Those Making Visits and Telephone Calls

The training and preparation for those making the visits and telephone calls should include prayer, sharing, and information. The *Invitational Ministry Handbook* for RENEW (available from Paulist Press) provides both the information and tools to offer good preparation.

The preparation and training needs to include

- shared prayer and the experience of sharing faith together
- an inspirational reflection on the place of small communities
- emphasis on the new evangelization that meets the needs of people today as a source of personal and communal joy
- how to invite
- whom to invite
- what people are looking for today
- how to do sign-up
- practical considerations

What Are We Inviting People To?

Ordinarily people are introduced to small communities through seasonal small groups. Seasonal small groups usually meet for six weeks beginning the week of Ash Wednesday or the first week of October. (Much of what follows though can also be applied to ministerial and especially small Christian communities.)

The three methods of the Invitational Ministry follow in the order in which the methods usually take place in the parish: personal and home visits, Sign-Up Sunday, and telephone campaign. Much of what is said in the section on personal and home visits applies also to the telephone campaign.

PERSONAL AND HOME VISITS

Seasonal small groups and small communities provide a wonderful opportunity for evangelization. Invitational Ministers can be very effective in this evangelization effort by reaching out to those who are inactive or have been "lost" in the parish. All ages, particularly young adults, should receive a personal invitation to participate in a small community. Experience shows that some young adults do not respond immediately to an invitation, but as long as they do not say "no," they are open to receive additional invitations.

How Do We Invite?

Our invitations will be most fruitful when the inviter is imbued with God's overwhelming love. We cannot invite with sincerity unless we ourselves have been sufficiently converted to God's love. If we are reluctant it may be because we feel as if it all depends on us rather than on the power of God. We need to be open to the fire of God's love in our lives and in the lives of those we visit.

The invitation we extend is not totally dependent on the words we say. It depends more on the communication of a sincere desire to see the person we are inviting included in something that we truly believe is wonderful. There has to be sincerity, love, and, above all, a listening heart. We must be fully present to the person we are inviting by listening with our heart as well as our mind. We begin with a prayer for that person before we even begin the invitation.

We always begin by listening to the person and finding out some aspects of the person's life. What struggles is he or she having? What joys? What problems? What fears? What pain? What excitement? What hopes?

The more we listen to the other person's concerns and where he or she is at in life's journey, the more open the person will become to the invitation of being part of a small community. It is best not to start with church talk, but together with them to explore the possible benefits of a small community experience. If we truly take the time to become personally involved in their lives, then we are "visiting" with a new friend. People are longing to become "befriended" in our impersonal world. Many times we are so busy dwelling on our own past or future that we don't take time to make friends. In fact, in many ways we, as a society, are losing the "art" of making friends.

A visit can occur anywhere—on the telephone, at work, in the supermarket, at someone's home, etc.

The important points to remember in inviting are

- Pray for the person
- Plant a seed by initiating a conversation
- Listen carefully and respond appropriately
- Talk about something of concern to the person (i.e., children, the neighborhood, sports, etc.)
- Share your own conviction about how the small community could help them and why you feel this is a wonderful opportunity for spiritual growth, community, support, etc.
- Invite the person to "come and see"
- Keep in touch
- Don't give up hope
- Keep praying for the person
- Hold confidences

Organizing Personal and Home Visits

Personal and home visits begin six to eight weeks prior to the beginning of small groups and continue until the small groups meet. The Invitational Ministers need to decide who will be visited and which visitors will be responsible to visit which people.

Most visits will take place in people's homes, but it is also good to look at other possibilities where an invitation could be given (e.g., parish activities, such as welcoming breakfasts, potlucks; talking with friends or acquaintances at a local health club or grocery store). Be as creative as possible.

Deciding What Groups To Visit

If at all possible, visit the entire parish. If, however, the parish is too large, target specific groups of people to ensure they receive a personal or home visit.

Today we need to look particularly at young people. As Pope John Paul II reminded us in his Apostolic Letter on the Third Millennium: "The future of the world and the Church belongs to the *younger generation,* to those who, born in this century, will reach maturity in the next, the first century of the new millennium" (58).

Therefore begin with young adults. Some may be coming to church on a regular basis but many may not. Try to reach all of them. Target specifically

- all parents of those who will be receiving their first communion
- parents who have children in school or religious education
- newly married people
- those who have just finished high school or college
- new immigrants
- those who no longer participate in the parish
- those who may be alienated or inactive

Give home and personal visitors a way to record their visits and responses, e.g., a notebook, paper, etc. Make sure that information from each visit is noted in order to ensure that important matters are followed up on and to avoid duplication.

Provide the following materials for visitors

- name tag with parish identification
- blank small community sign-up cards
- referral cards for pastoral needs to be given to the pastoral staff (see Sample A at the end of this chapter)

- flyers for small Christian communities
- a follow-up letter of thanks (from pastor and pastoral staff)
- envelopes to address after the visit (for follow-up)
- other materials specific to the parish that you wish to provide

Important Note . . .

Once in the home it is important to get into a conversation about the person's life before diving into the invitation. That will create a more relaxed situation where natural dialogue can occur. Getting invited into the house is extremely helpful. Be observant. If you are able to comment on the house or something that strikes your attention or bring up something you sense might be of concern or interest, it will frequently lead to an invitation to come in and sit down. Allow the conversation to develop as naturally as possible. There is no need to get immediately to the point unless you sense the person being visited wants it that way. Frequently connecting on a topic that happens to be of common interest like a town event, the neighborhood, children or sports will relax everyone and open up all kinds of doors.

The importance of personal invitations cannot be overemphasized. Invitational Ministers need to be alert to all kinds of opportune moments for inviting people to small communities.

SIGN-UP SUNDAY

Some of the Invitational Ministers work on organizing and carrying out a process of inviting parishioners through a day designated as Sign-Up Sunday. Key aspects of their ministry are highlighted in the following pages.

Sign-Up Sunday Talk

During the masses on Sign-Up Sunday, an invitation is extended to parishioners to sign up for small groups for the four- or six-week period. This invitation includes an explanation of why people join small groups, witnessing to the benefits of small-group participation, and the sign-up process.

The invitation can be made in the context of the homily or after the homily by one or two of the parishioners. It is desirable for the pastor to speak of his own conviction regarding the value of small communities and his desire to have everyone participate in small groups. He then introduces the person who will speak and encourages parishioners to participate in small groups.

Selecting the Right Speakers

Carefully choosing the right person(s) to invite parishioners to be part of a small group on Sign-Up Sunday is the single most important aspect of getting people to join a small group. Parishioners with high credibility in the parish who have been in a small group, who have good motivational ability, and who can speak clearly with conviction and enthusiasm ought to be selected. A team approach including a woman and a man will prove very effective, especially in order to encourage men as well as women to join small groups.

It is important to have the same speakers at all the Masses on Saturday and Sunday. This part of the Invitational Ministry is not to be divided among many. The very best motivators ought to speak at every Mass. They will not only gain confidence, but they will most likely improve their presentation the more frequently they speak.

Elements of the Talk

Small Groups

The speaker invites parishioners to consider a wonderful invitation to be part of a small group for a six-week period. He or she explains that eight to twelve people will gather in someone's home once a week during Lent (or October–November, etc.) and states the week they will begin (e.g., the week of Ash Wednesday, the first week in October, etc.). The speaker holds up the sharing material to be used and tells the people it will be available for small groups to provide prayer, Scripture reading, and sharing questions.

The speaker also stresses that the atmosphere for small groups is relaxed, that no one will be forced to talk and that each person will be respected. This will allay any fears that small-group gatherings are sensitivity groups.

Motivation

People are attracted to a direct spiritual approach. The factors that most effectively motivate people to join small groups need to be included in the presentation

- satisfying our hunger for getting to know God better
- meeting new people and being strengthened by these Christian friendships
- growing as persons and improving ourselves
- making the world a better place
- making a difference through God's gracious action in our lives

Witnessing to the Value of Small Groups

The most effective way to encourage others to sign up for a small group is through personal witnessing. When speakers share enthusiastically their experience of being a part of a small group, hearts are touched. Some starters that may be used follow:

"I've enjoyed the new friends I met...."
"At first I was afraid...."
"Being in the small group has given me more self-confidence."
"...has made Jesus more real in my life."
"...has given me the strength to cope with a specific situation."
"...has helped me live my faith at work."

Sign-Up Process

Toward the end of the talk the speaker pauses, holds up a sign-up card, and asks people to pick up a sign-up card and pencil in the pew. The speaker then invites all present to sign their names and indicate what day or night of the week is best for them to participate in this important activity. People are also asked to check if they are willing to host a small group.

- Allow time for people to fill out their card.
- Indicate that in a moment the ministers of hospitality will collect cards.

After an appropriate interval invite the ministers of hospitality to collect cards. (Comparisons show that collecting cards *after* Mass radically lessens the number of cards returned.)

Sign-Up Cards

Prior to Sign-Up Sunday, sign-up cards are designed and printed. Included on this card are spaces for people to write their name, address, telephone number, and the times small groups will meet. It is also wise to include on this card space for people to volunteer to host a small group. (See Sample B at the end of this chapter.)

In addition, if sign-up cards are to be mailed later to others who have not registered, the return address of the parish ought to be included.

Cards and pencils are placed in pews before each Mass and are collected by ministers of hospitality or other designated persons.

Support for Speakers

The person responsible for Sign-Up Sunday invites the other Invitational Ministers to gather together in a small room before or during part of each Mass to pray for the homilists and speakers and for the success of their efforts.

The Invitational Ministers can also meet with the speakers after each

Mass to give their critique. This allows for further refinement or development of the talk between Masses. This support usually encourages the speaker to improve the presentation as the day goes on.

Involving Others

Creative ways to involve parishioners can generate a good spirit in the parish. Existing parish committees/ministries might be helpful and also feel more a part of the parish-wide effort to hold the small-group experience if they are invited to help with some details of implementation. For example, the liturgical ministry might highlight the theme of "community" during the Sign-Up Sunday liturgy. The communication ministry might lend assistance with publicity, and the catechetical ministry might want to support the small-group experience as an adult enrichment experience.

TELEPHONE CAMPAIGN

While personal and home visits are the most effective means of invitation, telephoning is also an important way of inviting. Ideally much of the parish will have been given a personal invitation or will have signed up for a small community on Sign-Up Sunday. However, there will be those who have not been visited or have not responded. Thus a phone call will be one last way to offer this wonderful opportunity to everyone.

Therefore, it is important to organize a telephone campaign to try to call all parishioners who were not visited personally or did not sign up on Sign-Up Sunday. (Telephone callers will need training if they are different from the personal visitors. Additional helps are available in the Leadership Books for RENEW published by Paulist Press.)

Preparing for the Calls

The responsibilities of the Invitational Ministers working with telephone callers are as follows:

1. Pray personally and share faith together in order to grow into community.
2. Select, train, and prepare telephone callers.
3. Determine dates within which calls should be made. This time frame usually begins on the Sunday afternoon of Sign-Up Sunday and extends for seven to ten days. At this time the names of persons committed to being part of a small group are given to the Core Community.
4. Determine the location of calls. If possible, make the calls from a central location where everyone can be together when making the calls. This will allow callers to pray together before the calls are made and to discuss their strategies. Many parishes have done this from a real estate office or other places where there are several phone lines.
5. Strategize and make plans for the actual phone calling.
6. Provide callers with a way to record the calls and responses. (Keep a master list so you know exactly who has been contacted in order to avoid duplication.)
7. Provide the following materials for callers
   - sign-up cards
   - referral cards for pastoral needs to be given to the pastoral staff (see Sample A at the end of this chapter)
   - flyers for small groups
   - a follow-up letter of thanks (from pastor and pastoral staff)
   - envelopes to address after the visit (for follow-up)

Training

Callers will be asked to participate in the general aspects of the training sessions for personal and home visitors. In addition, the training of telephone callers should include an appreciation for the following:

- Have a clear understanding of small groups/communities.
- Employ good telephone calling skills.
  - A warm, friendly voice says more than words; be gentle, sincere, and clear.

- Your cordiality should not decrease when you receive a negative response.
- You are not a person just making a phone call; you are the representative of our parish, and that automatically adds a responsibility to your role.
- Act, don't react.
- Be kind, but don't dwell on problems.
- Should a personal problem or complaint surface, use the referral card.
- *Confidentiality* is of paramount importance.

Callers are asked to pray together before making calls and then spend a few minutes, individually, in prayerful reflection after making some initial calls.

A REFLECTION FOR ALL MINISTERS OF INVITATION

The following reflection can be used to motivate Invitational Ministers. It can be used in a talk during a training session, as a personal reflection, or as a group reflection followed by sharing.

What Makes for a Successful Invitational Minister?

Becoming a successful Invitational Minister is not just a matter of finding good approaches or techniques, no matter how good they may be. Becoming a successful Invitational Minister is a matter of motivation.

We must be people filled with the Spirit. The love and compassion of Jesus must flood our souls. We need to be sensitive to each person and empathize with their struggles, hopes, and dreams. Can we feel the human pain of broken marriages, of desperate loneliness or despair, of lives being lived without meaning or faith, of serious neglect and the experience of the loss of dignity for the unemployed?

Can we care enough to forget ourselves, to forget how we sound or look or whether we present ourselves as well as we would like? Can we have enough courage to reach out perhaps imperfectly but with a great amount of heart and love? Even more, do we recognize the spiritual hunger that is all around us in our secular society? Most of all, do we appreciate what we are offering to people? We are presenting people with an opportunity to meet the spiritual hungers in their lives and to help them find rich meaning in what otherwise may feel like meaningless circumstances. We are offering them the support of community and an opportunity to discover Jesus. "Where two or three are gathered in my name I am present in the midst of them."

We are not so much focusing on how many people actually come to small groups/communities. We are focusing on the fact that each person is of incredible value and that each contact is a sacred encounter. As we take on the mind of Christ, each person is "sacred" and is worthy of our greatest effort. It is not our responsibility to make others accept the Good News of Jesus; it is our responsibility to share the Good News.

As Invitational Ministers we need to throw caution to the wind. We need to take time to commit ourselves to this most important ministry, to sacrifice time and be willing to experience personal "failure." How can it really be failure if we are following Jesus? We follow the crucified Christ, but we also follow the risen Christ. We know that our efforts will be blessed because it is God's doing, not ours.

Let us forget ourselves and be moved by our deep love for God and our brothers and sisters.

A Final Word

An important aspect of the Invitational Ministry is to provide ongoing support and prayer for all who will be offering invitations. As the team grows in prayer and in sharing faith with one another, team members will also grow in confidence in their ability to speak God's Word to others.

Remember to record and share your "good news" stories of fruitful visits and calls. The same joy that the whole parish experiences when people return to active participation or when the newly baptized join the parish family is also truly felt in the successful visits and phone calls.

SAMPLE A

Referral Card

Name_____

Phone_____

Address_____

General nature of matter being referred

Person making referral_____ Date_____

Sign-Up Card

Please indicate your first and second choices for meeting times. (We will try our best to accommodate you.)				
	Adults			*H. S. Students*
	Morning	Afternoon	Evening	Evening
Sunday				
Monday				
Tuesday				
Wednesday				
Thursday				
Friday				
Saturday				

☐ YES, I would like the small group (8 to 12 people) to meet in my home. *(Scripture sharing materials will be supplied.)*

Name _____

Address_____

Telephone_____

† † † † † REFLECTION AND FAITH-SHARING QUESTIONS

Reflect on John 1:35–51.

1. Why do I believe that motivation is the key to becoming a successful Invitational Minister?
2. What invitational message do I believe is most important to extend?
3. Why do I need to forget myself and focus on the other person when inviting?
4. What are some of the "hungers" in our parish that the small communities will address?
5. What role does the Holy Spirit play in the lives of those who invite?

10. Ministry of Small Community Leadership

No book on the vision of small Christian communities would be complete without a rather extensive exploration of the kind of leadership necessary to help groups grow into Christian communities of faith. Each small community has a leader who is a person of faith and is trained in various skills.

What does it mean to provide the ministry of leadership for a small community? How does this leadership fit into the ministry of leadership of the entire parish and the larger church? These are questions that will be addressed in this chapter.

The ministry of leadership in small communities is a very specific service that lay persons can render. All persons, by virtue of their baptism,

Suegan Holmberg CSJ

receive a call, a personal vocation to holiness. Ordained ministers have a special sacramental and unifying role in the body of the church. However, it is not the responsibility of the ordained ministry to build up the church community and the responsibility of the lay community to transform the world. Rather it is the responsibility of both ordained ministers and the laity to build up the church and to help transform the world. It is a question of emphasis. The laity, as well as ordained ministers, are called to "communio,"[1] to building up the body of Christ.

It is not a matter of dependence or independence in ministry but rather a matter of interdependence. The church is not a mere organization, but the mystery of the Lord's continuing presence in and for the world. The church is the body of Christ in time and space. We are all responsible for bringing the awareness of the mystery of God into our world today. We can call it collaborative ministry or shared responsibility. It is that, but it is much more. As ordained ministers and laity, we all minister together for the purpose of living out "communio," making God's Word more alive in our world today.

Small community leaders share in the pastoral care of their small communities. What does *pastoral care* mean? The word *pastor* is taken from the Latin root word *pascere*, which means "to feed." *Roget's Thesaurus* offers another expression of the concept of pastoring or shepherding: "to guide" or "to show the way."

Very simply, for the leader, the ministry of pastoral care is caring for the small Christian community. The leader of the small community "feeds," "guides," and "shows the way." That is not to say that the leader is the only person responsible for pastoral care in the group. In fact, as the community grows, each person learns more about caring for others and the mystery of a communal church becomes a greater lived reality.

As was stated previously, priests and pastoral staffs often see great value in having others share in the ministry of pastoral care since even a very energetic staff cannot offer adequate pastoral care to everyone.

Every group needs good leadership. Let us look specifically at the significant role of the leaders of small communities.

ROLE OF A SMALL COMMUNITY LEADER

The leader is sensitive to each of the following responsibilities. However, the leader does not handle these totally alone, but also enables and encourages other members of the community to share in these responsibilities.

Welcoming

A small community leader is welcoming and hospitable to others.

In our culture, there are many "acceptable" signs of etiquette and politeness. Some of these may be motivated by a desire to please, to look good or to be accepted by others. While that is not entirely poor motivation, the kind of hospitality that a small community leader offers comes from a deep and honest love and respect for the other person, not mere politeness. Ideally, everyone is welcomed to be a member of the community—not only those of a particular social class, ethnic background, or educational status. The leader is constantly aware of any new person and gives special attention to introductions and welcoming to strangers.

The leader is conscious of the difference between being truly hospitable and being overbearing.

> The paradox of hospitality is that it wants to create emptiness, not a fearful emptiness, but a friendly emptiness where strangers can enter and discover themselves as created free; free to sing their own songs, speak their own language, dance their own dances, free also to leave and follow their own vocations. Hospitality is not a subtle invitation to adopt the life style of the host, but the gift of a chance for the guest to find his own.[2]

The leader knows that it is important to recognize each person every time a gathering begins. Each person is highly valued. As the small community grows in comfort the leader continues to offer hospitality, particularly if there is anyone in the group who may feel "left out" or uncomfortable.

Being Sensitive

A small community leader is sensitive and caring.

The leader is responsible for developing sensitivity to the needs of the other members of the community. If one member is hurting or unusually distressed, the leader notices and recognizes the pain. For example, one of the small community members has not been feeling well and is going for medical tests. In the course of the sharing, this person says that he or she is going for tests on Wednesday and acknowledges his or her anxiety. As a sensitive and caring response, the leader could call this individual on Thursday to inquire about the medical tests. The leader could also encourage others in the group to minister in a similar manner.

In another situation, a community member may be absent from the meeting without letting anyone know the reason. The leader would call after the meeting to let the person know he or she was missed and to find out if everything is all right.

Some community members may be more shy than others. Even after groups have grown together a long time, there may be some members who are still hesitant to speak. The leader will want to invite the shy or fearful person to share.

In some ways the small community leader may be likened to an orchestra leader. At times it is necessary to quiet down some of the trumpets and basses and at other times to bring in the quieter flutes and piccolos. At all times the orchestra leader is aware of the value of each instrument and how the song is to be played. The conductor is not a controller but rather allows the music to be played in harmony.

At some times, people may become discouraged, or fearful about some personal issues. Again the leader supports and allows for the sharing of feelings about personal crisis. Any response to someone's feelings is not conditioned by a judgment, but rather by acknowledging the validity of the feeling. Being sensitive to people is not always an easy task; however, it is very much a part of the pastoring role. Very simply, the leader serves the group by recognizing, respecting, and showing care for all members.

Because of the uniqueness of small groups and the open process of sharing personal experiences, it may happen that someone tries to use the sharing as an opportunity to unburden a deep-seated emotional problem. The leader ought to be ready to identify and respond to this possibility.

Faith sharing naturally involves the expression of personal stories and feelings. Tears are sometimes shed. But there is a point beyond which personal sharing becomes an attempt at therapy. How does the leader recognize that the group is going beyond that point? It will probably be evident to the leader that the group is feeling uncomfortable, embarrassed, or even fearful because someone is revealing aspects of his or her life that are inappropriate for this gathering. The sharing is no longer about faith at all. It does not stem from the Scripture reading or the focus of the meeting's theme. What may have begun as faith sharing has become an occasion for venting one's emotions.

An individual's use of the group for therapy is really unfair to everyone involved. This kind of sharing deters the group from its task, which is faith sharing. It discourages reluctant participants and prevents them from sharing their stories. It places an undue burden on the leader who is expected to respond as a professional helper. And finally, it is unfair to the troubled individual who obviously needs more help than the group can provide.

What is the leader to do? Here are six suggestions:

1. Try to prevent this kind of inappropriate sharing from happening in the first place. During the initial meeting of the group, an explanation of what faith sharing is and what it is not will establish ground rules and fix boundaries.
2. Anticipate dominating types who take control of the group and divert it away from faith sharing toward their own agendas.
3. When an individual sends signals for help, and if you feel personally capable of responding, meet or call that person. Express your concern ever so gently and give the other an opportunity to respond, e.g., "Joe, I noticed last evening that you seemed a little down. Am I correct? Is there something wrong?" This form of response and questioning is well within the role of leader and demonstrates effective pastoring.
4. If the preventative measures described above do not work and an individual begins to unburden a personal problem inappro-

priately during the meeting, try to stop the behavior before it goes too far. Use phrases or questions that redirect the group to faith sharing. When all else fails, simply stop the person carefully and gently, but firmly. For example, say, "Peg, you are really hurting. I want you to know that I care about you. Let's talk about it when our faith sharing is over, after the meeting. All right?"

5. Recognize the signs of deep personal trouble, such as the following:
   a. severe depression evidenced by the repeated admission of being depressed, sleeping disorders, and difficulty accomplishing ordinary life tasks
   b. uncontrollable tears in inappropriate circumstances
   c. serious parenting problems
   d. alcohol-related or drug-related problems

6. When a person is obviously in need of help and if you judge that you can be heard, arrange to meet with the hurting person. During the conversation, you can say, e.g., "I've heard you express a lot of pain in the last three weeks. You said that you've been very depressed. Have you thought about getting some help from a counselor?" This intervention can help the person recognize the need for help. You might refer the person to the pastor or a member of the pastoral staff. No matter what happens, confidentiality is observed.

Listening

A small community leader is a good and active listener.

In a world in which there is so much noise and activity, it is difficult to cultivate the skill of listening even in a small group of ten people. Good listening often means setting aside one's own thoughts in order to focus completely on the person speaking and what he or she is saying. The leader can best challenge the community to good listening by modeling it.

One important responsibility of the leader is to assure that there are no unnecessary outside disturbances. For example, if a telephone is constantly ringing, it is difficult for the group to pay attention to what is occurring in the group sharing. Quiet is a wonderful gift a group can be given, especially for prayer and reflection on the Scriptures.

Another responsibility is helping the community to listen to one another. Researchers in human communication tell us that over 80% of what is communicated is done non-verbally. The leader needs to be aware of non-verbal signals. If the non-verbal communication is very different from the words being spoken, the leader may wish to ask about it directly.

In one small group a young woman who had been divorced was speaking about how powerfully God had been working in her life. She shared about some of the earlier pain of her life, and how after a few years, she could feel that God had been with her all the time. As she spoke she began to cry. One group member assumed that she was crying because she was still upset with some of those earlier circumstances of her life. After the group member spoke to her and asked what she was still upset about, the leader asked the young woman why she was crying. Her response: "Because right now, as I am sharing this, I feel so loved by God. I don't feel sad, but I am crying because of the joy I feel." Good listening includes testing one's assumptions.

Challenging the Community to Growth

A small community leader challenges the community to growth.

No matter how long members of a community have known each other, there is the constant need to challenge one another to growth. The leader plays a gentle, encouraging role, does not dominate, but ensures that the group is growing in Christian community and not just becoming a comfortable "cozy" support group.

In some instances leaders would prefer to call themselves facilitators. Small community leaders certainly do facilitate the gatherings of the community, but there is much more that is asked of the leader.

The leader constantly evaluates with the community. If the community has moved into too much discussion and not enough real sharing about their lives, the leader invites the community to reflect on that reality. Perhaps they will take a full meeting to talk about sharing from the heart. Maybe the community has lost its prayerfulness, so there is need to bring that to the attention of the group.

A key responsibility of the small community leader is the ongoing spiritual development and learning of the community. The leader may wish to bring in speakers on particular areas of interest or share tapes that could help the community grow in knowing and utilizing various forms of prayer. As noted earlier, suggesting spiritual reading books or tapes as well as informing the community of opportunities for spiritual formation in the parish or community is also an excellent means of catechesis.

Small community leaders can encourage the community to share prayer experiences together. They can provide input on various styles of prayer and urge daily Scripture reading by community members. By inviting the members of the community to witness to their personal prayer, greater commitments to prayer can be generated in others.

The small community leader will also need to encourage community members to be prepared for the meetings and gatherings in which they share and support one another. Each person is called to be a contributing member, and thus preparation for the meetings is essential.

The area that is often most difficult for a community to remain faithful to is that of mission or action. For many Catholics there is a tendency to settle for a safe sanctuary, a privatized religion in which prayer and action are not integrated. The leader will constantly want to raise the question of action, application, and the integration of word and deed. Each gathering of the community should contain a time for planning action and evaluating past commitments to action.

As has been stated before, often these actions will take place within the daily circumstances of life, e.g., more patience with a child, reaching out to a neighbor whose wife recently died, making just decisions at the office, etc. At times they may also include some concrete action to help the parish grow, e.g., being greeters at some of the Sunday liturgies, planning a prayer vigil for the entire parish, hosting an evening of reflection on social concerns, etc. The community is strongly encouraged—particularly by the leader—to reach beyond the parish into the community or into the larger world.

One small community initiated a "twinning" experience with a Central American basic Christian community. They not only became acquainted and developed a prayer network between them, but actually got to know one another and offered needed support. They communicated through mail and some members visited the base community in Guatemala. As community members became more familiar and comfortable with one another, a special bonding took place. People were sharing as people. Now, in addition to watching the evening news and trying to sort out the "Central American situation," people were knowing and loving a group of Central American Christians.

The point of this reflection is that the leader is constantly growing in awareness of the needs of the church and world. While the leader is not totally responsible for the ideas and implementation of action, if the community is weak in that area, the leader challenges the group to growth.

The small community leader helps the community see that these actions are not isolated good deeds but rather a response to their call to mission. As members of the church we are all sent to transform the world, to be on mission. Thus, concrete actions are not an optional choice for Christians but a response to their baptismal call.

Setting the Stage

A small community leader sets the stage for growth in faith.

No detail is too minor for the leader. For the sharing itself, the arrangement of the room is important. A circle or some similar arrangement allows people to see and hear each other without strain. The Bible is given a place of prominence. A candle or a symbol reflecting the theme of the Scripture reading can also be utilized.

Most communities find that refreshments add to the social and communal bonding of the group. Serving coffee or refreshments during the sharing can often be distracting, but serving such refreshments following the sharing would be most appropriate. Again the leader may wish to arrange who will bring the refreshments or delegate this to some other members of the group.

Often the question is raised about the participation of children. The decision of how and when to include children may be dictated by cultural norms and preferences. Some groups may wish to include children in all aspects of the gatherings; others may wish to have a babysitter and include the children in the social part of the gathering. In some instances, it may be a difficult distraction to have children at the meeting itself because most adults cannot concentrate well when they have children to watch. (This issue will be addressed in greater detail in Chapter 13.)

Being Humble

A small community leader is humble.

As was stated previously, the leader of the small community is not in charge or in control. The small community leader has a humble heart, and like Jesus takes on the attitude of servanthood (Phil 2:6-8).

One human tendency a person may have when given authority or leadership responsibilities could be to control or "to make sure things happen the way I think they should." Since leaders in other areas of life sometimes focus on "taking control" and "moving up the ladder," small community leaders might be tempted to believe that the life and growth of the small community is totally dependent on them.

In fact, leaders do have a very unique role, but it is the type of leadership role that Jesus spoke of when he told his followers "not to lord it over one another," but rather to be servants, to be humble. Humble leaders constantly rely on the power of God. These leaders recognize that "nothing is impossible with God" and that truly loving relationships are possible only with the power of God in one's life.

Humble leaders do not believe that everything depends on them. In fact, with an attitude of humility, leaders know that others have good ideas, and also have very unique gifts to bring to the community. Humble leaders do not compare others' gifts, do not make judgments on the motivation of others, and are willing to share how they have worked out difficult situations and how God has helped them in their lives.

Humble leaders do not dominate and do not teach in the traditional sense of knowing more than others. Humble leaders are truly wise and share from life's experience and past learnings. These leaders are not threatened if others in the group share more experienced wisdom or even if others in the group have more natural leadership ability. Humble leaders pray constantly for guidance.

Let us look at two different reactions of a leader. At certain times, there may be the need for a new person to assume leadership in the small community. If the previous leader feels overly responsible for the group, it will not be an easy transition. The leader will find fault with the new ways things are being done. There may even be some undermining of the new leadership. This could all be very subtle and hardly recognized by the former leader.

Humble leaders, on the other hand, will undoubtedly experience some of the same feelings of "letting go," but will support the new leadership. If the previous leader finds things are not going the way that is most beneficial for the group, he or she takes a quiet, reflective stance and brings up the issues or concerns when appropriate. The humble leader does not govern the group. The leader is servant.

Being in Relationship with the Larger Church

The small community leader is clear about the small community's relationship with the parish and the larger church.

Small Christian communities are part of the parish. Small community leaders are clear that as leaders, they are a necessary link to the larger parish. Leaders know that these small communities exist in order to be at the service of the parish, the larger church, and the world. As leaders, they are sent to serve by the parish and they serve the parish.

Small community leaders are always encouraged to have respect for the teaching authority of the church, and recognize that it is through the body of the entire church that truths are revealed. To be truly pastoral means to have a firm commitment to the church and to look to the church for guidance.

Christian leaders are called to interiorize their Catholic heritage. According to Catholic teaching, each person has the right and responsibility to grow in one's relationship with God according to one's personal conscience, but the Christian conscience can only be properly formed through the Scriptures, tradition, and the teaching authority of the church. The Vatican II *Constitution on Divine Revelation* states:

> It is clear, therefore, that sacred tradition, sacred Scripture, and the teaching authority of the Church, in accord with God's most wise design, are so linked and joined together that one cannot stand without the others, and that all together and each in its own way under the action of the one Holy Spirit contribute effectively to the salvation of souls (*DV* 10).

Small communities are at the service of the parish. Leaders understand that a large part of the small community's mandate is to serve and to respond to the needs of the parish and larger community. Small community leaders recognize the importance of Sunday liturgy and active participation in the celebration of the liturgy. They encourage community members to see Eucharist as the center of their lives and the church building itself as a very important place of worship and welcome.

The leader assists the community members in learning they are to be hospitable not only to one another but to the parish as a whole. Small community members ought to be the first ones to extend a hand of welcome to a newcomer in the parish or to those visiting. Small community members ought to be the ones who circulate during doughnuts and coffee gatherings to meet and reach out to those who are not active in the parish.

A large part of the leader's role is to communicate with the pastor of the parish. The leader ought to strive to work within an open, respectful, and caring relationship with the pastor and staff.

Sometimes issues of doctrine or church teaching may arise. The small community leader need not handle these alone, but may take them to the pastoral staff for their input and expertise.

As circumstances change, a pastor who has supported the model of small Christian community in a particular parish may leave. Ideally, the new pastor would support this pastoral direction and the communities would continue to flourish.

In many instances, the new pastor will be coming from a parish background that did not include small communities. In time his experience in the parish may lead to a deep conviction of their value. In other instances, the new pastor may stress other priorities and be non-supportive of small communities. Dialogue and a welcoming invitation to small community involvement may in time lead him to be appreciative of the value of small communities. In all cases the leadership of small communities is encouraged to maintain an attitude of respect for the new pastor and to foster parish unity.

Being Prayerful

A small community leader is a person of deep prayer.

We have often heard the adage "pray always." What does "praying always" mean for leaders of small communities? Part of ministry to the community is to pray for each person regularly and for the entire group. Prayer helps leaders remember that God works in people's lives. The small community in its fullness is an experience of God. Only personal prayer and commitment to meditation will assure this.

Leaders play a large part in helping the community become and continue as a praying community. The meeting itself ought to have a conducive atmosphere for prayer.

Another aspect of the leader's role is to help community members become more comfortable with the Scriptures. Therefore, leaders themselves must know how to read and pray the Scriptures. Daily reading and meditating upon the Scriptures is of utmost importance for leaders. Through a daily commitment to the Bible, leaders learn first-hand the powerful way that the Word is able to transform lives.

Forgiving

A small community leader is open to forgive and be forgiven.

As the community matures, it will go through various stages of growth, some easy and some difficult. There will be moments of conflict and, as is true in any intimate human relationships, some alienation and fragmentation. No leader can be totally disengaged from the conflict. Small community leaders will recognize vulnerability, both their own and others', and will find it necessary to forgive and to be forgiven.

The small community leader takes Jesus seriously when he says that "if someone wrongs you seven times in one day, and returns to you seven times saying, 'I am sorry,' you should forgive him" (Lk 17:4).

This does not mean that the leader avoids conflicts; quite the opposite. Conflict and differences of opinion are not necessarily negative; they expand sharing. However, when conflicts elicit deep anger or emotion, they need to be addressed. Despite the fear of anger that many may have, conflict must be acknowledged by a leader. The challenge is to maintain a respectful atmosphere. If arguments ensue, the pastoral response is to clarify that opinions on many issues can be diverse.

It may be helpful for the leader to assess the symptoms of the conflict. Is the conflict the result of normal group growth patterns, a power struggle, personal insecurity or the threat to a person's self-image, transference from an area of someone's personal life, philosophical differences, or perhaps differences of method or approaches? If an assessment is accurately made, it allows the leader to deal directly with the conflict. If the situation concerns the group's growth or differences of approaches, it may be helpful for the leader to address the issues openly in the group setting. If, on the other hand, the conflict is the result of personal insecurity or transference from an area of personal life, the leader may wish to address the conflict with the concerned individuals outside the group setting.

Celebrating

A small community leader has a positive attitude, the gift of joy, and a celebrating spirit.

People create climates of acceptance and joy. For people to be open to the Spirit and the power of God's Word in their lives, the environment ought to create open hearts and souls so that God can speak. Sharing positive experiences of God and the beautiful world of the Spirit provides everyone with the personal knowledge of God's love in their lives.

Leaders help create this atmosphere by personal attitudes of joy and spiritual wonder. Leaders help the community in an awareness and acknowledgment of the power of God in its midst. This realization leads to a sense of joy and celebration. It may take the form of a party, of a prayer experience that celebrates some occasion, such as a birthday or significant anniversary. Cakes are baked, candles are lit, songs are sung. Leaders are sensitive to all aspects of life.

Much emphasis has been placed thus far on the meetings held by the small community. There are, however, numerous other means of celebrating, bonding, and creating communal experiences. Ideally, other gatherings include families of small community members, so that the bonding happens not only among adults, but among entire families and significant other people in community members' lives.

These could well include the following:

- Christmas parties
- summer picnics
- Sunday afternoon outings
- an annual weekend camping trip
- pilgrimage trips
- an annual retreat together
- vacations together
- apostolic endeavors, i.e., inner-city soup kitchen or a social justice response to an issue

This list is not exhaustive, but merely suggestive.

EXTENSIVE TRAINING FOR THE MINISTRY OF SMALL COMMUNITY LEADERSHIP

The development of leaders for the care of small communities is essential. Ongoing faith formation and leadership skills must be part of the total parish strategy for the initiation and nurturing of small communities. Nothing can compare to good preparation. Experienced small community leaders who have used the following practice of briefing over the years found it to be extremely helpful.

Briefing

Briefings are meetings in which there is an opportunity for small community leaders to prepare for their upcoming gathering of their communities. Through briefings small community leaders can dialogue about pastoral considerations for their communities, evaluate previous meetings, become better prepared in understanding the materials they will be using, and discuss any areas of concern they may have in regard to their community gatherings.

In addition to leadership development sessions, it is recommended that regular briefings be planned for leaders prior to each small community gathering. Members of the Core Community, a parish staff person or priest will hold the briefings or make arrangements for others to do so. On some occasions a member of the Core Community could meet with a group of small community leaders, although generally it is done on a one-to-one basis.

Since one of the responsibilities of the Core Community is to provide support and direction to the leaders of the small communities, these individual briefing sessions allow for that ongoing, regular support and direction. Briefing is especially recommended for these groups that are developing a more intense community life.

Aspects of Briefing

In a first organizational step, the Core Community decides who among them will assume the responsibility of briefing, to which small community each will relate, and how often. It is necessary to consider the number of small communities as well as the number of Core Community members who have the qualities, gifts, and time necessary for this role.

Geographic location and personal relationships among small community leaders and the Core Community members is also an important factor. It is necessary to have an openness to this kind of ministry as well as the positive support and recognition of the pastor and staff.

Specific qualities are important for those doing the briefing:

1. Respect for Diversity: Persons need a receptivity to different personalities and an openness to different expressions of spirituality.

2. Common Sense: Any person doing briefing needs an instinct for what seems appropriate or inappropriate in a given situation or relationship. In addition the person needs a facility to recognize and help small Christian community leaders acknowledge when a person's behavior is abnormal and requires care beyond their pastoral skills.

3. Emotional Stability: Those doing the briefing ought to be emotionally stable themselves.

4. Trustworthiness: Each person concerned must have the ability to keep confidences.

5. Credibility: Those doing the briefing must have a level of acceptance within the community.

6. Humility: "Briefers" need to realize that they do not have all the answers and must be willing to seek advice from others with more experience and knowledge.

7. Availability: Briefing will take time; it is important to be able to give adequate time and attention to small Christian community leaders.

8. Desire for Growth: Persons doing briefing also need a desire for continuing faith and skills development in their own lives.

What Happens in Briefings

The spiritual growth of the individuals and the group as a whole is key to developing as a small Christian community. Growth in personal relationship with Jesus and commitment to the gospel way of life is the foundation of any authentic Christian community. The briefing meeting gives the small Christian community leader time to discuss the needs for spiritual development experienced within the group and ways to meet those needs. The Core Community member can suggest resources that are available and also bring the needs of the groups to the Core Community meeting for long-range planning.

Suggestions that a Core Community member may offer to a small community leader include the following:

- simple instructions on how to keep a journal
- basic techniques for sharing faith at a deeper level
- resource persons who may be available for spiritual direction
- an evening of reflection on themes pertinent to the needs of the small community: God's love, forgiveness, prayer, ways to deal with feelings of jealousy and anger, etc.
- spiritual reading suggestions
- instruction and experience with different styles of personal and group prayer
- ways to do outreach and concretize mission

It is important that the Core Community person and the small Christian community leader have a good understanding of any content and materials that small communities are using at a given time. During the briefing session, small community leaders share their understanding of the content and the direction of the next small community meetings. During this time, any questions in reference to content could be raised. If the Core Community member is not familiar with the material, there is still time to consult a resource person or the materials for clarification.

Specific Issues for Briefings

There may be some things happening or not happening in the group that the small Christian community leaders need to discuss in the briefings that would help them better deal with the situation. The briefing meeting provides the opportunity to review the dynamics of a particular group, what might be causing certain behaviors and what the appropriate responses could be. Issues may be matters such as the following:

1. *People are not showing up for the meeting.* It is important that the individuals themselves be asked the reasons for this occurrence. The following questions may be helpful points of reference.

- Is the meeting location easily accessible to everyone?
- Is there a genuine atmosphere of warmth and hospitality?
- Is the content meeting the needs of those involved?
- Does the content relate to their life experiences?
- Do individuals realize that their commitment to be present at the meeting is very important to the growth of the group?
- Have expectations been discussed?
- Are meetings too frequent? Are meetings frequent enough to allow a true sense of belonging or commitment to growth?
- Is the leadership style meeting the needs of the group or is it too dominant or too non-directive?
- Is there a member that is too dominating or controlling?
- Are there personality conflicts?

2. *People in the group are in conflict; they have begun to wonder why things are not as "loving" as when they first joined the group.* The Core Community member could review with the leader some of the points regarding conflict resolution. Reviewing the stages of group development might help determine if the problem is emerging as part of the natural growth process. Should this be the case, encouraging the group to see their experience as a growing one and challenging the members to the next stage of growth is vital.

3. *Someone in the group is having a personal difficulty in some area of his or her life (e.g., sickness in the family, job loss, or other emotional upsets).* The best response might be to encourage the person to share the difficulty with the rest of the group so there can be a pastoral response (meals in time of sickness, suggestions about job opportunities, words of encouragement). It is crucial that sound judgment be exercised in this area. Small communities cannot provide for all of the therapeutic needs of their members; however, the person experiencing the difficulty might be helped by the leader, by some trusted person in the group, or by the group as a whole. In some cases, the person may be encouraged to go to someone or some organization outside the group who has a particular knowledge in the area of difficulty (counseling, Alcoholics Anonymous, Alanon, Weight Watchers, etc.). Naturally, it is everyone's responsibility, but in particular it is part of the role of the small community leader to pick up the signals that indicate someone is experiencing extreme difficulty. Briefing meetings can help a leader sort out various options.

4. *Someone in the group is dominating or being non-participative.* Reviewing some of the leadership skills and group dynamic insights and deciding which apply in the given situation may alleviate this problem.

Community Development

During the briefing meeting the Core Community member can help the small community leader explore various ways to increase the sense of community within the group as well as ideas to help with the bonding of families and close friends of the small community members. This is especially important if the group itself is not already taking the initiative in this regard. Some suggestions previously stated include an annual weekend retreat involving families and other significant people in the small community members' lives, parties, picnics, or even a mystery trip.

Relationship to the Parish

The briefing session provides time to relate to what other groups are doing also. It is important that each small group in the parish develop an appreciation and value for all the various types of groups in the parish. It is a time when the Core Community can assess with the small community leader the need for a large gathering of the small groups (or at least the leaders of the small groups) in order to network and develop a sense that each group is only a small part of a much larger vision. During the briefing session, small community leaders can better learn how to serve or be served by the larger parish community.

Support for Mission

As was stated previously, living out mission and ministry is an important component of the small community effort. The small community leader needs to be encouraged to call individual members and the community as a whole to a sense of mission to which the church has been entrusted by Jesus. Matthew 25 speaks strongly of the importance of living out our relationship to God through our relationships with one another. The briefing time provides the opportunity to reflect on ways to help people make these connections between their everyday lives and the call of the gospel. Briefings offer the opportunity to reflect together on the larger needs of the parish and the world at large. Briefers can help leaders be aware of the social justice efforts in the parish and other resources that would help the small communities respond to parish and larger community needs.

Briefing Summary

The areas covered during the briefing sessions relate closely to the five elements of Christian community: prayer, mutual support, sharing, learning, and mission. With the help of the leader, the small Christian community ought to have an opportunity to evaluate in an ongoing manner how it is developing in relationship to these elements. The briefing meeting provides leaders with the opportunity for mutual communication in which encouragement can be given, suggestions made, and resources cited that would help them assist the community in growth in certain areas.

THE GIFT

The call to ministry is ultimately the call to receive a great gift from God. The leaders of small Christian communities are truly gifted by God, for their call is to love people in a very real manner. They are invited to enter people's lives with humility, concern, and skill and to be vital links between the small community and the larger church. They are called to enable and empower others. Like all Christians, small community leaders are challenged to live a Christ-centered life, embodying the exhortation of Jesus: "Love one another as I have loved you." With their loving attention, communities will flourish and God's reign will be experienced.

✝✝✝✝✝ REFLECTION AND FAITH-SHARING QUESTIONS

Reflect on Philemon 4-7, which praises the leader who has concern for those in the community.

1. In this chapter we learn about the ministry of being a good small community leader. Share an experience of being in a group with an effective leader. What were the qualities of that leader?
2. A leader is asked to be sensitive, a good listener, humble, prayerful, and forgiving. Which one is my strongest point? How will I strengthen my weakest one?
3. Making the members feel welcomed, creating a prayer environment, and taking time to celebrate with the members are very important. How can other members in the small community assist me with these roles?
4. As a community matures it may experience tension, a natural and healthy sign of growth. When did this occur in our community? How was this opportunity used positively? How did it affect the ongoing life of the community?
5. Are we conducting briefing sessions? If not, how can I initiate this process? What are some concerns that I feel would be helpful to raise in a briefing session?

11. The Priest and Parish Staff

If this pastoral direction of the parish as a community of small communities is valued, then what kind of pastoral leadership is necessary to implement it?

In the local church, the bishop is the "source and foundation of unity" (*Lumen gentium* 23). Pastors minister to parishes on behalf of their bishop. In this service, pastors are assisted, first of all, by other priests and by deacons. By virtue of the sacrament of Holy Orders, bishops share their obligation to teach, sanctify, and lead the church with their priests.

Parish life is challenged to bring about deeper commitments to Christ and to enable faith life to be a leaven in our world. Today there seems to be more varied and increased expectations on priests. For the priest, there is often "a weariness that comes from 'standing in the breach' during a time of profound transition both in our culture and in the history of the Church."[1] Small parishes may no longer have the presence of a priest on a daily basis, and larger parishes try to expand their pastoral staffs in striving to meet the needs of parishioners.

The principal role of the laity is to give witness to Christ and his gospel in the world. Some lay people express this baptismal vocation by service to the parish community. Called to collaboration by their pastor, they offer their talents as teachers, musicians, business administrators, and in various other areas of expertise. "The use of the term 'lay ecclesial ministers' shows the following: first, that the immediate reference point of their ministry is the church community itself and, second, that their ministry is exercised not solely on their own in initiative, but as a publicly recognized and authorized action within a particular ecclesial community." "... It is important that the unique gifts, expertise, and insights of lay ecclesial ministers be fully incorporated into the life of the Church, in communion with the pastors of the Church (cf. *AA*, 3; *LG*, 12, c. 225)."[2]

Small communities offer great pastoral hope and promise. By utilizing the small community approach, the pastor can multiply a caring presence many times over through well-trained small community leaders. Small communities are an ideal place for parishioners to come to "know" God and be led to deeper conversion and mission.

ROLE OF THE PASTOR AND PASTORAL STAFF

With the increasing number of small communities developing in the parish, the role of the pastor and pastoral staff becomes crucial to the long-term success of developing the parish as a community of communities. In summary, the following are ways to support this development:

1. Be involved in a small Christian community. There is no greater witness than personal participation and there is no greater means of learning the value of small communities than a personal experience.
2. Visit small Christian communities. Pastors and staffs need to be aware of the small communities and their aspirations and needs and can learn a great deal from regular contact.
3. Encourage those involved in small Christian communities, e.g., by recognizing their efforts, giving feedback either publicly or privately. People need support from leadership.
4. Establish good lines of communication between small Christian communities and the parish pastoral council.
5. Recognize the leadership of small Christian communities as a ministry within the parish.
6. Express personal interest by visiting with people to find out how things are going.
7. Provide opportunities for the entire parish to understand the place of small Christian communities in the parish through the pulpit, the bulletin, a letter, and/or through a parish assembly.

8. Initiate the development of a Core Community as the first step to implementing this pastoral direction.

9. Be a part of and maintain ongoing communication with the Core Community.

10. Support all parish ministries in developing a more communal style (i.e., including all five elements in parish ministry groups).

11. Participate in a communal way in Core Community development and leadership development and providing ongoing support.

12. Participate in the yearly goal setting and evaluation session of the Core Community.

13. Help small Christian communities to be connected with each other and to the parish as a whole.

14. Challenge and support small Christian communities in outreach, mission and evangelization. Initially, small communities will need help in growing in this awareness and moving toward action.

15. Join in celebrations in which many small communities gather. When small communities celebrate, it is so important for staff to enter into the celebrations.

SMALL CHRISTIAN COMMUNITY PARTICIPATION

To be priest means to be part of the Christian community. Father Robert Lauder, in his book *The Priest as Person,* describes it this way:

A person's horizon or world is a network of meanings that are real to an individual. In other ages, the world or horizon of many people was Christian. Not so today. The contemporary priest functions in a post-Christian world. This reality puts special pressure on both him and those to whom he is ministering. No one can be a person alone. For better or worse, we need one another. We will influence one another. The crucial question is: how will we influence one another? Will we influence one another for better or worse? The answer for the believer is to enter as deeply as possible into the Christian community. The contemporary priest must experience Christian community in at least two ways: he must help to form a Christian community as part of his apostolate, and he must be part of a community if he is to grow or perhaps even survive as a Christian minister. In a Christian community, persons try to coexist precisely as Christians. The community is rooted in truth and love, and its members try to serve one another in these two areas.[3]

In the initial implementation, the priest and staff will need to spend time not only exploring the pastoral direction, but also adopting a communal style for all their staff meetings and retreat experiences. By so doing, their communication with the parish about the pastoral direction will be authentic because they will speak from experience and not mere theory.

In addition to incorporating this pastoral direction into all parish meetings, it is essential that all staff members themselves be participants in small Christian communities. There are many benefits to being a part of a small community. The most obvious is that personal experience is the best teacher. By experiencing small Christian communities first-hand, priests and staff members can encourage others with greater conviction. This will only enhance the development of the vision in the parish.

There may be some initial concern on the part of a few parishioners that one of the priests or other staff members is giving priority to a particular group of people (i.e., their small community), but if the staff members explain their own personal commitment to spiritual growth and how this is enhanced in the small community, fears will be quieted.

For any priest and/or staff members who are in small communities, the following **guidelines** may enhance their participation:

1. Communicate clearly why you will be a participant in this particular small community. Generally this would include the fact that one is free on a certain evening or at a certain time of the day. Thus, you joined this small community because it was available at a convenient time for you. You may wish to explain that you are not "playing favorites" but being a member of a small community is a top priority and this particular small community meets at a convenient time.

2. Don't allow the group to make you the "answer person." You may need to explain that there is a time and place for the important role of teaching, but in this instance you are there to share your own faith story and listen to others just as any other member of the small community.

3. Be yourself. It is not necessary to be anyone but yourself. People love people who are most truly and authentically themselves.

4. Follow rules of good participation, i.e., do not dominate. As a leader in the parish, it is sometimes difficult to be a member rather than the leader of the group. It will be necessary to be particularly vigilant in this area.

5. Be a good listener. Many times your responsibilities include imparting information to people. In a small community setting you have the opportunity to take a different stance—one of listening to the faith stories of your parishioners.

6. Be open to requests for priestly/staff ministry, i.e., evenings of recollection, retreats, etc. Being a member of a small community does not preclude providing reflection experiences for the small community or for a number of small communities. These requests frequently help priests and other staff members be what they are called to be.

It is essential that other small community members are clear about the role of the priest or other staff persons in their communities. Important **guidelines** for them include the following:

1. Understand the priest's or staff person's background. Understanding and acceptance are always the best ways to create an atmosphere of trust and warmth. Small community members need to understand some of the concerns the priest or staff persons may have, particularly coming from certain education styles and background preferences. This is true in regard to all participants in the community. Each person comes from a different background and needs understanding and acceptance.

2. Be welcoming but not pushy. It is easy when persons are in positions of authority to look to them for increased participation and with higher expectations than are given to the rest of the members. The priest or staff member is welcomed and encouraged as are others, but no special pressure needs to be given them. Constant pushing of anyone to become a participant is counterproductive. All people want to be with friends, not to be "worked on."

3. Respect their calendar and other responsibilities. It is essential that basic respect be given to the busy schedules of all concerned. In many ways this may be an opportunity to identify with the many responsibilities and demands of staff persons.

4. Love and support are key. Love draws people to involvement. For the priest or staff person, the message needs to be: "We would enjoy having you with us." Not: "You need this."

5. Do not make the priest or any staff member the "answer person." It is important for the entire group to recognize that in this particular setting the priest or other staff member does not want to be called on as the "expert" but rather as a regular participant in the community.

6. Be realistic in expectations. Others may need to miss meetings and so may the priest or staff member.

7. Do not be judgmental. Judgment is not appropriate for any member. In the final analysis, even though there are many benefits to small communities, the quality of participation or non-participation is not for one to judge.

MANAGING TIME

Obviously, new pastoral practices will not become a reality unless there is some change in the way ministry is carried out. A key element to reflect upon is the manner in which many priests or staff members spend their time. For many, ten to twelve hours a day of direct service could be the norm. But the questions become: "Is all ministry relating back to me? Am I making myself indispensable?"

Direct service ministry has many pluses, and for the priest and professional minister there are many positive returns for caring for the sick, counseling the troubled, solving problems for people who are needy and vulnerable. But is direct service in all instances the best way to create community? If others were empowered, could not many more people minister to one another and thus multiply the amount and quality of ministry?

The question is one of balance. We need both direct service ministry and a healthy balance of empowering. The old adage is appropriate here: "It is better to teach the hungry how to fish than to give them a fish."

Priests and staff members do not need more tasks; in fact, most are already overloaded. At a time when there are fewer priests and the median age is rising, it is impractical to suggest even higher expectations and demands on an already overburdened clergy. Rather, might not a restructuring of some current time commitments be helpful?

A dramatic change in time commitments is not suggested, but rather a gradual and clearly communicated change. Initially, the priest and pastoral staff will need to spend at least some percentage of their time in developing this pastoral direction as they work with a Core Community and with the leaders of the small communities. With a positive attitude and quality time commitment, they will begin to experience some success in the implementation of this pastoral direction.

As small successes are realized in becoming a parish community of many small communities, an appreciation of collaborative ministry ensues. The priest and staff understand that they are moving beyond "activating the laity" and "shared responsibility" to a greater sense of "the collaborative ministry of pastoral care" that is "to enable others to minister to one another, to become part of a people, and to extend their Christian commitment to everything they do."[4]

When small community leaders begin to assume their role within their small communities, a reduction occurs in the number of people the priest and staff need to relate to directly. Life becomes more manageable with a clear pastoral direction. While small community ministry will itself require time, the pastoral results are most encouraging. Priests and staffs experience great fulfillment from their efforts as they witness many parishioners growing spiritually. This approach to pastoring and management is a concrete way to avoid burnout and give needed hope and a morale boost to parish staffs.

Imagine how the efforts of one pastor could be multiplied if some quality time was devoted to developing a Core Community for small Christian community development whose members in turn would be at the service of twenty-five small-community leaders. These small Christian community leaders would, in turn, be at the service of small communities, each comprising about ten people. In effect, with this network, one person would be reaching 250 people in in-depth spiritual formation. It would be difficult to find another parish model in which so many could be benefiting in this manner. And these efforts themselves can be multiplied. Certainly at the initial stages of development, the Core Community needs special attention and involvement on the part of the pastor. However, once the overall direction is set and the Core Community is adequately prepared for this ministry, the pastor's role becomes less demanding.

The pastoral direction calls for developing ministry from a communal base. Let us say that the pastor spends ten percent of his time visiting the sick. During this visiting time, he can perhaps make ten calls per week, but is unable to spend much time with each person. If the pastor focused his efforts on the development of small communities, he could gather together small groups of people who feel drawn to this particular ministry and enable and support them in becoming ministers to the sick both at home and in the hospital. If ten people gathered for prayer, sharing, learning, and support, they could visit many more people each week and offer more quality time. At the same time, the pastor who also wishes to maintain direct ministry will himself have more quality time for the visits he is able to make.

Shifts of Time and Emphasis Maximize Pastoral Effectiveness

Obviously, it is not necessary to change time commitments in all areas of ministry. Initially it could mean only a five to fifteen percent change in the use of time. The key elements are supporting the Core Community, being a part of a community oneself, and making a firm commitment to personal prayer and spiritual development. As priests and staffs make their own deeper commitments to prayer and a more intimate relationship with Jesus, the vision will flourish. As the pastoral direction grows in the parish, priests and staffs will recognize that more and more of their ministry flows from a communal base.

Vatican II has challenged and encouraged priests not only to provide care to individuals, but also to provide for the "formation of genuine Christian community" (*PO* 6). Rather than weighing them down, formation of genuine Christian community can free priests and staffs. Meeting the current needs of people enriches the ministerial work of priests and allows them to move toward roles more fitting their priestly nature. Priests and other pastoral staff members want to see their people grow spiritually. They want to enable people to effectively live out the Christian life in their families and in the world in which they live.

Is this pastoral direction, this more communal style of church, that different from the early church? Not really; in fact it is very similar to the way Jesus and his disciples ministered. The Spirit continues to lead us in the ways of Jesus.

Part III will highlight concrete approaches in bringing about the fullness of the pastoral direction as well as the benefits that will occur in family life and in the faith life of all parishioners.

✝✝✝✝✝ REFLECTION AND FAITH-SHARING QUESTIONS

Reflect on Matthew 28:18–20 and Mark 16:19–20.
(Questions 1–4 are addressed specifically to priest and parish staff persons.)

1. How has faith sharing in a small community affected me personally?

2. Have any of the ways I behave in a small group changed as a result of my participation in a small community? What have these changes been? How has this affected me?

3. Jesus sent out his disciples two by two to every town and village saying to them: "Go and make disciples of all nations . . ." (Matthew 28:19). Have I been able to send out others to minister in my place?

4. "The eleven went forth and preached everywhere. The Lord continued to work with them throughout and confirm the message through the signs which accompanied them" (Mark 16:20). Have any "miracles" occurred as a result of my letting others minister in my place? Please share one with the group.

5. How many people are involved in direct service ministry in our parish? In my small Christian community? What kind of ministry have people chosen? Has their ministry been effective in bringing people closer to Christ?

6. What effect did the presence (or absence) of the priests and staff in small communities have on the whole parish?

PART III

Concrete Approaches

12. Helping the Parish Accept the Pastoral Direction

How can the pastor and pastoral staff most easily and effectively communicate the pastoral direction of a community of small communities to the parish? Communication, even in the best of circumstances, is a challenge. Webster defines the verb *communicate:* "to impart or to transmit knowledge, information, thought, or feeling so that it is satisfactorily received or understood." In this chapter, we will address not only ways to share about this pastoral direction, but also how to help parishioners receive and understand the concept of their parish as a community of small communities. We will look at methods of communicating the pastoral direction, and specifically three concrete ways to communicate: from the pulpit, with the parish pastoral council, and through a parish assembly.

METHODS OF COMMUNICATING THE PASTORAL DIRECTION

A. The pastor and/or pastoral staff members begin by introducing the concept of small Christian communities for the parish at a staff meeting and/or parish pastoral council meeting. The person initiating the idea must have both a clear sense of the pastoral direction as well as personal conviction about the importance of this approach.

B. The pastor assembles a group of people (hopefully this group will be or will develop into the Core Community), who are open to the pastoral direction, to gather information and plan for parish small community development. As this group is formed and begins the first steps of implementation, the group continues ongoing communication with the entire parish about its efforts.

C. It is essential to speak with the parish pastoral council about implementing the pastoral direction. They are a very important consultative group in the parish. Ideally, in the early stages of looking at the pastoral direction, the parish pastoral council is consulted. One practical way to help the parish pastoral council reflect on this pastoral direction would be to have someone explain the direction and the three approaches to implementation. If a Core Community has already been established, the Core Community could assist the council with this understanding. If no Core Community has yet been established, the council may wish to set one up.

D. In order to help the entire parish reflect on this pastoral direction, the Core Community may choose to hold a parish assembly. This assembly would be a gathering of parishioners for the specific purpose of gaining input into planning for the parish to move in this pastoral direction. It would also assist parishioners in their reflection and response to the pastoral direction. (*For assistance in developing this assembly, contact RENEW International, 1232 George St., Plainfield, NJ 07062, Telephone 908-769-5400.*)

Why have a parish assembly? The primary purpose of an assembly is to provide an opportunity for parishioners to listen to one another. It allows for shared responsibility, a time for the gifts of all to be used; it allows all parishioners to share their thoughts and feelings; it helps develop leadership; it can be a beautiful spiritual event. It is an experience of being church. The parish assembly can help parishioners connect with the pastoral direction and see its practical implications.

It is important for the pastor to take a key role in inviting the entire parish to participate in this assembly. The pastor could speak at all the

Masses, inviting people to pray for the upcoming assembly in which there will be more reflection on the parish's experience of small groups. Everyone interested is invited to come. The pastor will want to offer a great deal of encouragement and motivation.

E. Following the assembly, the pastor will again wish to speak from the pulpit and share the events of the assembly. He may wish to say something like this:

> I want to share with you the reflections from the parish assembly that was held last week to help us all better understand the small Christian community vision and what it could mean for the future direction of our parish.
>
> Over the years since Vatican II, our church has matured and gained a greater sense of its call to mission and ministry. We are truly aware of the power of the Spirit at work in the church, bringing parishioners into a growing, loving relationship with God and with one another.
>
> Now many more parishioners are better prepared to participate in the ministry of the parish. For example, in regard to baptismal preparation, we as a staff will be meeting with parishioners who will in turn be gathering with small groups of parents preparing to have their children baptized. We will be using a more communal model, with much of the preparation done in living rooms, sharing Scripture, praying, learning about the sacrament of baptism, and finding support from each other.
>
> I also want to give adequate time to my own small community in the parish. Some of my time will also be given to the development of the small community leaders. Again we're doing this in order to "multiply" the service that can be given in the parish. What I most want to say is that there will need to be some shift in the way the rest of the staff and I spend our time in ministering to and with you.
>
> Actually, the movement in this pastoral direction is not only happening here at _____ parish. Following our RENEW experience (or whatever small group experience has been a part of the

parish), the reflection of our parish pastoral council, and the input of the parish assembly, we know that our parish is not having an isolated experience. The development of small communities is happening in other parishes as well. Our diocese is helping and supporting these efforts, and it seems to be a strong reality, not only here, but in many parts of the world.

The question for all of us on staff is: how can we best serve the parish? Through your reflections and the call of the universal church, we feel this is the best way we can serve you now.

This is an exciting time in our parish. We will be learning together how to live out this call from our church in our everyday parish life.

THE PARISH PASTORAL COUNCIL AND THE PASTORAL DIRECTION

Parish pastoral councils differ from parish to parish, from diocese to diocese. A parish pastoral council is consultative. Its main purpose is to ensure the life of the parish reflects the mission of Jesus, and that all parishioners are provided the opportunity to share in that mission.

The parish pastoral council is called to invoke the Spirit to seek God's truth for the parish and to know more clearly how the mission and ministry of Jesus are to be lived out in the local community at this time. Councils are guided not only by their own "articles of understanding" or constitutions but also by the norms and directions of the universal and diocesan church.

When a parish becomes interested in implementing the pastoral direction, the parish pastoral council plays a key role. Therefore, parish pastoral councils need to be knowledgeable about small Christian communities and accept them as a pastoral direction. If a diocese has incorporated the development of small Christian communities in its pastoral direction, obviously a parish pastoral council needs to take this into consideration when planning to ensure that small Christian communities come to fruition in the parish.

The parish pastoral council can, through its own convictions and commitment, help parishioners realize the benefits of developing the parish as a community of communities. When it is understood that the pastoral direction is directed toward evangelization through small communities and is meant to enliven the faith life of all persons within the parish, enabling them to live fully the Christian vocation in the world, most parishioners are readily open to sharing in its implementation.

The parish pastoral council can be a key instrument in bringing the pastoral direction to reality. Its first task is to study and understand the concepts contained in the pastoral direction, to educate council members on its principles, and to enable these principles to become part of their life and ministry.

From a very practical standpoint, the council through its purpose, role, style, and structure can influence the acceptance of the pastoral direction in the parish. As a starting point, the council can begin as soon as possible to incorporate into its meeting format the elements necessary for the development of Christian community: prayer, learning, sharing, mission, and mutual support. Thus they will themselves model the communal style of meeting.

WHAT WE COMMUNICATE

In many different ways, we communicate what we believe! If the pastor, staff, and parish pastoral council truly believe in this pastoral direction, it will be communicated not only through means such as the pulpit, through the parish pastoral council's communications, and in a parish assembly, but also through less formal exchanges. It is extremely important to give clear, simple, direct messages about the implementation of this pastoral direction in the parish. The message is simple: God calls us to be a people who love and care for each other in community and live the mission of Jesus in the world. Together in all aspects of parish life we want to pray and grow spiritually, support and love one another, learn and deepen our faith, and reach out in mission and ministry.

In chapter 13 we will look at how families and small communities interrelate.

† † † † † REFLECTION AND FAITH-SHARING QUESTIONS

Reflect on 3 John 2–8.

1. What ideas from this chapter will assist me to help the parish receive and understand the concept of the parish as a community of many small communities?
2. What part do prayer and personal conviction play in this task?

13. The Family and Small Christian Communities

Anzqar Holmberg, csj

The family is the domestic church! What powerful implications that statement has for us as church. "The family is the basic cell of society. It is the cradle of life and love, the place in which the individual is born and grows."[1] According to Vatican II, the family will fulfill this "mission to be the first and vital cell of society . . . if it shows itself to be the domestic sanctuary of the Church through the mutual affection of its members and the common prayer they offer to God. . . . " (*AA* 11)

In many ways the family, the domestic church, holds the keys to a deeper understanding of what it means to be church today. Families share meals; families celebrate joys; they heal one another's hurts; families learn forgiveness first-hand; families are there when someone dies. Every day the sacred is revealed in the ordinary. God is at work among us, continuing our creation through the intimate relationship of family.

Small Christian communities are not unlike the family. They too provide an atmosphere in which stories can be shared and the stuff of life addressed. The intimacy and bonding in a small Christian community is in some ways like that which is experienced in the family.

Small Christian communities have a great deal to offer families and, in turn, families are the model and support for small communities. Those who participate in small communities are strengthened to bring communal values and the spiritual growth gained from the community more concretely into their family environments. Likewise, all discussion about the development of small communities ought to be done with a family perspective. Small communities need to be cognizant of the family roles and responsibilities of its members and build on those family support systems.

PARISH: A FAMILY OF FAMILIES, A COMMUNITY OF COMMUNITIES

The church has over the past years had very positive movements to support family life: Christian Family Movement (CFM), Marriage Encounter, Cursillo, all based very much on a communal model of church.

How do we enable the development of that spiritual vigor, commitment, and involvement of families? Small communities provide families with spiritual growth experiences and opportunities. Communities provide an environment in which families can come together or individuals can come separately, not to detract from the importance of the family, but to build the family.

Small Christian communities provide a place where Christian tradition and values can be better grasped and strengthened. If small communities commit themselves to strengthening their families, these values can be brought back to the domestic church renewed and revitalized.

In fact, many action responses of the small community directly relate to family life. Let us take, for example, the struggles of parents with teenagers. The small community provides a safe place for parents to look at how they are relating to their teens. It also provides support for parents in the hard decisions that they must make in fostering Christian values in their children. The small community has the capacity to assist single parents in action responses that enhance their relationship with their children. For example, community members could support a single parent's need for relaxation through providing babysitting assistance to a parent who is overwhelmed at times with all the responsibilities of being a single parent.

Action responses can relate very directly to family life in such areas as family affirmation, support, and reconciliation. Through sharing in a small community, a member may decide to reconcile with a child, a spouse, a brother, a sister, a parent.

If, in fact, parents are sharing what it means to be a parent in today's society and are receiving support from a small faith-filled group of people, they will be better parents. If couples share their faith in this larger arena, they will grow in intimacy with one another and God.

FAMILY/SMALL CHRISTIAN COMMUNITY MODELS

There are numerous ways that families and small Christian communities share similar values and are supportive of one another. Let us now turn to some concrete ways that small Christian communities can meet the needs of families.

Model I

The small Christian community meets regularly for prayer, faith sharing, support, learning, and outreach with only the adults attending these gatherings. Spouses are encouraged to be a part of the same community, but in some situations that may not be possible.

While children do not attend the regular gatherings, they are very much a part of the life of the community as parents share their daily joys, struggles, and experiences. Children are included in many other planned activities, such as Christmas parties, Advent gatherings, Lenten experiences, camping trips, summer outings, helping at a soup kitchen, etc.

Core Communities and small Christian community members need to have a clear understanding of the community members' preferences. In some cultures it would be inconceivable to have gatherings without children present for everything. In other situations, participants may feel it is easier to share without small children who need a great deal of attention. Some communities would want to include teenagers; others may wish to encourage teens to gather in peer groups.

Small communities plan activities to be done by families at home, such as the preparation and prayers for the Advent wreath, or gathering canned food for the needy. Small communities facilitate prayer experiences for families to utilize in their homes. Small communities allow the richness of family experience to be shared. They can help members learn to recognize the sacredness of their everyday family lives by reflecting on their vocation as mother, father, son, daughter, etc.

Model II

A second means of meeting the needs of families is by creating family small communities. In this model, entire families gather regularly for prayer, sharing, support, learning, and mission.

During the meetings, the families may break into various age groups with someone designated to be the group leader for the children. The theme and the reflection could be the same, but children would share and learn in a simpler form. The experiences for children are filled with more activities, perhaps songs and some sharing time. The entire family regathers for the closing prayer and social time. Time might also be given for family sharing or at least directions for continuing the experience at home as a family.

> Leah, 12, says her Kids RENEW Group "is a lot of fun!" She, along with brother Greg, 10, decided that they would meet in the living room and watch Christian videos with six other children while their parents met in the next room. After watching the videos together, Leah and Greg led the group in discussion, answered questions and just had fun with the Christian themes and Bible stories highlighted that evening. The Kids RENEW Group may be the first of its kind at St. Mary of Annunciation, Green Bay Diocese, but these siblings are already busy as leaders of a second group.

Adults in these small communities may share the role of working with the children. Some communities may ask just one person to take that primary responsibility.

The important point is to recognize the needs of all community members. In our diverse world today, we have many single and elderly persons who do not have children. We have families with small children and families with grown children. Families and small communities will grow with great diversity.

CALLED TO BE DOMESTIC CHURCH

In many ways the family is the ideal model for communities, and, in turn, communities can strengthen families to live in loving, supportive relationships with other family members. Small communities can help the family by providing an environment for sharing and support in dealing with difficult family problems. They provide an environment for adults and children to share and bond with other adults and children in a spiritual atmosphere. They touch into the heart of family life values of love, bonding, service, participation in the world, and evangelization in our world today. Small communities strengthen parents and children for their journeys in life.

In Chapter 14 some concrete approaches to prayer are explored to encourage small community members to vary the prayer forms used in their gatherings.

✝✝✝✝✝ REFLECTION AND FAITH-SHARING QUESTIONS

Reflect on Luke 2:46-52

1. In what ways has my family life been supported or strengthened since I have been a part of a small Christian community?
2. How have I experienced conversion (a positive change in my life) through a family member? In what ways am I not open to conversion (change and growth) experiences?
3. Have I ever "really invited" someone, particularly a family member, to return to church/join the RCIA/become a member of a small community? Why, or why not? If so, what was their response?

14. Concrete Approaches to Prayer

Prayer is not primarily doing something, it is being with someone we love. We are a people who place much emphasis on accomplishments. We are uncomfortable just sitting around, reflecting, observing, taking time to go over our commitments, our promises, our worries. For many of us, *to do* is to be worthwhile, to make a mark in life. To take time apart from seeking success in order to be with ourselves, with others, and with God in quiet attention and exchange seems irrelevant. However, the consequences of always rushing in order to perform are emptiness and boredom. We wonder why our life seems so unconnected! Prayer is a way of being with God. Connections are made through Scripture, through adoration and gratitude, through prayer for help. Connections are made when we take a long, loving look at the wonderful gifts God has given us—friendships, a marriage, children, nature—even in brokenness that seeks healing from our God. Prayer means lifting up our minds and hearts to God who is with us always.

> ...God tirelessly calls each person to that mysterious encounter known as prayer. In prayer, the faithful God's initiative of love always comes first; our own first step is always a response.[1]

Anegan Holmberg, csj

Prayer is a constant invitation from God and a willingness on our part to seek and make contact with God. Jesus is the very Word of God. He is the good news who communicates the love, mercy, and forgiveness of a loving God. We respond to that love by allowing God to live a life of goodness through us.

PRAYER FORMS

Prayer is an essential component of small Christian communities. Small communities themselves need to be praying communities. Shared prayer in the small community gatherings requires preparation and time.

As did the early Christians, we gather as communities to devote ourselves "to the apostles' teaching and fellowship, to the breaking of bread, and the prayers" (Acts 2:42). What kinds of prayers do we say? As did the early disciples, we pray prayers of blessing and adoration, prayers of petition, prayers of intercession, prayers of thanksgiving, and prayers of praise. (See *Catechism of the Catholic Church*, 2626-2643.) Sometimes we pray these prayers from rote and other times we pray them spontaneously.

Therefore, in this chapter we will be looking briefly at various prayer forms that small communities and individuals in small communities may be using or may wish to use in their spiritual life. Specifically, we will examine spontaneous prayer, official prayers of the church, shared prayer in small community settings, and personal prayer. While we can suggest different prayer forms, an important thing to remember is that the ultimate path to prayer is a desire for and openness to a close intimate relationship with God so we can respond to God's action in our lives.

Spontaneous Prayer

Spontaneous prayer is a way of praying that depends neither upon particular structures of prayer nor upon prayers composed by others. Rather, spontaneous prayer reaches out to God with a movement arising from concern or love or thanksgiving or sorrow. The gesture is always spontaneous and sincere. Spontaneous prayer can happen in a small community setting, in the quiet of one's heart, in a liturgical setting, or any place people attuned to God's presence find themselves.

Spontaneous prayer, speaking from one's heart, may be a difficult form of prayer for some, but a comfort level can be achieved if people understand that praying from one's heart is like speaking with a loving friend. Each of us has much to say about our lives, our needs, how we feel, what has happened to us. Speaking with God is essentially telling God about our lives—our fears, disappointments, joys, and dreams. It is not that God doesn't already know all of this; rather, it is that we need to communicate about our lives.

Sometimes we wait and listen as we would with any loving friend. Sometimes we are just grateful as we would be with a friend who just listened to us. Sometimes we may be overcome with joy and awe at the magnificence of God. We each need to speak with God as a "best friend," as one who understands.

Spontaneous prayer includes the recognition of the depth of God's love that is given freely and unconditionally. Acceptance of that love is not possible unless we also accept God's will in our lives. Many situations that we pray about are beyond our control. For example, parents may be praying desperately for the return of their runaway teenager. In essence, the parents have no power to control when the child will return. Prayer, however, can help. Prayer helps people with their legitimate worry to gain a sense of calm and hope, and to receive the inspiration of the Spirit helping them to respond in a particular situation. While their worry may not be resolved as they would have wished, a new perspective, a fresh start, a renewed sense of what is important can readily flow from a praying heart. God is with us through the power of the Holy Spirit in the ordinary and the everyday events of our lives.

We can call upon God to help us in any given situation. Likewise, we can turn to God as a loving friend in times of great joy and tell our friend how grateful we are for the depth of love. We can praise God whenever we become aware of great beauty, a sunset, the singing of birds, the love of a friend, etc. Sometimes we just want to sing songs of praise and thanks.

Spontaneous prayer in a small community or in a liturgical setting invites us to speak aloud our needs, our thanks, our praise. Spontaneous prayer alone, with family, or with one or two friends can happen at any moment; in fact, it can happen almost all the time. We are told by St. Paul to pray always! What a great gift to know we can have contact with God at any moment of our lives.

Prayers of the Church

The Tradition of the Church proposes to the faithful certain rhythms of praying intended to nourish continual prayer. Some are daily, such as morning and evening prayer, grace before and after meals, the Liturgy of the Hours. Sundays, centered on the Eucharist, are kept holy primarily by prayer. The cycle of the liturgical year and its great feasts are also basic rhythms of the Christian's life of prayer.[2]

The church has provided us with many helpful ways to pray. For our purposes here we will focus on two primary forms: the eucharistic liturgy and the Liturgy of the Hours. First, let us look at the power of prayer in the eucharistic liturgy.

Of all the possible forms of communal prayer the most esteemed, is liturgical prayer, especially that which occurs at the Eucharist. The Eucharist itself is the greatest prayer. In it we join our own prayer to that of the Eucharist's chief priest, Christ himself. There is a most intimate connection between our prayer which occurs outside the Eucharistic liturgy and our participation in the Eucharistic sacrifice or offering.

The Eucharist structures our prayer life. It instructs us concerning what should characterize the basic framework of our Christian lives, including the life of prayer. The liturgy is constantly teaching us that we go to the Father, in Christ, by the Holy Spirit. . . . The liturgy, by its communal, ecclesial setting, also instructs us that we are to live the spiritual life as members of the Christian community, the Church. The communal dimension of Christian existence, so vividly portrayed by the liturgical celebration, is to be operative at all other times also.[3]

Another great gift of the church is the Liturgy of the Hours. For centuries this has been the official prayer of the church used primarily by clergy and religious. Today many lay persons have found praying the Liturgy of the Hours to be an essential part of their day. Some parishes have the practice of using the Liturgy of the Hours for their morning prayer with parishioners and staff together.

The Liturgy of the Hours is a way of praying developed by the church that is celebrated at different periods throughout the day. The format for the major hours contains psalms, canticles, readings, prayers, and a song. As the official prayer of the church, it is a marvelous prayer to share with others, but can also be said alone. The Liturgy of the Hours attunes us to various seasons and feasts throughout the year. We are enabled to resonate more with the whole church's call to Advent expectation, to Lenten penance, to resurrection hope. The saints enable us to see courage, commitment, conviction in so many diverse situations in human history. What great power and unity to think of so many praying the same prayers at one time in the church.

Shared Prayer in Small Communities

An essential ingredient for small community gatherings is shared prayer. All community members will want to help create a quiet, peaceful, prayer environment. The atmosphere throughout the faith sharing needs to be prayerful and appealing to the whole person—head, heart, all the senses. The use of symbols and ritual can enrich our prayer experience. Silence too is important—as important, in fact, as the spoken word. It is a great asset for any community to be comfortable with silence. Generally, prior to the beginning of prayer, the community is invited by the leader to become mindful of God's presence. In developing prayer experiences for the community, the following elements are suggested:

1. Greeting: Acknowledging God's abiding presence within each one of us and God's promise to be with us. (An opening prayer or song may be used to help remind us of God's presence.)

(Leader) God, you are with us, in our midst and in our hearts. In the stillness and silence of this moment, help us simply to enjoy your company, to be with you, meet you, and welcome you.

(or)   An appropriate quieting song.

2. Readings: A psalm as well as another Scripture reading would be appropriate. (Keep in mind that more does not always mean better; sometimes the simpler, the better.) For variety, try praying the psalms in different ways. Have half the group read the first stanza, the other half read the next. Or have one person read the first stanza and all read the next. You could also have two people read and all respond with the antiphon. Sometimes you may wish to sing the psalms. There are many psalms that have been set to music, or perhaps someone from the small community has the gift of singing or playing an instrument to accompany the psalm.

3. Response: The response can vary in form. At times it may be good to have silence; at other times there could be another reading, sharing, etc. Since it is a response, give people the opportunity to reflect for a few minutes. The response should be structured in such a way as to allow all to participate.

4. Spontaneous Prayer: It is good to include time for people to share personally their needs, their praise, their thanks—whatever the Spirit is moving them to pray about. Let people know initially that after the response or reading they should feel free to share prayer spontaneously. Obviously no one should feel as if he or she has to speak; all are sharing by their very presence. Shared silence can also be a sacred time. The community will also wish to allow the Spirit to pray within a person at other times as well. For example, someone might be moved to pray immediately after the song. It is important not to rush prayer.

5. Closing: The time of prayer can be brought to closure in a variety of ways. One service might conclude with the sign of peace, another with a blessing using holy water, or with a song of praise or thanksgiving.

Like personal prayer, shared prayer is based upon a relationship. Thus in developing prayer experiences for the community, listening and sharing, appreciation and honesty are key elements.

Small community leaders may wish to develop their own prayer experiences or ask other members to take turns. It is also important to note

that there are many prepared prayer experiences available through publications that can be utilized as is or adapted to individual circumstances.
When looking for planned prayer experiences, it is helpful to make sure
that certain components are a part of the prayer: silence, a time for listening, a time for speaking to God, an appropriate prayer response.

Personal or Solitary Prayer

Personal or solitary prayer is essential to one's life of faith. Yet the term
solitary can be misleading.

> It suggests being alone by yourself in an isolated place. When we think
> about solitaries, our mind easily evokes images of monks or hermits
> who live in remote places secluded from the noise of the busy world.
> . . . On occasion this isolation is necessary to develop this solitude of
> heart, but it would be sad if we considered this essential aspect of the
> spiritual life as a privilege of monks and hermits. It seems more impor-
> tant than ever to stress that solitude is one of the human capacities that
> can exist, be maintained and developed in the center of a big city, in
> the middle of a large crowd and in the context of a very active and pro-
> ductive life. A man or woman who has developed this solitude of heart
> is no longer pulled apart by the most divergent stimuli of the surrounding
> world but is able to perceive and understand this world from a quiet
> inner center.[4]

All who are serious about the spiritual journey need to establish daily
prayer as a regular part of their lives. It is suggested that all small community participants set aside at least twenty minutes each day for prayer.
In some ways time has little meaning in prayer, yet it is essential to give
some structure to our day in order to give adequate time to God.

In their book, *Lord Jesus, Teach Me To Pray,* Sister Lucy Rooney and
Father Robert Faricy describe the conditions necessary for prayer: fidelity
and openness.

> Fidelity is spending time with the Lord regularly. I put time and effort
> into anything that is important to me. No relationship of love endures

and grows unless time is spent together. But the Lord is not a time-keeper. It is not the time itself that matters, but the fidelity to the time spent with him.

One cannot be fickle in friendship. That is what the Lord offers me. He said, "I no longer speak of you as slaves—instead, I call you friends" (Jn 15:15). The Lord is always present with me. I need to turn to him, to be faithful in meeting him each day. The first step to that is putting in time. Then I am saying to him: "You are important to me. My relationship to you is the most important thing in my life (and is the foundation of all my other relationships). I might have to miss a meal to come to our meeting—but being with you means more to me than eating or sleeping. I want to put nothing in your place, nor ahead of you in my heart."

So I come faithfully to meet the Lord. What do I do then? I am open, attentive to him—just being there, looking in love, knowing in my heart what his attitude to me is.[5]

In many ways personal prayer is taking a long, loving look at our God. It is perhaps more being than doing. In prayer I open myself up to God's love. I forget all my needs, my wants, my fears, and rest quietly in God's care.

In looking at personal prayer now, we will briefly describe six different prayer styles: meditation and meditative reading, contemplation, centering prayer, healing prayer, journaling, and devotions. We each have our own personality needs and preferences; one or two of these may seem more appropriate at certain times in our lives than others. Prayer practices are keys, nothing more, but they open the door to the room that is a relationship with God.

1. *Meditation and Meditative Reading*

"Meditation is above all a quest."[6] In meditation and meditative reading the style of prayer is reflective, imaginative, relation-centered. Frequently the Scriptures are used since we can most easily hear God speaking in Scripture. In meditation we can welcome Jesus into our lives and open ourselves to him. If we meditate on Jesus we learn who he is for us and what he wants to reveal to us.

Here is a simple process for meditative reading.

- Call upon the Holy Spirit as you take sacred Scripture in hand.
- Read the Word of God for five minutes or longer, listening as God speaks to you.
- Choose a word or phrase (or invite the Spirit of God to give you one) to carry with you throughout the day, and thank God for being with you and speaking to you.

A more detailed form for meditative reading follows.

- Ask the Holy Spirit to open your heart to be attentive to the Word of God.
- In a quiet place, read the Scripture passage. For our purposes, we will use Matthew 14:22–33 (Jesus responds to the fears and confusion of the disciples during a storm at sea).
- Imagine the scene as described in the passage. What do you see? What do you imagine Jesus to be like? How do you relate to Peter? What feelings do you have?
- Reflect on the following questions. What fears, doubts, losses, moments of despair have I experienced? What did I hear Jesus say to me in this passage? Do I really believe Jesus bids me to come to him? How might I reach out to others who doubt, fear, or are feeling hopeless or lost? How will I respond?
- Pray for the grace to know and do God's will.
- Ask the Spirit to fill your heart with gratitude for this time of prayer. Express thanks to God.

In meditation and meditative reading, then, we read over the passage slowly, stay with the words and images that especially catch our attention, stay aware of the feelings and images that are awakened, and read the passage lovingly, being grateful to our God for loving us.

2. *Contemplation*

> Contemplative prayer is the simple expression of the mystery of prayer. It is a gaze of faith fixed on Jesus, an attentiveness to the Word of God, a silent love. It achieves real union with the prayer of Christ to the extent that it makes us share in his mystery.[7]

Thomas Merton wrote a great deal about contemplative prayer. Shortly before his death Merton shared these reflections:

> In prayer we discover what we already have. You start where you are, you deepen what you already have, and you realize that you are already there. We already have everything, but we don't know it and we don't experience it. Everything has been given to us in Christ. All we need is to experience what we already possess.
>
> The whole thing boils down to giving ourselves in prayer a chance to realize that we have what we seek. We don't have to rush after it. It is there all the time, and if we give it time, it will make itself known to us.[8]

Merton goes on to talk about the importance of taking the presence of the Holy Spirit in prayer seriously. He says the purpose of contemplative prayer is to bring the presence of the Spirit in our lives into our awareness:

> ... to bring our hearts into harmony with his voice, so that we allow the Holy Spirit to speak and to pray within us, and to lend him our voices and our affections that we may become, as far as possible, conscious of his prayer in our hearts.
>
> For it is the Holy Spirit "who teaches us to pray, and who, though we do not always know how to pray as we ought, prays in us, and cries to the Father in us."[9]

In contemplation God wants to love us and asks that we come to know and love God in return. Contemplative prayer is characterized by a simple awareness of God's presence within us and around us in the ordinary and the everyday. This gift intensifies our desire to respond to the Lord through the service and love of others.

3. Centering Prayer

Centering prayer is so called because it focuses on the presence of God at the center of one's very being, one's spirit. In centering prayer, we open ourselves to rest in God's presence. Letting go of thoughts, insights, memories, reflections, sensations, etc., we consent to the presence and action of God who dwells within us.[10]

> Centering prayer is a very simple, pure form of prayer, frequently without words; it is an opening of our hearts to the Spirit dwelling within us. In centering prayer, we spiral down into the deepest center of ourselves. It is the point of stillness within us where we most experience being created by a loving God who is breathing us into life. To enter into centering prayer requires a recognition of our dependency on God and a surrender to His Spirit of love.[11]

How does one go about centering prayer? First, set aside about twenty minutes of time. Then settle yourself down in a quiet manner. Choose a comfortable position for yourself, usually sitting. It is best to keep the back straight. Then close your eyes. Once you have settled, turn your attention to God who is present within you by the indwelling of the Holy Spirit.

One way of becoming more attentive to God who is within is to choose a word as a symbol of your intention of openness to God. It could be a word from the psalms, a name for God, etc.

During the time of prayer, whenever you become aware of other things, simply use the word that gently helps you to return to the divine presence. Sometimes it will be important to use the word often; other times, you may not need to use it at all. It is simply a time when God can do with you as God likes. All your attention is on God.

End your prayer very gently. Praying the Our Father slowly and reflectively is a good way to close. Let each phrase come forth with all its meaning.

Fathers M. Basil Pennington and Thomas Keating have developed many materials and workshops on centering prayer that are extremely helpful to anyone who would like to make a commitment to centering prayer.

Father Keating summarizes the steps of centering prayer in the following guidelines:

1. Choose a sacred word as the symbol of your intention to consent to God's presence and action within.
2. Sitting comfortably and with eyes closed, settle briefly and silently introduce the sacred word as the symbol of your consent to God's presence and action within.
3. When you become aware of thoughts, return ever-so-gently to the sacred word.
4. At the end of the prayer period, remain in silence with eyes closed for a couple of minutes.[12]

Centering prayer allows us to go deeply into the place within which we can rest in God. In many ways centering prayer is learning self-surrender. It is letting go into a loving reality. It is more about intention (consenting to God's presence and action within) than attention.

In centering prayer one does not reflect upon images. One is not concerned with pleasant thoughts or reflections. One enters into the silence of one's heart wherein God dwells. As Father Keating expresses it

This awareness tells you that the core of your being is eternal and indestructible and that you as a person are loved by God.... Take everything that happens during the periods of centering prayer peacefully and gratefully, without putting a judgment on anything. Even if you should have an overwhelming experience of God, this is not the time to think about it. Let the thoughts come and go.

Don't judge centering prayer on the basis of how many thoughts come or how much peace you enjoy. The only way to judge this prayer is by its long-range fruits: whether in daily life you enjoy greater peace, humility and charity. Having come to deep interior silence, you begin to relate to others beyond the superficial aspects of social status, race, nationality, religion, and personal characteristics.

To know God in this way is to perceive a new dimension to all reality. The ripe fruit of contemplative prayer is to bring back into the humdrum routines of daily life not just the thought of God, but the spontaneous awareness of [God's] abiding Presence. . . . In this prayer we confront the most fundamental human question: "Who are you, [God]?"—and wait for the answer.[13]

4. Healing Prayer

All of us carry within ourselves painful memories. Some are conscious; others are not. Perhaps we do not recall exact circumstances, but we do know that a particular situation or type of personality usually causes us pain. Spiritual healing means being open to and receiving the forgiveness of our sins, thus coming to an inner wholeness. Emotional healing means the healing of hurtful feelings. Many of those painful feelings may go back to early childhood or even before. The healing of these memories may alleviate much of the spiritual and emotional pain.

Rooney and Faricy suggest some prayers for the healing of memories. Here is one example:

Prayer for Healing of Memories from Childhood

I cannot remember anything about my birth, Lord, but I know I suffered, that it was difficult for me. All that light, the noise, the strangers, the cold hostile world. Heal these buried memories. Let me hear your reassuring voice calling me to life, calling me by name. Take that little child I was in your hands, hold me up to your cheek and tightly to you so that I can hear the beating of your heart. Comfort and console me, give me the love that you desire so that I may be filled with your love.

I can see you, Lord, at home where I used to sleep and eat and play. Everything is bathed in your presence. You are looking at the child that I was. Moments of solitude, of sadness, of misunderstanding and of fear. . . . Heal me, Lord, from all the hurts inflicted on me during the first few years of my life.

Even if I have him no longer, I remember my father as I saw him then. I thank and praise you for his goodness, for everything he did and underwent for me. But he was not perfect. I want to forgive him now, in your presence, for the times he humiliated me and made me feel unwanted or inadequate, for the times he caused me suffering because of his absence, his misunderstanding and severity, or by ill-treating my mother or my brothers and sisters.

In my imagination, I move toward him and hug him, saying 'I forgive you!'. . . . Unite us, Lord, in your Spirit of love and forgiveness. Heal our relationship.

Help me, Lord, to remember in you all the unhappy moments of my childhood. I offer you everything you want to heal. When I was little it was difficult and often painful for me to socialize with other children. But you, Lord, loved me just the same . . . and now you want to heal those hurts and remove all those things which are rooted in my painful memories and constitute an obstacle between you and me, and between myself and others.

Heal me, Lord Jesus, and I shall be healed![14]

Numerous resources are available for the healing of memories. Prayers that speak to particular hurts in our lives can help heal our hurts.

5. *Journaling*

Journaling, or keeping a diary, is a very useful tool for spiritual growth. It is simply meditative writing when we sit down with a pen in hand and write our thoughts, feelings, hopes, and dreams to our God. In many ways journal writing is like writing a love letter. We recall memories, we clarify confusions in ourselves; we may discover suppressed emotions, hopes, or dreams.

Ira Progoff[15] has developed many helpful tools for good journaling. Again there are extremely helpful workshops and workbooks available to help in the beginning process.

Journaling can take various forms. Some will journal in the form of a letter addressed to God; others will write out a dialogue with a person, perhaps Jesus, another person, or even an event. It may be helpful to journal a response to a question, taking a line from Scripture, such as Jesus' question to Peter, "Do you love me?" Sometimes it is best in journaling just to allow Jesus or another person in the Scriptures to speak through the writing. Whatever the focus, journaling can provide a beautiful prayer experience.

6. Devotions

One of the forms of prayer with which many people in the church are familiar is the prayer of devotion. Devotional prayer is largely associated with forms of prayer that come to us from the lives of saints or from other ecclesial sources (e.g., novenas). Devotional prayer is a form of vocal or recited prayer which has enjoyed a long tradition in the church.

> Devotion "consists of emotions and affections which are common and appropriate responses to commitment to Jesus Christ and belief in his gospel within the church. Some components of Christian devotion are admiration at God's wonderful works, a feeling of familiarity with Jesus, abiding sorrow for sin, a sense of security because of God's providential care, the consequent habit of frequently praying about important events in one's life, and joy in companionship with other believers in the church. Devotion links Christian belief and Christian action."[16]

Devotions can also be utilized in ongoing spiritual growth and in coming to know God better. Not everyone is attracted to the same devotions but the church has endorsed a variety of devotions throughout history. Probably the most widely used has been the rosary. The rosary connects us to Christ through the various mysteries—joyful, sorrowful, glorious. The rosary continues to be a beautiful prayer to God with special attention given to Mary, the mother and first disciple of Jesus.

We can learn a great deal about prayer and can deepen our relationship with God by looking at Mary. Mary is the model of how we as human beings are called to respond to God. She teaches us how to say "yes" to the mysterious ways of our God, not always knowing the outcome, yet trusting in God's wisdom and goodness.

Mary was a simple woman, living a very ordinary life. With the angel Gabriel's call, God invited Mary into a relationship far beyond what she could have imagined. Her relationship with God grew within her busy life. Mary had many daily responsibilities, yet maintained an attitude of openness to God's presence. "Mary kept all these things, reflecting on them in her heart" (Lk 2:19). Like Mary, we too find much to reflect upon in the ordinary moments of our lives. Through reflection those ordinary moments become very extraordinary.

Devotions often repeat the central mysteries of the Christian faith. Novenas, prayers to the Sacred Heart, the Angelus, the Morning Offering, and the Memorare are all examples of beautiful and affirming prayers that keep our focus on the power of the divine in our lives and on our complete dependence on God.

SUMMARY

These reflections on prayer and its various concrete expressions are by no means exhaustive. Many books are available on the subject of prayer. Our tradition is rich and varied. Committed Christians know and experience the importance of being prayerful. Prayer to God transforms our own consciousness; we tend to grow more and more in terms of our discipleship of Jesus Christ. We sense the needs of our world and respond in gospel images of concern and action. Prayer binds together the love of God and the love of neighbor.

It is only appropriate that we close this chapter with a "faith story" of prayer. It is the letter of a layman included in John T. Catoir's book, *Enjoy the Lord.*

> I love to pray and I pray at any time, in any place, in any way. My day starts off with the reciting of formal prayers of the Church. Through these, I've come to know about many great Christians—not from the sense of history but because of their feeling and their love of God and His people. The Memorare was the most meaningful. . . . Many others followed. More than once I have suddenly realized that a part of my life has been transformed by one of these prayers, and just as suddenly, that that prayer no longer seems special to me and another suddenly speaks to my heart. I've come to recognize this as a way Jesus is leading and teaching me. . . .
>
> As time has gone on, I've been led into many different prayers and ways of praying. I've sat in silence just staring at the cross and Jesus until I thought my heart would break. I've sung for joy—shouted Alleluia! And then at times . . . I've found myself wording my own prayer to our God in ways that at times have astounded me. I've knelt, sat, laid down,

stood up, squatted; but it never seems to matter, Jesus always listens. Sometimes, it's with my arms ... extended to heaven, yearning to reach and hold my God.

The Rosary still holds a special place of prayer for me and has acted most often as a spring prayer for a variety of other forms of prayer during and after completing it, which at times has taken me an hour or more to do. My car has become an especially good place to pray and traffic and gas lines don't seem nearly as long.

At times, I've just sat or stood in awe looking out at [God's] beautiful world. ... I guess this is the best prayer—letting [God] speak to me. That, and the constant repeating of the name "Jesus" all through the day. What a beautiful and powerful name it is.

All in all, the most exciting thing about my prayer is its infinite variety and excitement as the Spirit leads me from and through one form to another.[17]

---

† † † † † REFLECTION AND FAITH-SHARING QUESTIONS

Reflect on some of the many instances in the gospels where Jesus prayed: Matthew 14:23, 26:36; Mark 1:35, 6:46; Luke 5:16, 6:12, 11:1–13.

1. "Prayer is not primarily doing something, it is being with someone we love." How would I describe the difference between "being" and "doing" when it comes to prayer?

2. "What kind of prayers do we say?" Is it possible to pray without "saying prayers"? An example of a time in my life when I found a particular prayer form or style the "best" way to pray was. ...

3. "All who are serious about the spiritual journey need to establish daily prayer as a part of their lives." How might a better prayer life help me on my own personal spiritual journey?

4. How has my prayer life changed since the time I was a child? Do I still relate to God in the same way as I did then?

5. "The most exciting thing about my prayer is its infinite variety. ..." Am I open to experiencing different forms or styles of prayer? What concrete steps could I take to learn new ways to pray?

15. Concrete Approaches to Evangelization

Charlotte Carter Attebery

In this chapter, we will look at how small Christian communities enhance evangelization and lead the parish to become a more evangelizing parish. We will also look at the relationship between the process of Christian initiation and small communities.

EVANGELIZATION AND SMALL CHRISTIAN COMMUNITIES

Small Christian communities provide an ideal vehicle to move the parish toward becoming an evangelizing parish. By restructuring the parish into a community of small communities, the parish could move beyond sporadic, periodic evangelization events to becoming a consistently evangelizing parish. Why this strong emphasis on the parish becoming an evangelizing parish?

There is and will always be a great emphasis in the Catholic Church on evangelization, for evangelization is the vocation of the church, her identity, her mission. Pope John Paul II spoke often about a "reevangelization" or a "new evangelization" of all Christians and called all Christians to renew their commitment and fidelity to the mission of evangelization.

Vatican II set the stage for this rejuvenation. Pope Paul VI then took the vision of evangelization articulated by Vatican II and clarified and explained it further in his Apostolic Exhortation, *On Evangelization in the Modern World*. This document provides a challenging and inspiring understanding of evangelization. Pope Paul VI writes: "The Church, 'striving to proclaim the Gospel to all people,' has had the single aim of fulfilling her duty of being the messenger of the Good News of Jesus Christ—the Good News proclaimed through two fundamental commands: 'Put on the new self' and 'Be reconciled to God.'"[1] This document, literally a long-term plan to help us become an evangelizing church, summarizes the direction of all evangelization efforts.

Evangelization! What Is It?

Evangelization is the essential mission of the church. As baptized Christians, we are called to the responsibility of evangelization, yet the word is still foreign to many Catholics.

The word *evangel* comes from a Greek root word, meaning "good news." *Evangelization* then means spreading the good news joyfully, sharing the story. What story? The story of Jesus and what he has done in our lives, the story of those who were healed and loved by Jesus, the story of how God has entered our lives, healed and loved us.

> Evangelization implies outreach to those who do not yet know and love Jesus Christ or realize how much he knows and loves them. It implies enthusiasm and apostolic zeal in the proclamation of the gospel, a passionate desire to help people fall in love with Jesus and commit themselves to him forever. More than a program, evangelization is an attitude. It is a mentality of sharing, of inviting, of welcoming people into the joy of communion with Jesus Christ.[2]

Pope Paul VI provides a broad definition of "evangelization." He states that "evangelization means bringing the good news into all the strata of humanity, and through its influence transforming humanity from within and making it new."[3] In Pope Paul VI's definition, "evangelization" is broader than "getting people to come back to church" or even converting the unbaptized. It is both of these, but so much more. Evangelization calls us to the transformation of humanity and making all of creation new.

How Did Jesus Evangelize?

Evangelization begins with each person accepting the Word of God. As we come to accept that Word more fully, deep, radical conversion happens, and not only do we speak that Word verbally, but we live it very concretely. We look to Jesus to see how evangelization occurs. Jesus evangelized through his life. He healed the sick and cared for the poor and downtrodden. People were attracted to him because he "spoke with authority." In other words, he spoke about God from his own knowledge and experience of God. He touched people where they were in their lives. If they were sick or hurting, he comforted them; if they were frightened, he reassured them; if they were self-righteous, he challenged them.

With What Slice of the World Am I Called to Share?

John Boucher, evangelist and author, calls us to look at the web of personal relationships through which we move. He invites us to think of this web as a fishbowl with us as fish who have other fish (family, neighbors, workplace/service, friends) swimming around us. These are the people with whom we are in contact at least every week. He says, evangelization is not so much a "thing to do," but a way we go through our everyday lives. We evangelize as opportunities present themselves in our everyday lives.

Who Are Most Open to Evangelization?

People are most open to evangelization or conversion when they experience a time of stress or hurt or are going through a transition. With God's help, we need to take greater care to notice and relate to those who are hurting, going through stress or transition. These are the people for whom the old answers are not working any more.

Small Christian communities offer some of the things most attractive to people in transition. Frequently, people in small Christian communities will be able to share a conversion story in their own personal lives that is most appealing and offers great hope. In all instances, people in small Christian communities are able to share an experience of community that also serves as a magnet for those searching.

Small Christian Communities: Greenhouses for Evangelization

In small Christian communities, God "grows evangelizers." For it is in small Christian communities that participants realize they can share stories of faith with one another, stories of how they live out the values of Jesus; those who listen seem interested. They feel more comfortable with the sharing, thus feeling more confident to share with others in everyday life.[4]

We give one another hope by telling how God is acting in our lives today. We share the wonderful miracles that are part of our everyday lives, the times we were blind, but now can see; the times we were downtrodden, but have been lifted up. Often those miracles will be in very ordinary, but powerful, experiences. How often have our broken relationships been healed or our tears wiped away! For small Christian communities to be most effective, they should be *intentional* about their evangelization efforts. Evangelization usually doesn't just happen. Through small Christian communities, we claim one another as brothers and sisters in Jesus Christ, take personal ownership of our faith, and take it out into the world.

As we come to know Jesus better and share his Word with others, we will also want to welcome new people and invite them to share their stories. There are so many stories of faith, but so few people who yet understand that that is what their lives are. Just as through the centuries the stories of Jesus have fed and nourished us, we can feed and nourish each other through our stories of faith.

Small Christian communities are an ideal way for the work of evangelization to be accomplished. It is precisely in small Christian communities that people are sharing their stories and seeing how God is acting in all aspects of their lives. These communities are able to reach out to the unbaptized and alienated with conviction and welcome them to their community of faith. The question is not, "Do we focus on evangelization *or* the development of small communities?" Rather we see that small communities provide a fertile environment for the overall task of evangelization to occur most effectively in the parish.

EVANGELII NUNTIANDI AND SMALL CHRISTIAN COMMUNITIES

In *Evangelii Nuntiandi,* Pope Paul VI speaks of the importance of small communities in the process of evangelization. He calls them "a hope for the universal Church." He then speaks of some important aspects of small Christian communities if they are to be truly evangelizing:

- that they seek their nourishment in the Word of God
- that they avoid the ever-present temptation of systematic protest and a hypercritical attitude
- that they remain firmly attached to the local church in which they are inserted, and to the universal church
- that they maintain a sincere communion with the pastors whom the Lord gives to his church
- that they never look on themselves as the sole beneficiaries or sole agents of evangelization
- that they constantly grow in missionary consciousness, fervor, commitment, and zeal
- that they show themselves to be universal in all things[5]

Paul VI describes the need for a radical conversion, a profound change of minds and hearts in people if they are to be effective evangelizers. He highlights key elements of evangelization: *interior change, renewal of humanity, witness of life, explicit proclamation, inner adherence, entry into community, acceptance of signs,* and *apostolic initiative.* We will explore each of these elements, and see how small communities can play a vital role.

Interior Change

Evangelization cannot happen without ongoing conversion in the lives of evangelizers. For Paul VI, this is *metanoia,* or a radical conversion that affects both the mind and heart of the believer.[6] This happens in such powerful ways in small communities. As people share about their life in faith, they begin to see their life in a new light. They break open the Scriptures and become aware of the discrepancies between how they live and the call of the gospel. They are inspired by the ways God is acting in their own life and in the lives of other community members. They are filled with gratitude, recognizing how God is working in every aspect of their lives. The Spirit is alive in the community and moves community members to a graced moment of metanoia.

> An excellent example is that of Jim, a man in his early thirties who lives in a tough neighborhood in New Jersey. Jim had little church or religious experience, but somehow got involved in a RENEW faith-sharing group. He took over some leadership responsibilities and his love for the Lord became real and obvious. When his pastor was asked about this new-found leader and where he got all his leadership skills, he smiled and said, "Jim was head of the local drug traffic here before RENEW." It was in the context of the small group that Jim had a real metanoia, a deep conversion.

There is story after story about changes in the lives of people who have participated in faith-sharing groups. Stories will only be multiplied and deepened as these groups grow into communities, where support for conversion becomes ongoing and normative.

Renewal of Humanity

Paul VI's vision of evangelization is interior change in order to transform society. The challenge is to bring the good news of Jesus into all parts of our culture and society.

In the sharing of their own stories and real-life situations with other people, those in small communities develop keener observational powers.

The caring in the group helps members become more compassionate toward people they interact with daily. Community members also grow in sensitivity to keeping abreast of world news events that influence human lives. Small communities, in fact, are the perfect context to connect the gospel message to any life situation. Communities not only help members "see" better, but also help them refine precise and explicit ways to act in complex life situations. Communities give people the courage to take concrete action and provide a context for accountability and evaluation of those actions.

> José crossed the border from Mexico into the U. S. with virtually nothing to his name. Through hard work and the grace of God, he eventually established himself as a budding entrepreneur in his new country, with millions of dollars in income and some three hundred employees in his factories. When José joined a RENEW small community, the sharing experiences opened his eyes to the struggles that face the immigrant Mexicans whom he employs. One day, while visiting one of his sites, José saw his foreman publicly berating a worker. While the situation humiliated the individual in front of his peers, José remained silent.
>
> For weeks the incident haunted him. Finally, through the strength he received from his small community, José located the worker and apologized for the foreman's action.
>
> Then, he approached the foreman at his home, asking him to remember that each worker is a child of God with dignity, and should be treated with respect. José recommended that the foreman relate to the employees in private, so as to avoid embarrassing them.

Witness of Life

The gospel will be best proclaimed by effective witnesses. The small community provides an excellent environment for people to become effective witnesses. It provides the kind of environment in which people can come, reflect, be healed, and know there is security and support as they live and work in a world that may seem hardened against gospel values. People offer an example to one another regarding concrete situations and allow the gospel to influence aspects of their lives that previously may have been unconnected to gospel values. Small community members begin to understand their responsibility to exemplify these values, and they begin to witness in a more holistic way.

> Hector and his wife, Alma, belong to a small community. Hector was impressed by the witness of one particular woman. "I learned from this lady who was like a good Samaritan. She picked up a woman who was on the street, who was homeless and brought her into her home. She offered her home to this woman until she could find a job and a home. That really broke my heart. And I thought, if this lady was capable and able to do this thing, why couldn't I do it?

Explicit Proclamation

How does the average parishioner proclaim the gospel in an explicit manner? Only through an authentic faith experience. Proclaiming the good news must come from a heart alive with the message of Jesus. The small community provides this type of formation. In communities people learn to speak about Jesus. What may have been fears or inhibitions start to break down and people begin to speak freely about Jesus and what he has done in their lives. The joy of discovering and the confidence that comes when small community members take ownership of their faith call for expression. This is carried beyond the community and leads to a natural expression of faith in everyday life.

Inner Adherence

Paul VI also speaks about the need for all Christians to develop an inner commitment to the gospel. As small communities gather, they come together as a group of believers. Because for many Catholics faith has been inherited, they need to think through and articulate their faith in order to assume personal ownership. The witnessing to one another builds up the faith commitment of each, and they begin to see that not only were most of them "born Catholic," but they have a deep conviction about their faith. Perhaps even to the surprise of small community members, they share their "beliefs" in conversations with family, friends, acquaintances, and co-workers.

> Jack, who was in a small community for years said, "I have used every opportunity to let people know I am in a group like this because usually when you say that—you find out there is a great depth of spirituality in a lot of people. But you just have to open up and talk about it."

Entry into Community

As the small community grows, members expand their understanding of mission. The tightly knit group realizes that it needs openness and expansion. The good news of Jesus cannot be contained. There is a growing desire to bring others to share the wonderful experience of being disciples of Jesus. The community is open to inquirers. In fact, it attracts others.

> An excellent example is the story of a man who approached the pastor of a large Catholic church. The man was walking down the corridor in the parish community center and asked if he could buy a ticket to the upcoming parish picnic. The pastor, not recognizing him as a regular parishioner, sold him a ticket and asked the gentleman if he was a member of the parish. The man said he was not and had not been to church for a long time, but his family wanted to come to the picnic. The pastor invited him to join a group that was meeting that very evening, the "Re-Membering" group, a small group adapted from the experience of Christian initiation. The gentleman seemed pleased to be asked and joined the group.
>
> As people began sharing their stories, the gentleman began to feel a bond with the group. He had a taste of a receptive and honest small community. One of the people said that she had been away from the church for many years, but had been back now for the past five years. Others had varying lengths of time of separation from the church. The gentleman who had come to the parish to buy a picnic ticket said, "I've been away from the church for twenty years and I've been back for fifty-eight minutes." In the experience a kernel of this man's faith had come alive!

Acceptance of Signs

Another key element that Pope Paul VI discusses is the acceptance of signs. As people change, they themselves become signs of transformation. They participate more fully in the life of the church. Any privatized view of faith begins to break down in the context of community sharing. Connections between difficult areas of life and faith are made. Small community participants not only participate in the church, but become living signs themselves, visible sacraments of salvation—something very attractive to others.

Apostolic Initiative

"Finally the person who has been evangelized goes on to evangelize others."[7] One of the important elements discussed earlier to help a group grow to become a Christian community is that of mission. True faith in Jesus cannot be "hidden" but must be shared.

Many Catholics grew up with the notion that faith is a personal matter. People's many personal needs can easily absorb their energy. As communities share, the message of the gospel compels people to greater concern for others. A sense of urgency is created as is compassion for suffering humanity and the suffering Jesus endured for the redemption of the human family. As people grow they become more open to the power of the Holy Spirit and allow that power to take root in their hearts, much like the Pentecost moment. As with the early disciples, they receive fire that cannot be quenched and begin spreading the good news of Jesus to the whole world. People who may previously have been fearful or passive begin taking apostolic initiative. Even the timid are transformed as they proudly boast of Jesus and his gracious and healing way of life.

Reflecting on Pope Paul VI's words, it is so apparent that small communities provide an excellent approach to evangelization. They provide an environment for sound growth, which allows many people to have a change of heart. What greater way to free people to proclaim the gospel! What greater hope for the universal church this could be!

GO AND MAKE DISCIPLES

The United States bishops have also offered us a very practical document entitled "Go and Make Disciples—A National Plan and Strategy for Catholic Evangelization in the United States." They articulate three goals and numerous strategies to implement these goals (emphasis added):

1. "To bring about in all Catholics such an enthusiasm for their faith that, in living their faith in Jesus, they freely share it with others." How?

   - "[F]oster an experience of **conversion and renewal** in the heart of every believer . . ." and ". . . in every parish."
   - "[F]oster an appreciation of **God's Word** in the lives of all Catholics."
   - "[M]ake the evangelizing dimension of the **Sunday Eucharist** more explicit."
   - "[F]oster an ever deeper sense of **prayer**."
   - "[F]oster active . . . religious experience through participation in **small-group and other communal experiences** in which the Good News is shared. . . ."
   - "[F]oster a sense of domestic church" in **families**.
   - "[D]evelop a **spirituality for the workplace**."
   - "[F]oster greater appreciation of **cultural and ethnic spirituality**."

2. To invite all people in the United States, whatever their social or cultural background, to hear the message of salvation in Jesus so they may come to join us in the fullness of the Catholic faith. How?

   - Make parishes more **welcoming**.
   - Help Catholics feel comfortable **sharing their faith and inviting others to share theirs**.
   - Help people learn to **evangelize**.

- Invite people into the church through **home visits, mailings, publicity, etc.**
- "[D]esign programs of **outreach** for those who" are no longer active Catholics.
- "[D]esign programs that reach out in particular ways to **those who do not participate in a church community**...."
- "[D]eepen **ecumenical** involvement" through "mutual dialogue and sharing; joint scriptural study and social justice projects"; and **shared groups.**

3. "To foster gospel values in our society, promoting the dignity of the human person, the importance of the family, and the common good of our society so that our nation may continue to be transformed by the saving power of Jesus Christ." How?

- "[I]nvolve parishes in ... the needs of their **neighborhood**."
- "[F]oster the importance of the **family**."
- "[D]evelop groups to explore issues of the **workplace** and lay spirituality."
- "[I]nvolve every Catholic ... in areas of **public policy**."
- "[I]nvolve the Catholic Church ... in the **media**."
- "[I]nvolve Catholics ... in questions of **economic systems**."

Small Christian communities are the ideal place to implement the three goals that the bishops enunciated. They provide an environment for solid conversion and renewal based on the Word of God to take place. Likewise they provide an ideal environment to invite people who may be searching for God in their lives.

WHY EVANGELIZE?

We live in a world desperately in need of the good news of Jesus. There are many who have not as yet been introduced to Jesus, and there are others who have been members of the church, but have disconnected themselves.

We hear the desperate cry from those seeking freedom from oppression and poverty. We hear the cry from those asking for freedom from domination and freedom of expression of their religious beliefs, and we hear the cry from those longing for spiritual meaning. No matter what the culture, there is a strong cry for the good news of Jesus.

CALLED TO BE EVANGELIZING PARISHES

In order to be an evangelizing parish, we need to call large numbers of parishioners to be responsible for evangelization. Like the universal call to holiness, the call to be an evangelizer is not an option for the Christian. Through small communities, we are able to have large numbers of people involved in evangelization efforts. A network of people will create a climate of evangelization for the entire parish. Imagine the impact of so many small communities actively engaged in evangelization.

All these small communities would provide members with courage and a sense of being sent forth. Successes and failures could be evaluated and people reenergized for evangelization outreach.

Whatever the focus of a particular small community might be, participants could be formed to see that they have an intrinsic call to evangelization. The key to successfully becoming an evangelizing parish is to move beyond passing and temporary efforts and create a style and structure of parish that is always carrying out the work of evangelization. The pastoral vision of the parish as a community of small communities would achieve this. "If evangelization is indispensable to the church, then small Christian communities are indispensable to evangelization."[8]

Recall that beautiful Pentecost moment in our church when the disciples were gathered as a small community, frightened and confused. The Holy Spirit came upon them and gave them the power to go out into the whole world to proclaim the message of Jesus. There was power and mystery. That moment is happening again today. We too are called to be transformed and changed. We too are called to go forth, as Christians supported and inspired by other Christians, to the whole world to **proclaim the good news that Jesus is alive, he is risen, he is here!**

CHRISTIAN INITIATION AND SMALL CHRISTIAN COMMUNITIES

The relationship between the process of Christian initiation and small Christian communities is readily evident. No Christian initiation effort can be totally effective if the parish itself is not striving to become a more faith-filled, evangelizing community. Small Christian communities are an effective means of creating such a parish. Small Christian communities and Christian initiation are a natural "fit." The catechumenal group itself is invited to become a small Christian community, and experience has shown that when it is implemented in parishes, it is an ideal model of small Christian community.

Charlie and Peggy Lockwood, catechumenate coordinators in Presentation Parish in Upper Saddle River, New Jersey, reflect upon the process of Christian initiation and small Christian communities:

> In September of 1978, our pastor invited us along with ten other parishioners to study the catechumenate in the hope of launching this conversion process one year later. We discovered the power of the Spirit of God at work in this process, evangelizing and forming everyone involved, not only the inquirers and candidates. Our study team evolved into a nurturing, faith-sharing small group, and we naturally have the small group model in all our Christian initiation outreaches.
>
> Now, we feel the call to evolve even more toward the integration of the Christian initiation process and the growing small community ministry that we are blessed within our parish. Through this, inquirers and catechumens benefit from more active concern and nurturing, not only from the catechumenate team and their individual sponsors, but from so many others in the parish.
>
> The sequential periods of the order of Christian initiation suggest that conversion happens in a prescribed developmental way with a beginning, middle and end. We feel from experience that this is somewhat artificial because evangelization, catechesis, conversion, discernment and service happen continually throughout the process of our lives, and they happen in all different orders. Thus to have a particular experience of Christian initiation grounded in an ongoing small

community environment frees the individual person to have conversion be an integral part of daily life with its differing rhythms.

The small community is a natural sponsor of the Christian initiation process and of all who are involved. Christian initiation and small communities not only need one another, they are part of the same Spirit.

Small Christian communities provide a big boost to the ongoing development of the total catechumenal process. Once the Christian initiation team has been developed, they too are called to become a community of faith. They welcome, initiate, instruct, and provide spiritual formation experiences.

The following schema is offered to show how small Christian communities and the process of Christian initiation might be integrated. The Christian initiation process can only be truly implemented within the context of a faith-sharing community. A movement in that direction is based upon the following conditions:

1. The parish has implemented or is moving toward the implementation of the process of Christian initiation in the fullest sense.
2. The Christian initiation team or catechumenal team is growing as a small Christian community itself.
3. A means of educating the parish about the process of Christian initiation and small Christian communities has been undertaken.
4. Small Christian communities are already operative or the parish is looking to foster their development.

When these conditions are present the integration of small communities and Christian initiation can occur in the following manner:

The Inquiry or Precatechumenate Period

The small Christian community itself is in an ongoing process of evangelization. Community members are called to reach out to people they know who are searching for something more in their lives and to welcome these people into their sharing. A living room in the home of one of the members of the small community may be a more attractive place for newcomers to be welcomed than a large church hall. If the small Christian community is indeed an evangelizing community, hospitality and welcoming of these newcomers will be a key component of the community's awareness and practice. Community members will share their stories of faith with those potentially interested and introduce the newcomer into the parish life and the process of the catechumenate.

In the case where an unbaptized or uncatechized adult comes to the parish on his or her own or through parishioners (who are not members of a small Christian community), it is ideal to have that person become a member of a small Christian community as a part of the initiation process. The community that would be most appropriate for the inquirer is discerned by the parish staff members, the inquirer, and the small community that will potentially receive the inquirer.

The small Christian community plays a very important role in the rite of acceptance which takes place as the inquirer becomes ready to make a declaration of intent to proceed further. The small Christian community is responding to its call to evangelize and the inquirer is given a loving community with which to share and from which to learn.

In some instances where there are no small communities in existence, the parish could organize a group of those parishioners who are interested in initiation ministry and then move forward with the establishment of small communities at large. In this situation: a small Christian community would be formed composed of "inquirers," their sponsors, and a group leader. Using the elements of a small Christian community they move toward the rite of acceptance.

The Catechumenate Period

Following the inquiry period, small Christian communities provide an opportunity for catechumens (and those seeking reception into full communion with the Catholic Church)[9] to be "one with" the faithful in experiences of Word, worship, service, and community.

In the *Rite of Christian Initiation of Adults* the period of the catechumenate is described as a time that "catechumens learn to turn more readily to God in prayer, to bear witness to the faith, in all things to keep their hopes set on Christ, to follow supernatural inspiration in their deeds, and to practice love of neighbor, even at the cost of self renunciation."[10] This, however, is not only the call of catechumens, but the call of the entire parish community.

The catechumenal community itself meets at various times, and the primary gathering point for the catechumens (and candidates) occurs when they are dismissed from the assembly at the conclusion of the Liturgy of the Word. While the catechumens (the candidates), their sponsors, and appropriate catechists form the catechumenal community, the intention of the initiation process is not to create a separate ongoing community. Instead, catechumens (and candidates) are encouraged along with their sponsors to be involved in other small Christian communities and/ or ministry groups of the parish. Participation in these small communities can provide opportunities for supplementary catechesis. In many cases, the most appropriate small communities for catechumens are the ones in which they began their early contact with the parish. That community may be the most appropriate one to offer continuing support since its members know and love the catechumen.

Period of Purification and Enlightenment

During the period of purification and enlightenment, small communities provide the occasion for the faithful and the elect (and/or candidates) to witness their faithfulness to Christ and to share their conversion stories.

During Lent, the entire parish community is focusing on the great Lenten stories of transformation. The whole parish is on a journey. For the catechumen this may be a "first time" journey; for others, it is a renewal of their baptismal journey into faith and deeper transformation. While the elect continue to meet together, they can also join with their small Christian community that would also be focusing on appropriate Lenten themes. Thus the catechumen and the small Christian community are sharing this Lenten journey.

During this time the faithful and the elect (and/or the candidates) are together and can share appropriate retreats, group meditations, and reflections. Again the most natural small community for catechumens could be the one with which they began. That community would be helpful in being a part of the reflection on the scrutinies to help the catechumen better appreciate them. (Scrutinies are special rites in which the community prays that the elect [and/or the candidates] will be enlightened and purified and that any evil influences within their hearts will be removed by the grace of God.) The small Christian community also has the opportunity to provide the catechumen a retreat experience in the small group itself.

Period of Mystagogy or Postbaptismal Catechesis

The entire parish now celebrates the Easter mysteries. Just as the entire parish focused on the Paschal Mystery in Lent, so the parish continues to look at what this transformation means for their call to mission in the world. It is an important time for parishioners to live out in all areas of their lives the values of the gospel.

Once the elect (and/or the candidates) become neophytes and share full membership in the universal church, the small Christian community continues to play a significant role in their faith journey. During the Easter season the neophytes together with the other members of their small Christian communities unfold the mysteries of our faith by "meditating on the Gospel, sharing in the Eucharist, and doing the works of charity."[11] This is to prepare themselves for entering anew the evangelizing ministry of the church celebrated on Pentecost.

In the year following the neophyte's initiation, the small Christian communities are instrumental in nurturing the faith of these newcomers and in helping them discern appropriate ministries both within and beyond their particular parish.

It is so easy for a new person to have a sense of being lost in the midst of a large parish. Many priests in the past may have wondered, "What ever happened to those to whom I gave instructions?" When the neophyte is a member of an already existing community of faith, there will be no need to wonder about what happened to the person.

MODELS FOR INTEGRATING SMALL CHRISTIAN COMMUNITIES AND THE PROCESS OF CHRISTIAN INITIATION

Father Thomas Caroluzza, former pastor of Holy Spirit Parish in Virginia Beach, Virginia, who has worked for a number of years with the catechumenal process, suggests three models that have been tried and proven successful. These models are based on the assumption there are small communities in the parish or at least the parish wishes to establish such communities.

Model I The small Christian communities of the parish learn how to listen to each other, care for, and support one another. They must reach out in their homes, their neighborhoods, where they work and recreate, inviting interested people to join them for prayer, faith sharing, ministry, or whatever is of concern that gathered them in the beginning. In essence, the **small communities are about the process of evangelization in their everyday lives,** with family, friends, co-workers, even strangers.

When someone indicates an interest, the members of **the community** into which the person is brought **helps the inquirer raise questions** and concerns. The community members need to be open to the newcomer/inquirer even as far as setting the agenda. In essence, this small community is doing the precatechumenate, that is: they are opening up the spirit of the community to the inquirer, the first proclamation of the living God.

When the small community **discerns the inquirer's readiness** to enter the catechumenate, they, as a community, present that candidate to the parish catechumenal team and offer sponsorship. In this particular model, the small community does not have to participate in the catechumenate itself. In most cases, one of the members of the small community would be the sponsor for the catechumen and have a greater role in the person's faith development.

That particular sponsor would share with all the members of the small community the progress of the catechumen. The community would continue to offer support from afar as well as more intimate friendship and informal contact with the catechumen.

During Lent, **the elect** (or the candidate) **returns to the small community** where prayer, fasting and the works of charity could be practiced with the small community. All members of the small community who have come to know the elect (or the candidate) will want to give testimony at the parish rite of sending and to be actively involved in the Lenten rites and the Easter vigil.

During the Easter season, the small community **helps discern the gifts of the neophyte** and how those gifts could be exercised in the parish and the world. The tender faith of the neophyte continues to be nurtured and nourished in the small community in the months and years ahead.

In this model, there is little need for follow-up programs for new members. The new Catholic is nurtured and supported by friends known intimately over many months. When ten, twenty, or fifty small communities are exercising their responsibility for evangelization in this way, there will be not only larger numbers of inquirers and catechumens each year, but greater numbers of the parishioners directly involved in the process and the rites.

Model II Some parish communities focus specifically **on pre-catechumenate and evangelization** while **others** focus **on catechesis** and still **others** on the **content of the Lenten and Easter seasons.** In this model, the sponsor takes the inquirers and the catechumens to various communities at different times for different reasons. After the Easter season, the neophyte chooses one of those communities with whom to continue to share and grow.

The advantage to this second model is the greater number of parishioners that the elect (or the candidates) come to know over the many months of their journey. The disadvantage is that this experience is less intimate, and therefore less bonding takes place between the candidates and the members. Those who have used this model feel that this kind of bonding will take place when the neophyte chooses a stable community after Easter.

Model III The small **communities provide supplementary and individualized catechesis.** In this model the catechetical needs of each catechumen are the primary concern. Various communities develop a **specialized area of catechesis** in order to help the catechumens learn about the Catholic faith. The parish designs a plan to assure that all areas of catechesis are provided.

The catechumenate group meets each Sunday after dismissal. The special needs of this group are supplemented by a small community that takes a particular formational focus. Each sponsor assumes responsibility for bringing the catechumen to those communities for one or more sessions. In other words, the catechumenate community itself would be the primary community, but catechumens would have the opportunity to meet many parishioners and become "formed" in a community model by visiting different communities. After Easter, the neophyte would be encouraged to become a regular member of one of the already existing small communities.

SMALL CHRISTIAN COMMUNITIES SUPPORT THE PROCESS OF CHRISTIAN INITIATION

Obviously, there are many more possibilities, and great creativity can be utilized to implement the process of Christian initiation in a parish which is structured as a community of small communities or where there is some focus on the development of small communities. Small communities provide both the environment and the opportunity for formation that is essential to the process of Christian initiation. Just as we are all called to evangelization, we are all called to implement the process of Christian initiation in our local parishes.

A small community structure for the catechumenate helps meet many parish challenges: sponsorship, follow-up, working with varying backgrounds of inquirers and catechumens, just to name a few. In the small communities model of the catechumenate, the catechumenal team benefits from working with small Christian communities and is assisted in exercising the functions, roles, and responsibilities in the process of initiation.

An understanding of the importance of meeting the needs of alienated and returning Catholics has also emerged from the experience of the catechumenate. This process of reconciliation is known as the "re-membering church." Like the process of Christian initiation, the re-membering church is brought together as a small faith-sharing group.

All that has been said about initiating new members into the church can be underlined when we speak of returning Catholics. If a person who has been alienated is coming back to deepen his or her faith, what better place to begin than in a small community where intimacy is possible and questions and concerns can be dealt with? Any one of the three models discussed above could be utilized equally well with returning Catholics.

Since all small communities are responsible for the work of evangelization, having a new or returning Catholic will not only enrich the community, but will offer the newcomer support and love in a faith-sharing environment. "See how these Christians love one another." What greater invitation will there be than to see that truth in action!

✝✝✝✝✝ REFLECTION AND FAITH-SHARING QUESTIONS

Reflect on 1 John 2–3 and the excerpt from *Evangelii Nuntiandi* on page 236.

1. "Evangelization" means spreading the Good News joyfully, sharing Jesus' story. What story/stories of Jesus particularly touch me?
2. In what ways has my family life been strengthened since I have been a part of a small Christian community?
3. How have I experienced conversion (a positive change in my life) through a family member? In what ways am I not open to conversion (change and growth) experiences?
4. Have I ever "really invited" someone, particularly a family member, to return to church/join the RCIA/become a member of a small community? Why, or why not? If so, what was their response?
5. Small Christian communities are indispensable to evangelization. Why is this statement true? How have I experienced it in our parish?
6. As a parish or small community, what opportunities are present for serving the rejected, the poor, or the marginalized?

16. Concrete Approaches to Outreach

A VARIETY OF GIFTS
BUT ALWAYS
THE SAME SPIRIT

We are all called to live the reign of God in our everyday lives. The practice of faith is not restricted to Sunday worship or special times of prayer. Our faith is to permeate our entire week and to be reflected in all human activity. Because the full practice of our faith may conflict with the customs and mores of society, we have a tendency to avoid tension in our lives by compartmentalizing religion to special times of prayer. As a result, religion can become insipid and lack real impact in our daily lives.

The Second Vatican Council projected a more holistic view when it stated:

> Christ's redemptive work, while of itself directed toward the salvation of people, involves also the renewal of the whole temporal order. Hence the mission of the Church is not only to bring people the message and grace of Christ but also to penetrate and perfect the temporal sphere (Vatican II, *Decree on the Apostolate of Lay People*, #5).

Why is it difficult to get people involved in concrete actions? Perhaps many people equate action, mission, or outreach with involvement in particular activities that they would find difficult or questionable. While some Christians are called to be involved in picket lines or marches, others may address the same problem through political actions such as writing their congressional representative. Still others may find their greatest challenge in their family and work relationships.

People react to the call to outreach in a variety of ways. They may be afraid. They may be tired. How often have we heard the statement: "I'm already too busy. The kids have so many things going on, I can't keep up with everything I have to do now."

Gregory Pierce reflects on the difficulties of motivating any religious congregation to action:

> How many congregations have a "social action" or "justice and peace" committee made up of an assistant pastor or rabbi and six lay people who are involved in everything from migrant farm workers to nuclear disarmament? Despite countless sermons and leaflets, this committee has difficulty producing more than a yawn or a paternalistic pat on the back from the rest.
>
> There are three very good reasons for this. First, people tend to have a healthy respect for existing institutions and leaders. For this reason, they are not about to make fools of themselves or those institutions by grabbing a picket sign and protesting every issue.... Second, people do not like to waste their time on unattainable goals. If they don't think that they can win or at least make a difference, then they don't tend to get involved.... Third, people usually have a clear sense of their own self-interest. If something doesn't affect them pretty directly, they feel that they should leave it alone and let those whom it does affect deal with it.[1]

The three reasons cited by Pierce explain well why people may have difficulty becoming involved in social action. While we are not necessarily suggesting that everyone join a picket line, we do want to look at the three difficulties he proposes.

We, as Christians, are challenged to grow beyond these three roadblocks to action. In regard to the first reason, the church and its leaders tell us that we have to critique our institutions, their structures and systems and condemn what is not conducive to human life. "[The] social order requires constant improvement. It must be founded on truth, built on justice, and animated by love; in freedom it should grow every day toward a more humane balance. An improvement in attitudes and widespread changes in society will have to take place if these objectives are to be gained" (GS 26). Attitudes change and positive values are supported in small communities. A small Christian community may be the only place a person can honestly look at changes needed in the social order. Here a person can share doubts and be supported in taking concrete actions in unjust situations.

In regard to the second reason for the difficulty in motivating congregations to action, people have to feel they can make a difference. If the goal is unattainable, people feel overwhelmed. Thus it is important in our social involvement that we set attainable goals and means by which we can have clear successes. In small communities people help one another discern a concrete action they can achieve. The focus is on concrete and measurable actions, steps that are attainable.

Regarding the third reason, when something is suggested as an action response to the gospel or a ministry or mission, unless it touches people's lives directly there is not a great response. In small communities people are moved to act when they can see the connection between a certain action and their everyday lives—neighborhood, family, job, political life, the environment, etc.

An action step, or concretely living out the mission of Jesus, is something each Christian is challenged to do in every aspect of life. Too often people think of an action step as an extra thing to do.

> John chose as his action to help monthly in the local soup kitchen. He came from a wealthy background and found a great deal of satisfaction in helping the poor. While that action was good, John had not as yet begun to think through how he could more clearly live out the mission of Jesus in the decisions in which he was involved as an executive of a major United States company. As vice president of public relations for a utilities company, he had responsibility for the "public image" of that corporation. Gradually, through his sharing in his small community and their mutual reflection on the bishops' economic pastoral, *Justice for All,* John began to see that responding to the needs of the poor by not shutting off people's gas in the winter would be the Christian response and would also help with the company's self-image. By working out a plan in the company, he was able to bring about more flexibility in providing heating fuel to the poor. John's action response, his living out the mission of Jesus, was becoming very much a part of his daily life.

OUTREACH—NOT AN OPTION

For small Christian communities to be worthy of their name, carrying out the mission of Christ must always be the primary focus. Faith sharing that tends to turn in on the self-interest of the group will, in time, have the effect of atrophy on the group. God's Holy Spirit should be a fire vigorously moving a healthy community to a ministry of loving service. Many issues are somewhat difficult to face and to grasp. Experience shows that they are seldom addressed without a certain amount of challenge, guidance, and assistance. Good materials can help small Christian communities to realize better their great potential for participation in God's reign on our earth.

Small Christian Community Materials

The most valuable materials the small communities can use are those that lead people to action. Usually these materials will follow the time-honored process: Observe, Judge, Act. In summary—

- What is happening in my own life and the world in which I live?
- What does Jesus or my Christian tradition tell me about how I am to respond?
- What will I do differently to respond with Christian values to the various situations in my life?
- How can my action be specific?

1. The IMPACT Series aims to connect faith to the wide range of human concerns and personal issues.
2. The Observe, Judge, Act methodology is the basic process of this series. Assistance is available from RENEW International (888-433-3221).
3. In the process, participants will not only be led to prayerful reflection and fruitful sharing, but also to concrete actions that positively influence attitudes and behaviors.

Faithfulness to living Christian values in contemporary society requires vigilance, courage, and conviction, and yet more than ever we are called to act with Christian values in all areas of our lives. The small Christian community is an invaluable resource in supporting individuals in such fidelity. As communities help each person grow in knowing the call of Jesus in their personal lives, they also need to help individuals grow in living out the values of Jesus.

The success or failure of small Christian communities may very well depend on a deep interior relationship with the Lord and outreach from the community that has impact on the world and society in which we live. Communities that merely live to be a support system to one another—however friendly, comforting, and enjoyable this might be to members—falls far short of what a small Christian community should be.

The strength gained in our common exchange is not intended to keep us inwardly directed, but to give us the courage to bring our faith outward into our daily lives. All life—from that within our own families to the lives of distant people struggling for the basics of life—must be the concern of small Christian communities. Christ's injunction is to bring the gospel to all people. He places no limits in our untiring efforts to help all experience the reign of God.

In the small community gatherings, it is essential to reflect on action responses and outreach efforts. During each meeting, there should be some initial time to listen to each person's outreach commitment from the previous meeting—what it was, how it was implemented in life, what further areas of outreach are needed. Likewise, in each meeting there needs to be time to have each person or the entire community decide on an area of outreach.

Very simply, the purpose of outreach is to help persons grow in their ability to respond to the call to love one another and to live out the Christian life in a concrete manner. In this way they will be fulfilling the mission of Jesus that enlightens the world with the saving action of God. What persons have received as gift, they must give as gift! (See Mt 10:8.)

THE "HOW" OF OUTREACH

No two small communities will respond in exactly the same manner in the area of outreach. Some may focus more on individual outreach; others may do more outreach together as a community. For example, an individual in the community may make a concrete decision to do something differently in work-related areas. That will be an individual response. On the other hand, an entire small community may wish to begin working on a serious concern they may have about people who are hurting in their parish or about world hunger or about homelessness.

The outreach or action may be affected by the type of community. Action is essential for the **seasonal small groups** that meet. It may be a temptation to omit that part of the sharing because it is the most difficult, but small group leaders need to give special attention to this aspect of the group meeting. If the community is primarily ministerial, then the action may focus on that particular ministry. For example, with a community of teachers in a school, the outreach may focus primarily on relating to students or other teachers. However, one of the areas of growth for **ministerial communities** may be to have ministers also look at responding to and living the mission of Jesus in other areas of their lives. If the group is a **small Christian community,** then the action response needs to be ongoing and stronger in all aspects of life.

The important thing to recognize is that actions flow from the very "stuff" of life.

- Tina, who was in a small community, had a six-month-old child. In her small group was a single mother who struggled to be patient with her two small children. Through sharing, the first mother became aware of the need to assist the other woman with child care that could reduce stress and lower the possibility of abuse of a child. Her action response was to take the two children one afternoon a week to give the single mother some time for herself.

- José was struggling with a fellow employee at his place of business. Because of some negative history, competition over the job and just some general dislike for the other person, there was a constant strain in their work relationship. For his action response, he decided that Jesus' words to "love one another" were much more powerful than his dislike for a certain employee. His first concrete attempt to live out his faith in this situation was to greet the man each morning with a friendly hello. He also decided to pray daily for this gentleman. He was able to share that after a few months his dislike for the other fellow had lessened and from his perspective God had intervened.

• Julie, who had been working for many years in a professional capacity, became aware of the needs of the homeless whom she saw every day. She became involved in efforts to develop low-income housing and reduce crime in her neighborhood.

Sometimes the stuff of life is not as obvious. Direct service can be more obvious than an action for systemic change. For example, it is easier to gather clothes for the poor than to work for adequate housing for the poor or even to address the economic realities that keep people poor in our society.

Small communities can help people begin to see structural injustices with new eyes, and to take concrete action steps to change systems. In small communities the sharing and interchange not only help people accept gospel/church values, but also produce prudent, sensible, and realistic action responses. The small community gives people the courage to act, and it builds in accountability. Each time the small community meets there is an accountability time for participants to share their success or failure with outreach. With support and commitment to living out the mission of Jesus in all aspects of their daily lives, small community members will continue to grow together as disciples of Jesus.

The point is that there is a serious need for all Christians to choose just actions on every level of life. Each time someone chooses to respond with Christian values—faith, hope, and love—the world becomes a better place. Each time a choice for Christian action is not made, we lose the opportunity for the message of Jesus to be more real. Christian mission then flows from our ability to observe a situation realistically, judge it in light of gospel values and act in accordance with that judgment.

Outreach has to do with **changing behavior** and a **concrete action**. For example, if I say, "I want to be your friend," but never call, write, or make any effort to get to know you, my words are empty. If I say to myself and to others, "I would like to become more prayerful," but do not allot any time in my daily schedule for prayer, then I will not grow in that area.

Outreach needs to be **specific** and **measurable**. Little will happen if a small community says, "For our action we will become more aware of the poor." Instead, the community would need to set some specific and measurable goals to become more aware of the poor. For example: "This week we will volunteer at the local soup kitchen on Wednesday night." Or, "This week we will write to our congressional representative about the need for low-income housing."

Whether it be a seasonal small group, a ministerial community, or a small Christian community, it is helpful to move beyond the community itself at times and collaborate with others in outreach. The parish social concerns community or a local interfaith council may be helpful to small communities in networking. Learning what other churches or community groups are doing in a particular area of need may be of great benefit. For example, many city and church groups work cooperatively in meeting the needs of the poor and homeless in their area. In fact, in many small towns, it is essential to collaborate with other congregations in meeting needs in order to be effective and not duplicate efforts.

AREAS OF MISSION

In many ways when we use the term *mission,* we could substitute other words such as *justice* or *evangelization.* To reach out in justice is to do the mission of Jesus. Evangelizing is promising the good news of peace and justice, "to bring good news to the poor ... proclaim release to the captives and recovery of sight to the blind, to let the oppressed go free, to proclaim the year of the Lord's favor" (Lk 4:18-19). Outreach, action, justice, is living the beatitudes (Mt 5:3-10).

Through social encyclicals and explication of social mission, the church has indicated the kind of actions that are incumbent on a Christian. Pope John XXIII outlines clearly the standard for basic human existence to which all human beings are entitled.

> Every person has the right to life, to bodily integrity, and to the means which are necessary and suitable for the proper development of life; these are primarily food, clothing, shelter, rest, medical care, and finally the necessary social services. . . . A human being also has the right to security in cases of sickness, inability to work, widowhood, old age, unemployment, or in any other case in which he is deprived of the means of subsistence through no fault of his own. . . . Every human being has the right to respect for his person, to his good reputation; the right to freedom in searching for truth and in expressing and communicating his opinions, and in pursuit of art . . . to share in the benefits of culture . . . to a basic education and to technical and professional training in keeping with the stage of educational development in the country to which he belongs to honor God . . . to choose freely the state of life which he or she prefers . . . to establish a family . . . to work . . . to private property, even of productive goods . . . the right of assembly and association . . . to freedom of movement and of residence . . . and when there are just reasons for it, the right to emigrate to other countries and take up residence there . . . to take an active part in public affairs and to contribute one's part to the common good of the citizens . . . to a juridical protection of his rights.[2]

These basic rights, other social teachings of the church, and the Scriptures are standards by which we can judge our action and outreach.

It is also important to note that the small community leader can help the community grow in its awareness in many areas of need. The leader might encourage members to become aware of parish, city, and global concerns by working closely with the social concerns community of the parish. The social concerns community itself is an excellent vehicle for providing information and resources on parish needs, local, and global concerns.

Direct Action

Wherever someone is hurting, action is needed. It may be some very obvious hurt like a hungry homeless person or someone with a serious illness, or a not so obvious hurt like the tears of a child who got in a fight with a friend, or the pain of a broken relationship. Responding to someone who is hurt may be comforting a spouse when he or she comes home from a disappointing day at the office or consoling a friend in emotional pain. Many of the action responses we do as Christians are not things we do, but rather are a normal response to God's children who are hurting. There are numerous organizations that can also offer ideas and opportunities—food pantries, Hospice, clothing centers, Catholic Charities, nursing homes, to name just a few.

Systemic Change

A second area of action and perhaps a more difficult one, is critiquing systems and structures and working to change them when they are unjust and oppressive. Individuals and small communities together can begin to look at what actions they can take to begin to transform unjust systems. Possibilities include the following:

- work to assure just policies in the business world
- write letters to or visit legislators
- be informed on political issues
- invest in companies/enterprises whose policies are based on solidarity and justice
- become involved in community organizations
- change spending patterns
- work for issues that concern equitable food distribution and just international monetary systems
- work with national and international groups (e.g., Pax Christi, Bread for the World, Network[3])
- learn and implement different models of parenting through such resources as Kathleen and James McGinnis' *Parenting for Peace and Justice* and *Helping Families Care*[4]

Networking

There are many ways a small community can convene or network around a social concern or need in the parish or broader society. It is important to link with other individuals or groups for support. Where a large number of people are linked together in a common cause, there is usually greater strength and the group can exert greater influence.

Networking can be done for direct service and/or systemic change. An example of direct service was experienced in Northern Ireland.

> Catholics and Protestants forged a common bond for the refugees in Kosovo. "A number of our faith-sharing groups organized a cross-community effort," explains Fr. Arthur McAnerney of Beragh in the Archdiocese of Armagh, Ireland. "Through this joint effort, clothing and other goods were collected and stored in the Presbyterian church hall. The Beragh parish itself collected approximately $30,000 to send to Kosovo. The faith-sharing groups were able to identify a need that people were ready to do something about."

People need other people for support. An important action step may be to meet and join efforts with others who have similar concerns.

Within the small community itself, there may be the opportunity for action in creating networks of support. When that is not possible, however, because of different interests, schedules, etc., individuals within the small community can continue to glean support from their community in order to network with other groups.

Perhaps the important point here is that it is not always necessary to participate in more actions, but rather that the daily networks and connections we already have can be strengthened and nurtured with Christian values. If all Catholics lived out their faith today, we would have very different parishes, towns, cities, and countries. We would see significant change in the world, since so many Catholics hold key positions in the political, economic, and social arenas.

SUMMARY

The call of the gospel is clear; the message of Jesus is challenging. We are to bring the good news to the poor, liberty to captives, sight to the blind. We are called to be evangelizers. But we know from our experience that those things do not just happen. In order to translate knowledge of the gospels into practice, each person needs support, help, and discernment. Each time a small community gathers, each participant is encouraged and supported in outreach. Only through the loving interaction of disciples of Jesus committed to living out the gospel in everyday life will there be a true transformation of the earth.

---

††††† REFLECTION AND FAITH-SHARING QUESTIONS

Reflect on Luke 4:14–21.

1. Are our small communities moving beyond sharing into action? How can I or we encourage this to happen? How will we ensure that strong action steps are taking place?
2. What have been some of the challenges for me personally or for us as a small community in moving toward action?
3. "For a value to be present, life itself must be affected." How have I experienced this in my own life or as part of a small community?
4. Have the experiences of outreach in my small community been more personal or communal?
5. The chapter mentions three roadblocks to getting involved (p. 258): institutions will do it; 2) the goal is unattainable; and 3) it doesn't serve our self-interest. Do I identify with any of these? How can I break down some of these barriers?

17. Paths to Implementation: Parish and Diocesan

Marion O. Flowers CSJ

How, then, does a parish go about beginning this process of implementing the vision of their parish as a community of small communities?

Each parish has its own history, its own composition, its own concerns. However, following some of these simple steps will help and greatly support an individual parish.

1. Establish a parish Core Community.
2. Help the parish gain ownership of the pastoral direction through articulating it as a diocesan/parish vision.
3. Keep prayer as a priority (staff, parish pastoral council, Core Community, entire parish).
4. Hold a parish assembly.
5. Speak about the pastoral direction from the pulpit.
6. Begin leadership development of small community leaders.
7. Coordinate all activities relating to community development (e.g., seasonal groups, ministerial committees growing into communities, small Christian communities).
8. Continue to pastor the groups, communities, leaders, staff.
9. Keep clear lines of communication open with all concerned.
10. Network with other parishes and national and international small community efforts.

DIOCESAN VISION AND SUPPORT

A convinced and strong supportive diocesan leadership is a powerful asset in the implementation of the vision of the church as a community of many small communities. A diocese wishing to implement this vision would do well to develop a pastoral direction highlighting the importance of small Christian communities. Some concrete ways a diocese may wish to go about developing both the vision and a support system include the following:

1. Setting Up a Diocesan Structure

If the pastoral direction of small communities is truly to take root in a comprehensive manner, it has to have a wider base and more authoritative sanctioning than is found in an individual priest or parish. In order to foster the acceptance of this vision, dioceses may wish to do one or more of the following:

a) establish a diocesan office of small Christian communities;
b) designate one diocesan staff person to concentrate on small communities;
c) set up a Diocesan Core Community;
d) ensure that the entire diocesan staff has reached a common understanding and commitment to this pastoral direction and that it is utilized in all areas of ministry.

Currently more than fifty dioceses in the United States have designated a person or team to work with the ongoing development of small communities.

2. Offering Help with Accepting the Vision

Meeting regularly with priests, parish staffs, and parish Core Communities to support them in developing a vision for the parish is crucial for diocesan leadership. If diocesan leadership has experienced the impact of small communities in people's lives, they will recognize that realistically parishes will need support in furthering this development.

3. Providing Leadership Development

Providing leadership development is an important resource service a diocese can provide for parishes. Many times parish leadership will not feel themselves sufficiently qualified to provide all the leadership development necessary. The diocese can be most helpful in providing this resource to their parishes.

Ideally, diocesan personnel will be assisting in the training of the parish Core Communities as well as in the development of small community leaders. (Six sessions for developing Core Communities are contained in *Resources for Small Christian Communities: A Vision of Hope*, available only through RENEW International. Sessions for leadership development for small community leaders ought to be ongoing based on the experience and needs of those leaders.)

4. Providing Reflective/Growth Opportunities

Diocesan staff members serve a most helpful purpose when they are ready and available to offer nights/days of reflection for small communities and for leadership groups. Many parishes hunger for these spiritual growth opportunities.

5. Providing Help with the Development of Materials

A diocesan office assists parishes in researching small community materials that will be most beneficial for small community use. There is a great need to do good researching of faith-sharing materials on the market. Developing a library of small Christian community materials where parishioners can preview resources and perhaps even borrow some would be extremely helpful. It is important to provide a wide variety of good materials that will help small communities grow in all areas, including vision.

6. Encouraging All Diocesan Offices and Agencies To Become Part of the Fabric of This Pastoral Direction

When all diocesan offices and agencies collaborate and work in a unified fashion toward a common vision, it is not only helpful to parishes but also a wonderful model of church unity. At times parishes feel there is an over-abundance of directives and ideas coming from diocesan offices. While diocesan offices may provide good opportunities, parish staffs sometimes feel overwhelmed by various workshops and programs. With a clear statement of what it means to be church and a pastoral direction to which all offices and agencies will be accountable, parishes will have a greater opportunity to focus their efforts and initiate an invitation for diocesan assistance based upon their particular needs.

7. Networking with Other Dioceses

Networking with other dioceses in fostering the vision of the parish as a community of small communities can be a real benefit. Through networking, diocesan leaders can continue to articulate the vision and support one another. Diocesan leaders could participate in the North American Forum for Small Christian Communities, an organization composed of representatives from almost sixty dioceses and organizations in the United States and Canada who gather annually to share their experience and expertise in mutually building this style of church (Web site: www.nafscc.org).

A DIOCESAN OFFICE FOR SMALL CHRISTIAN COMMUNITIES OR A DIOCESAN CORE COMMUNITY

One of RENEW's greatest learnings is the importance of a diocese working together for the spiritual development not only of individual people, but of all parishes and the entire diocese. In the RENEW process, the diocese adopts a vision of spiritual growth for all its people. It agrees that for three years the primary emphasis will be helping people learn and witness to the power of the Word of God in their lives, helping parishes become more vibrant faith communities, and assisting parishioners in their ability to act justly. Following the RENEW process, or any clearly defined spiritual growth effort, it is extremely helpful if the diocese sets forth a clear pastoral direction in order to continue to focus and foster this spiritual growth.

A diocese committed to developing small Christian communities as an ongoing style of parish life embraces its present and future with enthusiasm and hope. But this cannot be done blindly. A tremendous amount of commitment and creative planning is required. It is essential that certain questions be addressed: Who will assume responsibility for bringing form to the vision? How will it happen? Who will nurture it? That which is everyone's responsibility is easily in danger of becoming no one's responsibility. What may become one more added responsibility to an already unrealistic list of responsibilities for an office will probably never be addressed. RENEW International's experience confirms that unless a person is specifically named to direct the efforts of small Christian communities, the task will likely go unattended.

The creation of a diocesan office and/or a Diocesan Core Community for small Christian community development speaks clearly to the kind of commitment the diocese gives to such a vision. However, due to financial constraints, it may be necessary to assign these responsibilities to an already existing office. Let us look at how a diocesan office for small Christian communities (SCCs), Diocesan Core Community (DCC), or another office assuming the responsibilities could operate.

DEVELOPING A SMALL CHRISTIAN COMMUNITIES OFFICE OR A DIOCESAN CORE COMMUNITY

The staff for small communities or the DCC can serve parishes throughout the diocese in a number of ways. First, there is the visiting of parish staffs and leaders in order to better understand the current pastoral life of the parish. Second, the parish is helped to articulate a pastoral direction of small communities as an ongoing part of parish life. Third, parishes are assisted in developing a step-by-step realistic plan to serve their individual needs.

The specific goals and objectives of a diocesan office for small Christian communities or a DCC flow from the conviction that a diocese serves its people most faithfully when it not only responds to their expressed needs, but also offers the visionary gift of leadership to discern a way of moving together toward the "not yet" where the reign of God will be more fully realized.

Ideally the diocese will articulate its own pastoral direction. Many dioceses have mission statements. This pastoral direction could be incorporated within the diocesan mission statement, or the pastoral direction could be written separately and seen as a means of living out the mission statement.

One concrete way to assure concrete implementation in parishes is to establish a diocesan office for small Christian communities. Having a specific office is most ideal but in some situations it may only be possible to have one diocesan staff person designated to work in this area with parishes.

Another model is the development of a Diocesan Core Community. This Diocesan Core Community could be composed of eight to twelve people, depending upon the size of the diocese. It needs to include a diocesan coordinator, preferably a diocesan staff person, as well as other people who represent different geographic locations and ethnic groups of the diocese.

The role of the Diocesan Core Community is the following:

- to understand and embrace the vision of the role of small communities in the ongoing life of parishes
- to model a communal style of leadership through collaboration, faith sharing and prayer
- to work closely with and assist individual parishes, enabling them to develop strong leadership for small communities (generally each member of the DCC is responsible for four to five parishes)
- to work with parish Core Communities and to provide ongoing formation for them and for small community leaders
- to share information and communicate regularly with pastors, parish staffs, and the parish Core Community in order to enable small communities to grow in their ongoing development

- to communicate regularly with the diocesan coordinator and other members of the DCC

DEVELOPING A PLAN

Whether a diocese chooses to set up a full-time diocesan office for small Christian communities or a Diocesan Core Community, it will be important to develop a clear plan of action. The following seven-point outline is one model that could be used. Individual circumstances will account for its being fleshed out.

1. Articulate a vision of church after the RENEW process (*or, if the diocese has not implemented RENEW, at an appropriate time following a synod or some spiritual growth opportunities*).

    A. Develop a process for formulating a pastoral direction . . . evaluating one's experience.
        a) Discern those components of RENEW (or related spiritual activity) that had the greatest impact on parish community life.
        b) What would you like to see endure and grow?
        c) Explain the need for small communities from theological, sociological, and pastoral perspectives.

    B. Develop a process for the diocese to gain ownership of this pastoral direction.

2. Articulate approaches for organizing the diocesan office for small Christian communities or Diocesan Core Community (*or the diocesan office that will assume responsibilities for small community development*).

    A. Purpose of the Diocesan Office for SCCs or DCC
        The office for small Christian communities or the DCC exists to bring about the acceptance and support of small communities as an ongoing way of parish life.

The office for SCCs consists of one or more full-time persons who assume responsibility for parish visitations and ongoing support, securing materials for use by small Christian communities, surfacing needs, and working with diocesan offices and agencies.

B. Goals and Objectives of Staff

To support the attitudes and behavior of parish staff in implementing this pastoral direction.

Rationale: The office for SCCs or DCC accepts and affirms its primary role as a change agent, both promoting and providing for a new way of being church (envisioning the parish as a community of communities) among parish staffs.

Objectives

a) to phone and visit each parish staff person to discuss this pastoral direction

b) to assist parish staffs in assessing the needs of their parish in relation to the small Christian community vision

c) to establish ongoing contact with parish staffs and encouragement for them

d) to develop a plan of action with staff

e) to encourage staff persons to recognize and develop a Core Community for small community development

f) to encourage staff prayer and faith sharing on a regular basis

g) to develop clusters of parish staffs who gather to share witness stories and provide support systems among parish staffs

h) to strengthen skills and resources of parish staffs through workshops and ongoing education about the pastoral direction

i) to encourage parish staff members to join a small community to experience its possibilities and witness its credibility

j) to promote the visitation of small communities by parish staff members

3. Have the diocesan office for small Christian communities or DCC model a faith-sharing community.

Rationale: The office for small Christian communities or DCC accepts its call to model to local parishes and to the entire diocese a style of community that is rich and life-giving.

Objectives

a) to be God-centered as individuals and as a community of faith; to express this faith ecclesially in a liturgical and sacramental way

b) to share one another's life events, faith stories, and ministerial experiences

c) to support one another through caring, listening, encouraging

d) to be personally committed to one another through daily prayer for and with one another as an ecclesial priority

e) to continue ongoing education through sound catechesis, reading, workshops, and shared learning experiences with other staff members

f) to ensure outreach as vital to Christian ministry by providing for ongoing development and sharing of ministerial gifts with others

g) to come together as community on a regular basis with importance given to prayer and faith sharing

h) to celebrate life together with days of prayer/fun/relaxation

i) to be loyal to one another

j) to have a clear understanding of each member's role within the group

k) to devise both individual and communal evaluation tools for the office for SCCs or DCC

l) to assist one another in the process of ongoing conversion to Jesus Christ

4. Enable parish-based small Christian communities.

Rationale: Recognizing and rejoicing in the rightful place of the laity in the renewal of church, the office for SCCs or DCC looks to the commitment and strength of small communities as the hope and creative energy for parish life in the present and in the future.

Objectives

a) to visit parish staffs

b) to visit small groups and small communities within the parish

c) to provide training for small Christian community leaders and group members on a regional and parish basis

d) to assist parishes in establishing Core Communities as the means of promoting the small community model

e) to work with parish pastoral councils and assemblies

f) to provide materials for small communities

g) to develop and broker good ideas among parish small communities

h) to nurture the development of small Christian communities among various cultural and ethnic groups

i) to encourage small communities to celebrate together as a united larger parish community

j) to work with parish staff in surfacing small community leadership

k) to maintain ongoing contact with the ministerial development center or similar diocesan structures

l) to encourage and enable existing parish committees to become more communal in their style

m) to establish a mailing list of small Christian community contacts

n) to facilitate parish assemblies as opportunities to reflect on this pastoral direction

5. Foster ownership of the small Christian communities pastoral plan as an ongoing way of parish life among diocesan agencies, organizations and their personnel.

Rationale: The office for small Christian communities or DCC understands that the diocesan pastoral direction will be realized only to the extent that all diocesan organizations and agencies demonstrate commitment to it through implementing the small Christian communities concept in their plans and programs.

Objectives:

a) to develop an ongoing relationship with other diocesan agencies by meeting with them regularly

b) to work with the diocesan pastoral structures in implementing the pastoral direction through parish, deanery, vicariate, and diocesan pastoral councils

c) to provide a process for commitment to the small community pastoral direction

d) to offer direct assistance to offices and agencies, helping them to develop their own initiatives and connections with the pastoral plan (e.g., the religious education office may design sacramental programs with small community components for parents and children)

e) to assist other agencies in designing new materials that are small Christian community-related and using existing materials to serve their needs

f) to support initiatives taken by other diocesan offices to further the pastoral direction

g) to maintain a priority commitment to ongoing communication with the bishop/vicars/directors of diocesan offices, etc.

h) to cooperate with responsible offices integrating the pastoral direction with the process of Christian initiation

6. Select and/or develop materials for small Christian communities.

Rationale: The diocesan office for small Christian communities or DCC realizes the need for the selection and development of materials consistent with the components for and growth of small Christian communities.

Objectives

a) to select materials that will help small communities grow (e.g., the IMPACT Series and/or the *Catechism* Series, both available through RENEW International)

    b) to ensure that the materials being used provide a balanced approach to the Christian vocation, e.g., ecclesial, sacramental, ministerial, etc.

    c) to maintain continuous dialogue and share experiences with small communities to meet their needs effectively

    d) to connect with needs of special groups, i.e., youth, young adults, family life, etc.

    e) to develop an expanding library relating to small communities

7. Evaluation.

    Rationale: Evaluation is an essential tool for learning. Regular evaluations will be helpful to diocesan and parish personnel in monitoring how the pastoral direction is being implemented.

(As stated earlier, the above plan is one suggestion of how a diocese may outline responsibilities for implementing this vision. Each diocese will want to consider components like those listed above in developing an appropriate plan for itself.)

QUALITIES OF DIOCESAN STAFF OR DCC MEMBERS

While a specific job description for the staff of a diocesan small Christian communities office or a Diocesan Core Community can be gleaned from the above goals and objectives, we would now like to suggest qualities to look for in selecting staff for a small Christian communities office or for a Diocesan Core Community who would assume responsibility for the development of small communities.

1. Highly Relational The office for small Christian communities or the DCC exists to be of service to people. The gift of relating well with a wide spectrum of persons, individuals and groups, lay, religious, and priests, is critical to the development of small Christian communities as a pastoral direction for parish life.

2. Initiating The diocesan coordinator of small communities needs to be an initiator—one who can assess the present reality of a given parish and respond to the felt needs of staff and people with concrete and creative ways of initiating small communities as an ongoing means of promoting vibrant parish life.

3. Visionary One entrusted with the ministry of small Christian community development must be in touch with the present, aware of the past, and alert to the future in order to shape the future church in faithful continuity with its gospel roots. The members of the diocesan staff and/or DCC will ideally have some theological expertise and be committed to the growth of the church.

4. Persevering Moving toward the "not yet" requires a high degree of patience. Flexibility, light-heartedness, and untiring commitment contribute to a spirit that will not give in to discouragement. The quality of perseverance in people who are in the role of nurturing small communities is important since much of their contribution may not be known until sometime in the future. Perseverance will enable a person to continue in the significant work of developing small Christian communities.

5. Motivational An important quality for a diocesan staff member or a member of the DCC is the ability to inspire and motivate others in developing small communities. Often this quality is best nurtured through the person's own small Christian community experience.

6. Organized In addition to intuitive, relational gifts, the coordinator and staff of a small Christian communities office and/or the DCC need to be well organized. The pastoral direction has many tasks and the ongoing task is to clarify, concretize, and strategize realistic goals and objectives and then measure the outcomes so that movement is observable.

IMPORTANCE OF A DIOCESAN APPROACH

In closing, we reiterate the importance of a diocesan approach. A diocese without a dream, a vision, a pastoral direction can become cold and businesslike. The diocese "constitutes a particular church in which the one, holy, catholic, and apostolic Church of Christ is truly present and operative" (*CD* 11). This local church needs a clear pastoral direction in order to carry on the mission of Jesus.

The vision of the church as a community of small communities was very much a part of how Jesus related to his disciples and how the early church developed. But for many, it is new. Diocesan leadership is in a unique position to provide spiritual and structural support for developing the parish as a community of many small communities and thus be an expression of the reign of God today.

✝ ✝ ✝ ✝ ✝ REFLECTION AND FAITH-SHARING QUESTIONS

Reflect on Habakkuk 2:2–3.

1. What initiatives will we take to help the parish become "a community of many small communities"? Who will follow through?
2. RENEW International has a dedicated and skilled Small Christian Community Team to help you as well as a wide range of small community publications and videos. Phone: 908-769-5400.
   Phone: 888-433-3221 **(Orders Only).**
   Fax: 908-769-5660. E-mail: Resources@renewintl.org
   Who in our community will further explore these possibilities?
3. How can we network with local parishes that share the vision?

Appendix

IMPLEMENTING THE PASTORAL DIRECTION OF THE PARISH AS A COMMUNITY OF SMALL CHRISTIAN COMMUNITIES

The following premises are foundational when implementing the pastoral direction of the parish as a community of many small communities.

- that the pastoral direction of the parish as a community made up of many small communities is a way of being church that is rooted in Christian tradition

- various types of small communities exist to support people in living their Christian lives

- five elements of Christian community—prayer, sharing, mutual support, learning, and mission—help to strengthen people's commitment to each other, to God and to the world

- transitions have taken place in our society and church, and have helped to create the need for new support systems

- when implemented, the pastoral direction leads parishioners to be actively involved in the mission of Jesus

Types of small communities that may exist in a parish

- **Small Christian Communities:** Face-to-face gatherings of six to twelve people who invest time with one another for the common purpose of applying gospel values to every aspect of their lives. These usually involve three or more years' commitment with prayerful discernment. They commit themselves to the mission of Jesus in the world.

- **Seasonal Small Groups:** Groups that meet for six weeks twice a year e.g., in the fall and during Lent. During their periodic gatherings these small groups pray, share faith and life experiences, engage in learning, mutual support, and outreach.

- **Ministerial Communities:** Committees, ministries, organizations, and special interest groups with a communal style of meeting that integrates prayer, sharing, ongoing learning, and mutual support within a particular outreach or ministry. Participants frequently commit themselves for two years, renewable after evaluation and discernment.

ESSENTIAL ELEMENTS OF COMMUNITY

In developing small communities we emphasize five essential signs of communal life: sharing, learning, mutual support, mission, and prayer. These elements express a spirituality that acknowledges complete dependence upon God for creation of community while providing a structured format for meetings.

These elements are certainly not all-inclusive, nor do they attempt to fully define small Christian communities. They are listed not as static qualities but are intended to convey a sense of movement. The dynamic of small Christian communities is living, ever growing, and always deepening.

Sharing Sharing means talking freely about God and about life experiences and reflecting on these in the light of Scripture and tradition.

Learning Because small Christian communities are part of the wider church they are called to an ever fuller knowledge and understanding of the gospel, of the Catholic Church and its teaching on faith and morals, and of the relationship of that teaching to the circumstances and issues of their lives.

Mutual Support In a society in which gospel values are all too frequently ridiculed and rejected, the believer needs a community that is supportive of these values. The small Christian community encourages fidelity to the gospel and also challenges itself and its members to a more profound and authentic commitment to Christian living.

Mission Authentic Christian communities are, like Jesus, committed to a life of loving mission or service. As a group and through its individual members, the community will work for compassion, justice, reconciliation, and peace within the group, in the family, in the workplace, in the neighborhood, and within the wider society.

Prayer The element of prayer emphasizes the centrality of God's active presence in each small Christian community member's life and in the life of the community itself.

By incorporating these five elements the small Christian community becomes a place where Christians can hear their baptismal call and participate in continuing the mission of Jesus.

SEASONAL SMALL GROUPS

Pastoral Reflection

1. Are there any seasonal small groups and/or RENEW groups ready to become small Christian communities? (That is, meeting regularly and with a long-term commitment of approximately three years.)

2. If there are seasonal small groups and/or RENEW groups that do not want to become small Christian communities at this time, are there individuals in these groups ready and interested in being part of a small Christian community?

3. Which seasonal (RENEW) small groups prefer at this time to become ministerial communities? (That is, bereavement, service to the elderly, Invitational Ministers, etc.?)

4. How will the individuals in seasonal small groups be given opportunities to join a ministerial community?

5. How will the parish continue to provide opportunities for people to join seasonal small groups in the parish?

   - Who is pastoring these seasonal small groups at present?

   - Who will minister to their development?

Key Leaders

SMALL CHRISTIAN COMMUNITIES

Pastoral Analysis

- How does each small Christian community demonstrate the following:
  - Sharing
  - Learning
  - Mutual Support
  - Mission
  - Prayer

- Which of these elements is strongest?

- Which element needs further development?

- Who is pastoring these communities at present?

- How can we continue the growth of small Christian communities in the parish?

- Who will minister to their development?

Key Leaders

MINISTERIAL COMMUNITIES

Pastoral Analysis: Parish Organizations, Committees, Ministries

- Is faith sharing a regular part of the meeting?

- If not, would any of the groups be open to faith sharing as a part of their meetings?

- How will we bring this about?

- Who is pastoring the groups at present?

- Who will minister to their development?

Key Leaders

PASTORAL OVERVIEW OF
THE PARISH AS A COMMUNITY
OF SMALL COMMUNITIES

This form is a tool to give the Core Community an overview of the parish in terms of the parish as a community of small communities. Do this page after completing the forms that precede.

	Present	*Goal by*_____
Number of seasonal small groups	_____	_____
Number of small Christian communities	_____	_____
Number of ministerial communities	_____	_____

Key leaders who are possible candidates for Core Community

Name	*Group affiliated with*
_____	_____
_____	_____
_____	_____
_____	_____
_____	_____
_____	_____

Notes

Chapter 1

1. Various contemporary scholars have named the times in which we live "the post-modern era." Among them is Joe Holland. See "The New Debate Over Faith and Culture," in *American & Catholic: The New Debate* (South Orange, NJ: Pillar Books, 1988) 1-14.

2. Max Delespesse, *The Church Community: Leaven and Lifestyle* (Ottawa: The Catholic Centre of Saint Paul University, 1968) 16.

3. Delespesse, 18.

4. Albert J. Nevins, MM, *The Maryknoll Catholic Dictionary* (New York: Grosset & Dunlop, 1965) 260-61.

5. Robert C. Broderick, *The Catholic Encyclopedia* (New York: Thomas Nelson, Inc., 1976) 249.

6. *New Catholic Encyclopedia* (New York: McGraw-Hill, 1976) Vol. XIII, 409.

7. David C. Leege, ed., "Parish Organizations: People's Needs, Parish Services, and Leadership," in *Notre Dame Study of Catholic Parish Life* (Notre Dame: University of Notre Dame, July 1986) 8.

8. Nevins, 610.

9. Nevins, 126.

10. Chuck Mathey, *Successful CFM Leadership* (Ames: Christian Family Movement, 1988) 1.

11. Thomas Aquinas, *Summa Theologica, 11,* Question 47, Article 8.

12. Bernard J. Lee and Michael A. Cowan, *Dangerous Memories: House Churches and Our American Story* (Kansas City: Sheed & Ward, 1986) 37-45.

13. In addition, the Congregation for the Doctrine of the Faith has issued two documents on liberation theology: "Instruction on Certain Aspects of the Theology of Liberation," in *Origins* (September 13, 1984) 193-204 and "Instruction on Christian Freedom and Liberation," in *Origins* (April 17, 1986) 713-28. In the first document there is a concern about the formation of base communities without sufficient catechetical and theolog-

ical preparation. Since catechetical and theological preparation is essential for small Christian community development, RENEW International has incorporated a greater emphasis on catechesis and theology in its materials. See, especially, *Why Catholic? Journey through the Catechism.* The second document touches upon the reality of small groups in diverse ways.

14. Joseph Healey, "Comparing 'Basic and Small' Christian Communities," in *AMECEA Documentation Service* (Nairobi), 284, May 8, 1984, in "Communities," *Ministries and Communities* (Leuven, Belgium: Pro Mundi Vita, 1984) 3, 2.

15. William D'Antonio, Dean Hoge, and John McCarthy, Loyola University Institute for Ministry, Preliminary Report on "Small Christian Communities in the U.S. Catholic Church" (New Orleans: Loyola University, June 30, 1995) 6.

16. Bernard M. Lee with William V. D'Antonio, et al., *The Catholic Experience of Small Christian Communities* (New York/New Jersey: Paulist Press) 10.

17. William D'Antonio, memo to Mary McGuinness from Life Cycle Institute, The Catholic University of America, January 29, 1997, 1.

18. Bernard M. Lee with William V. D'Antonio, et al., *The Catholic Experience.* 10–11.

19. Ibid. 168.

20. Bernard Lonergan, "Dimensions of Meaning," *Collected Works of Bernard Lonergan,* eds. Frederick E. Crowe and Robert M. Doran (Toronto: University of Toronto Press, 1988) 235.

21. Vatican Secretariat for Promoting Christian Unity, *Sects or New Religious Movements in the World: Pastoral Challenges,* United States Conference of Catholic Bishops, May 3, 1986, 12.

22. Ibid. 12–13.

23. Robert Wuthnow, *Sharing the Journey: Support Groups and America's New Quest for Community* (New York: The Free Press, 1994) 45.

24. George Gallup, Jr., "Evangelizing the Unchurched American," in *Pentecost '87 Supplement, A National Satellite Celebration of Catholic Evangelization,* Saturday, June 6, 1987 (Washington, DC: Paulist National Catholic Evangelization Association) 4.

25. RENEW evaluations from bishops, pastors, and diocesan staff support this testimony. In addition many other sources could be listed. To

name a few: the testimony of leaders from nineteen dioceses gathered at the National Forum for Small Christian Communities, October 24-27, 1988, in Cleveland, Ohio; Bernard J. Lee, S.M., with William V. D'Antonio, et al., *The Catholic Experience of Small Christian Communities,* published by Paulist Press; numerous articles, e.g., "Illinois Hispanics Put on Clinic for the Church" by Robert Johnson, *National Catholic Reporter,* Vol. 25, No. 4 (November 11, 1988).

Chapter 2

1. Wilfred Ward, *The Life of John Henry Cardinal Newman,* 2 (New York: Longmans, Green, 1912) 147.

2. Peter Coughlan, *The Hour of the Laity: Their Expanding Role* (Philadelphia: E. J. Dwyer, 1989) 33.

3. John Paul II, "Los Angeles Meeting of the Pope and U.S. Bishops," *Origins,* 17 (October 1, 1987) 257.

4. United States Conference of Catholic Bishops, *Called and Gifted for the Third Millennium: Reflections of the U.S. Bishops on the Thirtieth Anniversary of the Decree on the Apostolate of the Laity and the Fifteenth Anniversary of Called and Gifted* (Washington, DC: USCCB, 1995) 11.

5. A Statement from the U.S. Bishops' Committee on Hispanic Affairs, *Communion and Mission: A Guide for Bishops and Pastoral Agents on Small Church Communities* (Washington, DC: USCCB, 1995) 6.

6. Vatican Secretariat for Promoting Christian Unity, ibid. 13.

7. Avery Dulles, SJ, *The Reshaping of Catholicism: Current Challenges in the Theology of Church* (San Francisco: Harper & Row, 1988) 23.

8. Ibid. 31.

9. John Paul II, *On Social Concern of the Church* (*Sollicitudo Rei Socialis*), Encyclical Letter, December 30, 1987, Washington, DC: United States Conference of Catholic Bishops, 72-73.

10. Synod of Bishops, *Justice in the World* (Washington, DC: USCCB Publications Office, 1972) 34.

11. Philip J. Murnion, "Parish Renewal: State(ments) of the Question," *America* (April 24, 1982) 317.

12. Avery Dulles, SJ, *A Church to Believe In: Discipleship and the Dynamics of Freedom* (New York: Crossroad, 1986) 17.

Chapter 3

1. Coughlan, 37.

2. Libreria Editrice Vaticana. *Catechism of the Catholic Church, Modifications from the Editio Typica* (Washington, DC: USCCB, 1994, 1997) 2014.

3. Joe Holland, "Beyond a Privatized Spirituality," *New Catholic World* 231 (July/August 1988) 176.

4. Ibid. Holland cites testimony from Bishop Paul Cordes, a Vatican official at the Pontifical Council on the Laity, Dolores Leckey formerly from the Office of the Bishops' Committee on the Laity, and Reverend Robert Kinast, author of one of the official reports from the consultations of the laity in preparation for the October 1987 Synod.

5. Catholic News Service, Wire Report, November 11, 1988.

6. John Paul II, "Christifideles Laici: Apostolic Exhortation on the Vocation and the Mission of the Lay Faithful in the Church and in the World," *Origins* 18, no. 35 (February 9, 1989) 29.

7. Lee, 10.

8. John Paul II, *The Gospel of Life* (*Evangelium Vitae*) 42, Encyclical Letter, Rome, March 25, 1995, Boston, MA: Pauline Books & Media.

9. John Paul II, *On Social Concern* 72-73.

Chapter 4

1. Joseph Cardinal Bernardin, "Evangelizing the Active Catholic," in *Pentecost '87 Supplement, A National Satellite Celebration of Catholic Evangelization,* Saturday, June 6, 1987 (Washington, DC: Paulist National Catholic Evangelization Association) 17.

2. John Paul II, *Redemptoris Missio,* December 7, 1990, 51.

3. United States Conference of Catholic Bishops, *The Parish: A People, A Mission, A Structure: A Statement of the Committee on the Parish,* November 1980 (Washington, DC: USCCB, 1981).

4. United States Conference of Catholic Bishops, *Our Hearts Were Burning Within Us: A Pastoral Plan for Adult Faith Formation in the United States* (Washington, DC: USCCB, 1999) 38.

5. Bernardin, 16.

6. Ibid. 36-37.

7. United States Conference of Catholic Bishops, *The Parish: A People* . . . 11.

8. Ibid. 17.

Chapter 6

1. Permission given by Father Michael Hammer and Paul to use Paul's story.

Chapter 7

1. Henri J. M. Nouwen, *Behold the Beauty of the Lord, Praying with Icons* (Notre Dame: Ave Maria Press, 1987) 65.

2. United States Conference of Catholic Bishops, *Called and Gifted for the Third Millennium: Reflections of the U.S. Bishops on the Thirtieth Anniversary of the Decree on the Apostolate of the Laity and the Fifteenth Anniversary of Called and Gifted* (Washington, DC: USCCB, 1995) 12.

3. Donal Dorr, *Spirituality and Justice* (Maryknoll: Orbis Books, 1984) 8–18.

4. Staff to the Committee on the Parish, United States Conference of Catholic Bishops, *Parish Life in the United States, Final Report to the Bishops of the United States by the Parish Project* (Washington, DC: USCCB, November 1982) 61.

Chapter 10

1. John Paul II, "Apostolic Exhortation on the Laity" 19.

2. Henri Nouwen, *Reaching Out* (Garden City: Doubleday & Co., 1975).

Chapter 11

1. United States Conference of Catholic Bishops, "Bishops' Committee on Priestly Life and Ministry, Reflections on the Morale of Priests" (Washington, DC: USCCB, 1988) 18.

2. United States Conference of Catholic Bishops, *Committee on the Laity, Lay Ecclesial Ministry: The State of the Questions* (Washington, DC: USCCB) 16–17.

3. Robert E. Lauder, *The Priest as Person: A Philosophy of Priestly Existence* (Whitinsville: Affirmation Books, 1981) 97–98.

4. United States Conference of Catholic Bishops, *The Parish: A People*...ibid.

Chapter 13

1. John Paul II, *Apostolic Exhortation on the Laity* 40.

Chapter 14

1. *Catechism of the Catholic Church* 2567.

2. Ibid. 2698.

3. Edward Carter, SJ, *Prayer Perspectives* (Staten Island: Alba House, 1987) 85–86.

4. Henri J. M. Nouwen, *Reaching Out* (Garden City: Doubleday & Co., 1975) 25.

5. Lucy Rooney, SND, and Robert Faricy, SJ, *Lord Jesus, Teach Me To Pray* (Garden City: Doubleday & Co., 1988) 5.

6. *Catechism of the Catholic Church* 2705.

7. *Catechism of the Catholic Church* 2724.

8. David Steindl-Rast, "Recollections of Thomas Merton's Last Days in the West," *Monastic Studies* 7 (1969) 2–3.

9. Thomas Merton, *Spiritual Direction and Meditation* (Collegeville: Liturgical Press, 1960) 78–79.

10. Thomas Keating, *Open Mind, Open Heart* (New York: Continuum Publishing Co., 1995) 36.

11. Jacqueline Bergan and Sr. Marie Schwan, *Forgiveness: A Guide to Prayer* (Winona: St. Mary's Press, 1985) 4.

12. Thomas Keating, *Open Mind, Open Heart*...139.

13. Ibid. 114–15.

14. Lucy Rooney, SND, and Robert Faricy, SJ, 33–35.

15. Intensive Journal Program, 80 E. 11th St., Room 305, New York, NY 10003, 212-673-5880.

16. Joseph Komonchak, Mary Collins, and Dermot Lane, eds., *The New Dictionary of Theology* (Wilmington: Michael Glazier, 1989) 283.

17. Catoir, 54-55.

Chapter 15

1. Paul VI, *On Evangelization in the Modern World* (Washington, DC: United States Conference of Catholic Bishops, 1976) 2.

2. The Catholic Bishops of Texas, "Mission: Texas: A Pastoral Letter on Evangelization" (March 1989) 3.

3. Paul VI, *On Evangelization in the Modern World* 18.

4. RENEW International, *Parish Core Communities: Renewing the Face of the Earth,* Tape 3: "Small Communities Reaching Out," videocassette.

5. Ibid. 58.

6. Ibid. 10.

7. Ibid. 24.

8. Archbishop Dennis Hurley, "Address to the International RENEW Convocation" 1989.

9. Although the Rite of Christian Initiation of Adults is intended primarily for unbaptized adults, it envisions including uncatechized baptized adults (either in the Catholic Church or in other Christian communities) in an adapted process. To reflect this inclusive vision of the document both categories of people are used in this section. The references to baptized adults will be placed in parentheses to indicate our understanding that an adapted process can be used.

10. International Commission on English in the Liturgy and Bishops' Committee on Liturgy, *Rite of Christian Initiation of Adults: Study Edition* 75.

11. Ibid. 37.

Chapter 16

1. Gregory F. Pierce, *Activism That Makes Sense: Congregations and Community Organizations* (Mahwah: Paulist Press, 1984) 24-25.

2. John XXIII, *Pacem in Terris,* David O'Brien and Thomas Shannon, eds., *Renewing the Earth* (Garden City: Doubleday and Company, 1977) 126–30.

3. Pax Christi, USA, (National Catholic Peace Movement), 532 West Eighth Street, Erie, PA 16502-1343, 814-453-4955, Web site: www.paxchristiusa.org; Bread for the World, 50 F Street, NW, Suite 500, Washington, DC 20001, 800-82-BREAD, Web site: www.bread.org; Network (A National Catholic Social Justice lobby), 801 Pennsylvania Avenue, SE, Suite 460, Washington, DC 20003-2167, 202-547-5556, Fax: 202-547-5510, Web site: www.network lobby.org.

4. Kathleen and James McGinnis, *Parenting for Peace and Justice* and *Helping Families Care* are available from The Institute for Peace and Justice, 4144 Lindell Blvd., Suite 408, St. Louis, MO 63108, 314-533-4445, Fax: 314-715-6455, Web site: www.ipj-ppj.org, E-mail: PPJN@aol.com.

Bibliography

Abbott, Walter M., SJ. *The Documents of Vatican II.* New York: Guild Press, 1966.

Bergan, Jacqueline, and Sr. Marie Schwan. *Forgiveness: A Guide to Prayer.* Winona: St. Mary's Press, 1985.

Bernardin, Joseph Cardinal. "Evangelizing the Active Catholic." *Pentecost '87 Supplement, A National Satellite Celebration of Catholic Evangelization.* Saturday, June 6, 1987. Washington, DC: Paulist National Catholic Evangelization Association.

Breña, Jess S., SJ. *Christian Faith Communities: A Do-it-Yourself Manual of the Chinese Bishops Conference.* Taipei, Taiwan: Jess S. Breña, SJ, 1989.

Brennan, Patrick. *The Evangelizing Parish.* Valencia: Tabor Publishing, 1987.

Carter, Edward, SJ. *Prayer Perspectives.* Staten Island: Alba House, 1987.

Catholic Bishops of Texas. "Mission: Texas: A Pastoral Letter on Evangelization." March 1989.

Catoir, John T. *Enjoy the Lord. A Path to Contemplation.* Staten Island: Alba House, 1988.

Coughlan, Peter. *The Hour of the Laity: Their Expanding Role.* Philadelphia: E. J. Dwyer, 1989.

Cowan, Michael A., and Bernard J. Lee. *Conversation, Risk and Conversion: The Inner and Public Life of Small Christian Communities.* Maryknoll, NY: Orbis Books, 1997.

Davis, Kenneth, OFM, Conv. "Base Communities: Changing the Chemistry of the Church." *The Catholic World,* November/December 1990, 281-85.

Delespesse, Max. *The Church Community, Leaven and Lifestyle.* Ottawa: The Catholic Center of Saint Paul University, 1968.

Dorr, Donal. *Spirituality and Justice.* Maryknoll: Orbis Books, 1984.

Dulles, Avery, SJ. *A Church to Believe In: Discipleship and the Dynamics of Freedom.* New York: Crossroad, 1986.

———. *The Reshaping of Catholicism: Current Challenges in the Theology of Church.* San Francisco: Harper & Row, 1988.

Ferguson, James, CSC. "The Demise of Mission." International Papers in Pastoral Ministry. Notre Dame: University of Notre Dame. February 1990.

Gallup, George Jr. "Evangelizing the Unchurched American." *Pentecost '87 Supplement,* A National Satellite Celebration of Catholic Evangelization, Saturday, June 6, 1987. Washington, DC: Paulist National Catholic Evangelization Association.

Gannon, Thomas M., and George W. Traub. *The Desert and the City: An Interpretation of the History of Christian Spirituality.* Chicago: Loyola University Press, 1969.

Healey, Joseph. "Comparing 'Basic and Small' Christian Communities." *AMECEA Documentation Service* (Nairobi) 284, May 8, 1984. In "Communities," *Ministries and Communities,* Leuven, Belgium: Pro Mundi Vita, 1984, #3.

Hoge, Dr. Dean R. *Converts, Dropouts, Returnees: A Study of Religious Change Among Catholics.* Washington, DC: United States Catholic Conference, 1981.

———. *The Proceedings of a Symposium on Renewal in Catholic Evangelization.* Gainesville: Koch Foundation. 1986.

Holland, Joe. "Beyond a Privatized Spirituality." *New Catholic World* 231, July/August 1988.

International Commission on English in the Liturgy and Bishops' Committee on Liturgy. *Rite of Christian Initiation of Adults: Study Edition.* Chicago: Liturgy Training Publications, 1988.

Ivory, Thomas P. *Conversion and Community: A Catechumenal Model for Total Parish Formation.* Mahwah: Paulist Press, 1988.

John Paul II. "Address to the Hispanic Community in San Antonio, Texas," 1987.

———. "Apostolic Exhortation on the Family." Washington, DC: United States Catholic Conference, 1981.

———. "Christifideles Laici: Apostolic Exhortation on the Vocation and the Mission of the Lay Faithful in the Church and in the World." *Origins* 18, February 9, 1989, 561-95.

———. "Los Angeles Meeting of the Pope and U.S. Bishops." *Origins* 17, October 1, 1987, 253-76.

————. *On Social Concern,* Sollicitudo Rei Socialis. Encyclical Letter, December 30, 1987. Washington, DC: United States Catholic Conference.

John XXIII. "Pacem in Terris." David O'Brien and Thomas Shannon, eds., *Renewing the Earth.* Garden City: Doubleday and Company, 1977, 117-70.

Keating, Thomas. *Open Mind, Open Heart.* (New York: Continuum Publishing Co., 1995).

Komonchak, Joseph, Mary Collins, and Dermot Lane, eds. *The New Dictionary of Theology.* Wilmington: Michael Glazier, 1989.

Lauder, Robert E. *The Priest as Person: A Philosophy of Priestly Existence.* Whitinsville: Affirmation Books, 1981.

Lee, Bernard J., and Michael A. Cowan. *Dangerous Memories: House Churches and Our American Story.* Kansas City: Sheed & Ward, 1986.

Lee, Bernard J., S.M., with William V. D'Antonio, et al., *The Catholic Experience of Small Christian Communities.* Mahwah, N.J.: Paulist Press, 2000.

Leege, David C., ed. "Parish Organizations: People's Needs, Parish Services, and Leadership." *Notre Dame Study of Catholic Parish Life.* Notre Dame: University of Notre Dame, July 1986.

Libreria Editrice Vaticana. *Catechism of the Catholic Church.* Washington, DC: United States Catholic Conference, 1994. English translation of the *Catechism of the Catholic Church* for the United States of America Copyright © 1994, United States Conference of Catholic Bishops. English translation of the *Catechism of the Catholic Church: Modifications from the Editio Typica* Copyright © 1997, United States Conference of Catholic Bishops.

Marins, José, and Team (Teolide Maria Trevisan & Carolee Chanona). *Basic Ecclesial Communities: The Church from the Roots.*

Mathey, Chuck. *Successful CFM Leadership.* Ames: Christian Family Movement, 1988.

Merton, Thomas. *Spiritual Direction and Meditation.* Collegeville: Liturgical Press, 1960.

National Center for Family Studies at the Catholic University of America. "Contemporary American Families: Facts and Fables." Washington, DC: 1985.

National Conference of Catholic Charities. "Toward a Renewed Catholic Charities Movement." Washington, DC: 1972.

Nouwen, Henri J. M. *Behold the Beauty of the Lord: Praying With Icons.* Notre Dame: Ave Maria Press, 1987.

———. *Reaching Out.* Garden City: Doubleday & Co., 1975.

O'Halloran, James, SDB. *Small Christian Communities: A Pastoral Companion.* Maryknoll, NY: Orbis, 1996.

———. *Signs of Hope. Developing Small Christian Communities.* Maryknoll, NY: Orbis, 1991.

Ott, Bishop Stanley J. "Bringing the Christian Message to Modern Men and Women." *Catholic Evangelization,* January/February 1988, 22-25.

Paul VI. *On Evangelization in the Modern World.* Washington, DC: United States Catholic Conference, 1976.

Pierce, Gregory F. *Activism That Makes Sense: Congregations and Community Organizations.* Mahwah: Paulist Press, 1984.

RENEW International. *Parish Core Communities: Renewing the Face of the Earth,* Tape 3: "Small Communities Reaching Out," videocassette, Plainfield, N.J.: RENEW International Publications, 1998.

RENEW International. *Why Catholic? Journey through the Catechism.* Plainfield, N.J.: RENEW International Publications, 2002.

Rooney, Lucy, SND, and Robert Faricy, SJ. *Lord Jesus, Teach Me To Pray.* Garden City: Doubleday & Co., 1988.

Staff to the Committee on the Parish, National Conference of Catholic Bishops. *Parish Life in the United States, Final Report to the Bishops of the United States by the Parish Project.* Washington, DC: United States Catholic Conference, November 1982.

Steindl-Rast, David. "Recollections of Thomas Merton's Last Days in the West." *Monastic Studies* 7, 1969.

Sweetser, Thomas, and Carol Wisniewski Holden. *Leadership in a Successful Parish.* San Francisco: Harper & Row, 1987.

Synod of Bishops. *Justice in the World.* Washington, DC: United States Catholic Conference, 1972.

———. "Message to the People of God." *Origins* 19, November 12, 1987, 385-99.

———. "The Final Report of the 1985 Extraordinary Synod of Bishops." *Origins* 15, December 19, 1985, 441-56.

U.S. Bishops' Committee on Hispanic Affairs. *Communion and Mission: A Guide for Bishops and Pastoral Leaders on Small Church Communities*

(Comunión Y Misión: Orientaciones para Obispos y Agentes de Pastoral Sobre Pequeñas Comunidades Eclesiales). Washington, DC: United States Catholic Conference, 1995.

United States Catholic Conference. Bishops' Committee on Priestly Life and Ministry. "Reflections on the Morale of Priests," 1988.

———. *Family Centered Catechesis.* Washington, DC: United States Catholic Conference, 1979.

———. *Go and Make Disciples: A National Plan and Strategy for Catholic Evangelization in the United States.* Washington, DC: United States Catholic Conference, 1993.

United States Conference of Catholic Bishops. *Called and Gifted for the Third Millennium. Reflections of the U.S. Catholic Bishops on the Thirtieth Anniversary of the Decree on the Apostolate of the Laity and the Fifteenth Anniversary of Called and Gifted.* Washington, D.C.: United States Catholic Conference, 1995.

———. *Called and Gifted: Reflections of the American Bishops. Commemorating the Fifteenth Anniversary of the Issuance of the Decree on the Apostolate of the Laity. Origins* 10, 1980.

———. *The Hispanic Presence: Challenge and Commitment, A Pastoral Letter on Hispanic Ministry.* United States Catholic Conference, December 12, 1983.

———. *The Parish: A People, A Mission, A Structure: A Statement of the Committee on the Parish.* November 1980. Washington, D.C.: United States Catholic Conference, 1981.

Vandenakker, John Paul. *Small Christian Communities and the Parish.* Kansas City: Sheed & Ward, 1994.

Vatican Secretariat for Promoting Christian Unity. *Sects or New Religious Movements in the World: Pastoral Challenges.* United States Catholic Conference, May 3, 1986.

Welch, John, O. Carm. *Spiritual Pilgrims.* Mahwah: Paulist Press, 1982.

Wuthnow, Robert. *Sharing the Journey: Support Groups and America's New Quest for Community.* New York: The Free Press, A Division of Macmillan, Inc., 1994.

Index

More Praise for *Small Christian Communities: A Vision of Hope for the 21st Century*

I came to St. Austin Parish to form small Christian communities and developed them by following Small Christian Communities: A Vision of Hope *religiously. I used it to educate staff, to discern Core Community members, and to form pastoral facilitators. I have recommended it to others who want to start small Christian communities. It's that good!*

Sr. Sharon Groetsch, D.C.
Austin, TX

. . . well-written and surprisingly pleasant-to-read manual. . . . The authors offer a clear "vision of hope" in direct terms, with recognition and respect for the realities and demands of daily life. . . .

Robert Dylak, Publisher
The Catholic Advocate

Small Christian Communities: A Vision of Hope for the 21st Century *is a classic. It's a how-to manual for SCCs that encourages members to develop an "integrated spirituality," one that combines a deeper personal spirituality with service to God's world. I use this book because it convinces me time and again that we are participating in the reign of God.*

Mary Ann Jeselson
Core Community member, author

10-12 Min DVD reflects on Ave SCC exp. Explore the Chall. 9

Need to hear Friars speak about fin from Ave pulpit

SCC Sunday

Mission Weekend

Ambassadors — go to groups to speak / PPT

Bulletin ← Articles
         ← Advertising
         ← Testimonials

Web

Mailing (Letter, postcard, brochure

Email

Liturgy

Mission communications? Telephone?

Stewardship Center

Prayers of the Faithful